FLATNESS

FLATNESS

B. W. HIGMAN

REAKTION BOOKS

Published by Reaktion Books Ltd
Unit 32, Waterside
44–48 Wharf Road
London N1 7UX, UK
www.reaktionbooks.co.uk

First published 2017

Printed and bound in China by 1010 Printing International Ltd

A catalogue record for this book is available from the British Library

ISBN 978 1 78023 729 9

CONTENTS

Frank den Oudsten, interior of the Schröder House, Utrecht, by Gerrit Rietveld, 1924.

ONE

CONCEPTUALIZING FLATNESS

'Planar surfaces and variants of planar order are so pervasive
and so encompassing, so fundamental to our behaviour and
thought, that it is easy to think of them as natural.'
David Summers, 2003[1]

Wherever you find yourself reading these words, you very likely
inhabit a space dominated by flat surfaces. This is a condition of the
modern world. The words themselves are formed by flat characters
on flat paper or on a flat-panel display. The room you occupy is
almost certainly a box defined by its flat floor, walls and ceiling,
perhaps furnished with a flatweave rug or carpet, tables, bookshelves
and cabinets, and decorated with pictures and posters or maps, all
of these things dependent on external and internal flatness for their
efficiency and functionality. Perhaps you are lying down, stretched
out in the horizontal, the orientation adopted for about a third of
your life.

When you stand to leave the room, you assume there is an even
surface beneath your feet – including steps and stairs – or watch
warily for hazards like sudden drops or random toys. Walking
confidently, you scan the flat screen of your phone or watch. If you
leave your home or office to ride or drive, you move swiftly and
smoothly along flattened roads, rails or pathways, perhaps travelling
to play sport on a level playing field, and parking in a level car park.
For many of us, a wide variety of daily activities are performed on
a flat screen: everything from sending and receiving text messages
to paying bills, reading books, checking the news and weather,
watching television and viewing videos. In the United States, adults

spend about ten hours each day staring at such screens. We can fly from Madrid to Mexico City, sitting in a chair, our feet firmly planted on a flat floor, watching movies or playing games on a flat screen, and finally landing on a flattened runway, every surface on which we step 'unnatural'.

All of these surfaces are crafted or engineered, placing 'manufactured' or 'artificial' flatness at the centre of the everyday experience of modern life. However, as the art historian David Summers argues, we hardly notice this pervasive planarity, seeing it as inevitable or almost natural. Flatness is fundamental to the Anthropocene, the recently recognized era in which human beings have taken a leading role in the shaping of the Earth. Our experience stands in strong contrast to the structure of the natural world and the spatiality of the greater part of human history. Today, for instance, more than 50 million kilometres of roads, with their annexed driveways and vast car parks, dominate the daily movement of most of the world's people; and 1 million kilometres of railways link levelled croplands with architecturally planar cities. In the 1960s and '70s, before the advent of the multi-storey car park (parking garage), more than two-thirds of the land space in downtown districts of major U.S. cities was taken up in streets and car parks. All of these locally levelled landscapes are the product of forest-clearing and earth-moving projects designed to carve out and build up flat surfaces. The Earth has been given a new skin, notably concrete and asphalt, designed both to obliterate what beauty had existed previously and to inhibit natural processes of change – to install flatness as a permanent condition.

We tend not to notice that more than two-thirds of the planet remains covered by water, finding its own natural level. Even in the era of the Anthropocene – when hubris crowns humans as the great movers and shapers – we have done nothing to alter the local flatness or global curvature of the ocean surface, however much or little we have raised sea levels through our contribution to global warming. Thus, although the physical transformation represented by the modern flattening of the world is profound, it must be qualified and limited to terra firma. Indeed, it can be argued that the many advantages of

Escalators enable movement from one flat surface to another, along a slope, while standing vertical on a flat platform: in the Berlin Hauptbahnhof, 2011.

the flatness of the ocean surface have been applied to activities on land, most obviously lower transportation costs and increased speed and comfort.

Variations in scale and perspective bring ambiguity to our perception of flatness. At sea, a ship sits on the flatness of the surrounding ocean, a perception only weakly belied by the curvature of the horizon; in contrast, viewed from a space station, Earth's curvature erases all notions of flatness. In the same way, we would experience the surface quite differently if we had the stature of an ant or, perhaps, a giraffe. Because things look different from different perspectives and at different scales, it comes as no surprise that when the spatial concept of flatness is allowed to take on metaphorical, philosophical and spiritual meanings, it shares the ambiguity found in perceptions of the material world.

Flatness is a quality that is highly desired yet frequently disparaged. The tension lies in the word itself. On the one hand, 'flatness' indicates smoothness, evenness, levelness and predictability, all useful characteristics that facilitate movement and activity, things that contribute to social and economic efficiency. At the same time, it identifies corollaries such as monotony, homogeneity, sameness, emptiness, absence, lack, insipidity, dullness, deficiency, tedium, boredom and even deadness. It describes the degradation of social and individual experience under modernism, the levelling associated with the commodification and commercialization of cultural life.

Flat lands are often dismissed as featureless, boring, uninteresting and depressing because they seem to represent the antithesis of the scenery that modern humans appreciate, lacking natural beauty and majesty. On the other hand, human beings fear change and desire stability. No one wants a bumpy ride. So flat pathways are good to walk or drive on, level playing fields allow fair contests in sport, and flat sites are good for building secure and stable structures. It is distressing when these are 'flattened' by storms or warfare.

To feel flat is to feel down, but to be level-headed and even-handed is to behave in a fair and consistent manner. In fiction, flat characters keep popping up in the same guise, dependable and predictable, never developing complex profiles. Flat affect exhibits a lack of emotion or perhaps its suppression; it is an attitude attributed to Barack Obama, for example, by political opponents who believe that anger and fury are more appropriate responses to certain situations. Societies with a relatively flat distribution of wealth and income are seen as egalitarian, flat societies – sometimes based on a flat tax – but a flat economy is undesirable. Being flat broke is a bad financial situation. Flat beer and flat champagne are no good. A flat note is not music to the ears. It is exhausting to go flat out, but to fall flat is to fail.

Historically, flat-footed, flat-chested, flat-faced, flat-nosed and flat-headed people have often been subjected to derision. However, in some cultures, such physical features were, in the past, considered beautiful, as, for example, the traditional high regard for the flat face in East Asian women and the widespread deformation of the skull. A flat belly has become desirable, particularly in the West, but earlier generations preferred a generous fatness. In England, the expression 'flat as a witch's tit' was taken to indicate a lack of fertility in women, but was also applied negatively to level landscapes. The oval-shaped hieroglyph for 'Egypt' indicated, with pride, 'a flat slice of fertile black soil', set apart from the fringing, rugged world.[2] In the contemporary world, to flatline is to demonstrate an absence of growth and development, or the absence of heartbeat and imminent death. On a seismograph, however, it is the variations from the flat line that are troubling.

These few examples are enough to suggest the apparently contradictory variety of ways in which the concept of flatness can be used literally and metaphorically to describe fundamental aspects of the real and imagined world. However, it does appear that the positive features of flatness have to do mostly with the practicalities of everyday life and the engineering of the physical world. As a conceptual metaphor, the pattern is more clearly negative, or, at best, neutral. Thus Richard Trim, in his study of the evolution of metaphors, takes 'flat' as an example of the most basic category of conceptualization, arguing that 'The general notion of flatness is linked to a pejorative quality that lacks significant points of interest, as in a flat landscape which might appear more monotonous than rugged or mountainous terrain.' In essence, he finds 'flat' equivalent to 'uninteresting'. It is difficult, argues Trim, to imagine 'flat' evolving completely different or opposite meanings – setting aside irony – to connote, for example, excitement or enthusiasm.[3]

In spite of its apparent variety, flatness serves as a consistent spatial concept, with an underlying unity of meaning. Whether positive or negative, literal or metaphorical, the essential element of flatness is the notion of invariance. This is not the same thing as being uninteresting. Further, it is clear that metaphorical and literal meanings of flatness overlap and interact, sharing always the essence of the term as an indicator of invariance, thus ensuring the coherence of the idea across varied contexts. Indeed, the idea of flatness obeys the 'invariance principle' applied in linguistics to the portability of terms used in both everyday communication and more refined conceptual metaphors.

Most modern languages possess an equivalent of the English noun 'flatness', and in some colonized cultures – in Africa, in particular – the word has been borrowed in its English form. More broadly, the concept of invariance is commonly associated with the condition of being flat. According to the *Oxford English Dictionary*, 'flatness' entered the language in the fifteenth century, and was used to indicate the quality of being flat or level, but the roots of the word are much deeper. The modern English adjective 'flat' probably derives from the Indo-European base which contributed to ancient Greek – in which the Oxford scholar S. C. Woodhouse found equivalents for flat, level, smooth, insipid and plain, as well as 'flatness' itself, glossed as smoothness – and Sanskrit's *pṛthu* ('broad').[4] These and related words for plane and its allies were distributed in the form *plat* or *platt*, through Old French, German, Dutch, Danish and Swedish, into Old English; they referred by the twelfth century to horizontal surfaces and, by the fourteenth, to flat, level land. In English, 'plat' came quickly to be used to indicate bluntness and survived in remote places as a synonym for flat or level into the twentieth century. According to Trim, in English, the flatness metaphor was dormant between 1200 and 1500 CE, and then actively used in language to the present.

In French, *plat* provides the prefix in platitude, first used in the seventeenth century to indicate dullness or banality, but entering English in the eighteenth when its meaning was broadened to include trivial expressions that fail to rise above the mundane. *Plat* also means plate, broadly attributed, and creates directly 'platen' and 'platter'. A 'platform' is a good surface to stand or build upon, and French threw up 'plateau' in the eighteenth century. In Spanish, 'flat' translates as *plano* or *aplastado*. German has flatness as *Ebenheit* or *Plattheit*, sharing associations with physical levelness and lowness, as well as the usual dullness, insipidity and vacuity. These characteristics are shared by the Indonesian *kebosanan*, combining flatness with tedium and boredom.

The richness and variety of the meanings and uses of the word 'flatness' reflect the fundamental role of spatial reference in language. Systems of categorization and classification vary – in/out, left/right, north/south, seaside/mountainside, upper/lower, superior/inferior – and some cultures employ absolute frames of reference, typically the cardinal directions, whereas others depend on relative frames.[5] These differences are significant and relate to social practice, but everywhere spatial reference appears primal – rooted in the orientation of the body and sensed through the pull of gravity. This may seem unsurprising and indeed inevitable, but space itself (like time and number) is not something we can perceive directly. It is simply taken for granted. It is probably as difficult to conceive pure empty space as it is to imagine a universe in which things exist in the absence of space. Surely everything has its place – every object its location in space? Flatness partakes of both space and place, at once an abstract construct of the mind yet immanent.

In the world of mathematics, the West had to wait for non-Euclidean geometry to reject the notion that space is an empty container and begin to acknowledge its curvature, something Buddhism had long understood. Although emptiness is a fundamental spatial concept, suggesting absence and negation, in Buddhist philosophy, it refers to the illusory appearance of the world, the paradox and mystery that underlies the practical reality of our daily lives. It also indicates the emptying of the self and the making of the non-ego, and connects with practice, such as chanting and the repetition of mantras. In this sense, emptiness is a way of being, a way of existing, knowing and acting. The negation may go further, however, if the illusory character of the world extends to the very concepts used to describe its form. In these ways, Buddhist notions of emptiness are closely associated with Western ideas of the philosophy of nothingness, as developed by Jean-Paul Sartre, for example. The implications for flatness are that although boundless empty space is often thought equivalent to emptiness – featureless and measureless – nothingness (non-being) is not a replacement for being.[6]

Our perception of space depends on the perception of the layout of objects and surfaces, in relation to one another and to a fundamental surface (typically the ground). When we move around the space, these relations change, enabling the construction of a picture of its topography. Empty space, lacking stimuli and landmarks, cannot be perceived, whether by sight or touch.[7] It is in this sense that flatness is associated with the notion of emptiness, an absence of content and spatial clues. However, in the case of flatness, it is not that spatial perception is impossible. Rather, it is the more limited claim that vertical spatial clues are absent. Thus the 'emptiness' of a landscape – such as a sandy desert or salt lake – is defined by the lack of verticality and the homogeneity of its physical content.

In spite of the supposed modern lack of enthusiasm for flat landscapes, the world's population is increasingly concentrated into coastal zones and urban settlements in which the landscape is more likely to approach flatness than mountainous peaks. When human beings attempt to remake their geophysical environments, they frequently work hard to level the land in order to enjoy the practical benefits that come with flat surfaces. And when archaeologists seek clues of past human occupation of a place, they look first for straight lines and right angles, since these features are more likely to be human traces than products of nature, just as geometrical figures drawn in the sand – according to the classical tale – alerted shipwrecked ancients to the presence of philosophers.[8] On the other hand, modern digital image analysis, essential in science and medicine, often depends on enhancing sharply localized features by diminishing slowly varying elements, or the 'flat fielding' of background intensity.[9] Here, 'background' flatness is exaggerated in order to illuminate spatial nonconformities in natural systems.

What is it about flatness that makes it so desired in everyday life yet often unattractive in landscape and metaphorically negative? Why have open, flat places replaced the mountain and the forest as the most frightening habitat? Certainly the peoples who have inhabited such flat places for millennia understand their countries differently. They possess an awareness of local nuances and relativities; they perceive splendour rather than any notion of lack or absence, and often hold the land sacred. They belong to the land. Its elements are not derived from a typology of natural features but from respect for the individual and unique, written on the landscape in the naming of each. On the other hand, the desire to categorize, classify and rank – to generalize and simplify the complexity of the natural world – may be understood as part of a project to impose order on the world, as

Aristippus Philosophus Socraticus, naufragio cum ejectus ad Rhodiensium litus animadvertisset Geometrica schemata descripta, exclamavisse ad comites ita dicitur, Bene speremus, Hominum enim vestigia video. *Vitruv. Architect. lib. 6. Præf.*

delin. M.Burghers sculpt. Univ. Oxon.

Shipwrecked, Aristippus senses the presence of civilized beings, proved to him by the plane figures drawn on a sandy shore of ancient Greece. Frontispiece from David Gregory, *Euclidis quae supersunt omnia* (1703), engraving.

an intellectual exercise but also as a means to the exercise of political power, writ large in imperialism and globalization. The categorization of landscape into types is a central element in this way of seeing the world, including the abstraction of physical flatness and its extension into the imposition of systems of uniformity.[10]

Because absolute flatness is rare in nature and may appear an abstract idea, it proves a surprisingly challenging spatial concept. Rather than a feature of the natural order or a simple convention, the idea of the plane represents a conceptual invention, raising fundamental questions about the nature of space, the very fact of landscape and its relationship to nature and culture. It also raises questions about the meaning of absence and emptiness, both in the world as experienced and in terms of representation in pictures and sound, art and music.

In spite of its capacity for abstraction, and its seeming simplicity, flatness is an intensely practical thing with ramifications spreading far and wide throughout everyday life. It is the very foundation on which we stand, and build, and absolutely vital to the making of the modern world. It is essential to everything from architecture to the development of literate cultures. Without a writing surface there can be no text, and without pages, no reading; without a canvas, there can be no painting; without a screen, no moving picture can be shown. The flat surface is essential to the conceptual vision of science and technology. Modern life would be inconceivable without flatness, both physically and conceptually.

What explains the centrality of flatness in modern life? To try to answer this question, I look at flatness from three contrasting perspectives. In the first part of the book (chapters Two, Three and Four), the emphasis is on the ways human beings have *perceived* flatness in the world around us. The second part (chapters Five, Six and Seven) is concerned with the ways we have *created* flatness, and the third (Chapter Eight) with the *representation* of flatness. The question of perception takes at least two forms: (a) how do we understand the flatness we see in the natural world – particularly, but not only, the landscape – and (b) how do we understand flatness as an abstract spatial concept? Underlying these questions are issues of dimensionality and measurement. The second major topic of this book, the creation of flatness, also has two major components: (a) how and why have human beings devoted so much energy to the flattening of the natural world, and (b) how and why have we become obsessed with the manufacture of artificial flat things? The third part of the book asks why flat surfaces dominate in the representation of information and our pictures, particularly in cartography, art, music and literature.

These questions rarely worry us. Probably this lack of concern derives from the complicated relationship between what we see as simple everyday inevitability – something rooted in practicality and not in need of explanation – and the apparently intuitive status of fundamental spatial concepts in a three-dimensional universe. The significance of flatness lies in the intertwined functional and abstract facets of the idea that define its power to organize space. However, the dominance of flatness, in both its literal and metaphorical meanings, is very much a creation of modern human experience. Its impact has been profound. We see it wherever we look, in the places we now most often live: in the flattened landscape smothered by concrete and asphalt that conceals the natural shape and texture of the earth; in the engineered architecture of urban settlement; in level playing fields and computer gaming screens; and in the flat information surfaces covered by pixels or print that dominate our visual lives. It represents the victory of abstract and artificial spatiality over the natural forces of terrestrial diversity. Some of it brings beauty to the eye of the beholder; some of it is responsible for appalling eyesores. Flatness is at once a symbol of civilization and a prime indicator of human disrespect for a living, breathing Earth.

TWO

THE DIMENSIONS OF FLATNESS

'Imagine a vast sheet of paper on which straight Lines, Triangles, Squares, Pentagons, Hexagons, and other figures, instead of remaining fixed in their places, move freely about, on or in the surface, but without the power of rising above or sinking below it, very much like shadows . . .'
Edwin Abbott, 1884[1]

How many dimensions does flatness possess? We may think of it as the perfect two-dimensional surface, yet flatness inhabits a universe in which space is perceived as three-dimensional. Seeing the world in three dimensions seems intuitive, rooted in sensation and imagination. Indeed, ancient philosophers believed that spatial concepts are essentially innate, and modern branches of neuroscience agree.[2] Although 'empiricist' philosophers have, to the contrary, sometimes assumed that concepts of space (and time) derive from experience and inductive experimentation, recent studies – among indigenous Amazonian communities, for example – suggest that people spontaneously make use of basic (Euclidean) geometric concepts.[3] The debate is more complex and subtle than this simple nature/nurture dichotomy might seem to suggest, but the outcomes are much the same for dimensionality. Thus a spatial system possessing measurable length, breadth and height – but no other dimensions – may appear to be a pre-scientific certainty that has its roots in deep time, yet is acceptable in science as well as everyday life.

The origins of dimensionality

In spite of this certainty, how we came to embrace the three-dimensional model is by no means clear. It has been argued that human ideas – including the abstract conceptual metaphors underpinning symbolic logic, geometry and trigonometry – have their roots in sensory-motor experience.[4] The French mathematician Henri Poincaré (1854–1912) pondered these questions in terms of cognitive psychology as early as 1907, arguing that although space is an essentially meaningless concept and all measures of distance are relative, human intuitions of 'the unintelligible concepts of distance, direction, and straightness' are so strong that they must spring from 'a complicated system of nervous impulses in the depths of the unconscious' that enable us to function in three-dimensional space. Any other model would seem artificial. Through natural selection, the human mind simply adopted the geometry most advantageous to the species.[5]

Certainly the human body is a vital and primary source of spatial reference, but as a model for flatness it is problematic. In addition to its incomplete rotational symmetry, the body's components are typically cylindrical. The same applies to many other animals and to plants. In vertebrates, left/right symmetry is an evolutionary rule that is rarely broken, but flat body parts are rare.[6]

Most important is the fact that the structure of the human body evolved to maintain an upright posture against the force of gravity, regardless of the slope of the terrestrial surface. The priority of this terrestrial surface as the point of reference is equally significant: human beings evolved to live *on* the Earth, not underground or in or on the sea, and we are held in place by gravity. We are very aware of the significance of this surface and the striking difference between the earth under our feet and the breathable atmosphere that envelops us, but our knowledge of what lies even a few metres beneath our feet is severely limited. Our perception of the Earth is superficial. Thus there is every good reason to perceive the terrestrial surface as the surface that really matters in the development of concepts of spatiality.

Humans are the only fully bipedal mammals, and this fact has been important in their evolution, placing a premium on the capacity to stand up straight. When we stand upright, the axis of the body points directly towards the very centre of the Earth, and the tangent on which we stand – that surface that to our feet feels flat and therefore stable – is at right angles to our axis. However, we do not spend all our lives standing. Today, a great deal of time is spent sitting down, and in the past various other postures were commonly adopted in farming and hunting. More importantly, humans have always devoted about one-third of their total lifetimes to sleep, and most often this has been in the horizontal. Cribs, cradles and cots – and hammocks – deviate from the model, but sleeping on the ground was always safest on level surfaces, and the modern sleeping mat and bed are designed flat, to match the body in the horizontal. Through most of history, sleep was matched to darkness, a time to dream and fear, to surrender to the forces of nature. In death, in most cultures, the final surrender has always been horizontal.

Whether we are standing up, sitting or lying down, gravity provides the fundamental principle of spatial orientation, and a physiological warning system of hazards which may be encountered when the body strays or is misled by false spatial clues. No doubt the world is experienced differently by bats and sloths, but hanging upside down has little appeal for humans. Falling down can be dangerous, whereas standing upright creates the conditions for an abstract appreciation of verticality in an unseen plane. However, although crawling on all fours is abandoned by humans as soon as they can stand, and reverted to only in constrained spaces, children have difficulty dealing with the complexities of dimensionality. Especially for children, and because of the top-down asymmetry of the body, inverted images (in the vertical plane) are more easily interpreted than mirror-image (horizontal) transformations.

When an infant sits up, argues Yi-Fu Tuan, she sees a horizon quite different from the visual field of the supine. 'Standing' means more, the word itself related to stature and status, giving the grown individual both commanding height and verticality. These perspectives are enough to create a differential between things that are high and low, superior and inferior. God inhabits the heavens. Mecca is closer to heaven than any other place on Earth. In everyday language, the 'horizon' differentiates between what can be viewed and what is hidden, and its shape can be varied. It is the point where earth and sky meet. Strictly, however, the word 'horizon' indicates the circle of the Earth's surface that might be viewed in the absence of obstructions, and to be 'horizontal' is therefore to be parallel to the plane of the horizon, and hence flat, level and uniform. The distant horizon can be level and the intervening terrain roughly dissected. Only at sea or on a great plain, where sight is unhindered, will the two be the same.[7]

Horizontality is also more difficult to comprehend because this is the normal plane of locomotion. Thus vertical spatial referents (up or above, for example) are the same for individuals wherever they are located in a plane, whereas horizontal referents (left, front) differ according to where they are placed, and change when they move. Children learn words describing vertical relationships before they acquire words for the horizontal, and draw pictures with multiple horizontal frames. More broadly, it is certain that spatial information is fundamental to the learning of global concepts in infancy, the quite small number of 'innate spatial primitives' – including the idea 'surface' – that enable early language and contribute to the later learning of more abstract conceptual systems.[8]

Although the body's symmetry contributes to our three-dimensional image of the world, this symmetry is imperfect and lacks the elements required to establish the plane as an abstract surface. Only in modern times have anatomists employed the concept of 'body planes' equivalent to the cosmic planes that underlie geometry and geodesy. Three planes or axes of the human body are identified – vertical (up/down), frontal (front/back) and lateral (left/right) – but these can be reduced to just two fundamental dimensions, vertical and horizontal, and of these only the vertical is common across activities because it is the only dimension specified by gravity. As the psychologists David R. Olson and Ellen Bialystok argue, 'no counterpart reliably describes a horizontal.'[9] In every case, the supporting surface is crucial to how dimensionality is perceived. Typically, it is assumed that the person is standing on a relatively flat and stable surface. Tests of walking trajectories are similarly made on flat, open sites, in which it is found that in the absence of points of orientation – with the sun hidden behind clouds – people walk in quite small circles, whereas with the sun visible they walk an almost perfectly straight course.[10] Any more complex topography introduces too many unmeasurable variables. Standing on a rough or sloping surface – concave or convex – can create a different feeling and perception, as does vertigo or, for some, agoraphobia. The same fundamental principles apply to robots, which, when not bolted to the floor, work best if they have flat bases that move smoothly across flat surfaces.

The ability to stand upright depends both on the actual slope of the surface stood upon and our perception of the steepness of the slope. A horizontal, flat and rigid surface is preferred for standing, and the same applies to walking, running and dancing. The sole and heel of the human foot itself consist of two relatively smooth, flat surfaces, and their flatness is accentuated by the wearing of shoes that create an artificially continuous flat bottom, or flat heel and sole, designed to even out any roughness in the surface stood upon. Exaggerated high heels and the ballerina's pointe shoes have the opposite effect, but these are generally perceived as uncomfortable and are indeed prone to induce injury. In bare feet, humans expend very little energy in walking on a level surface because the negative mechanical work required to raise the centre of gravity with each step is partly recovered when the centre of gravity falls again. When slopes become steep, it is difficult to walk or run, or even to stand. It is possible to resort to climbing, but only if the surface has irregularities which can be grasped or stood on. Smooth slopes greater than about 30° are typically perceived as not walkable. Solutions can, however, be found in engineering, by building stairs, escalators and ladders, typically with a flat surface for each step.[11]

The same principles apply to other activities, notably the movement of vehicles controlled by humans. In tight situations, such as car parks (parking lots), the surface needs to be quite flat

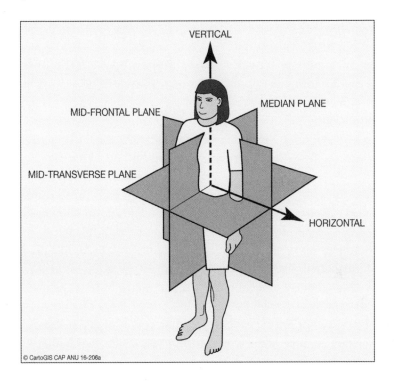

Body planes.

(maximum 8°), and the tolerance is not much greater in driveways (maximum 10°), whereas on the open road cars can climb more steeply (up to 20°). With the aid of a rack, railways can be even steeper (up to 25°). Beyond these limits, accidents become increasingly common: vehicles turn over and brakes no longer hold. Steep slopes are often climbed by following a winding route, but this technique also has finite limits.

Beyond an awareness of potential hazards, standing upright on the ground offers the possibility of a largely unconscious perception of abstract vertical and horizontal planes, situated within pure space that we cannot see or touch. We maintain this upright stance with the help of sense organs usefully located in the head. More or less at right angles to the vertical axis, a line runs through the ears and the eyes, matching the horizontal of the perceived external world. The brain maintains an estimate of three-dimensional motion in space, receiving constantly updated geometrically consistent data from the visual and vestibular sensory systems – the latter located in the cavities of the inner ear – and sends messages to our muscles and joints to keep us upright and spatially oriented. When asleep, it is wise to lie on a flat surface or have secure boundaries, as in a hammock or cot.[12]

Our eyes, the most visibly spherical parts of the body, depend on their mobility to enable spatial resolution. They have no fixed axes of rotation but, just as for the geometry and cartography of the Earth, science has created systems which ascribe to the eye a variety of spherical attributes – poles and equator, latitude and longitude, meridians – and planes, similar to the symmetry of the body. The dichotomies up/down and left/right are conceptual simplifications of these myriad lines of sight, dictated by the structure of the body as a whole. Eye movements might seem to give birth naturally to the dimensions of height and breadth, but we do not have eyes in the backs of our heads, so the visual perception of depth depends on geometric clues available in two-dimensional images. If our eyes were on the sides of our heads, as those of cows are, we would have superior spatial cognition but poor depth perception, and would easily be spooked moving forwards. These facts of human physiology also contribute to our notions of time. Looking ahead, and moving forwards, we occupy a place in the present: the past lies behind us, while we look forwards to the future, scanning visible space for clues to what might come next.

Regardless of physiology, vision is always limited to the available light cone. To see an object, it must be illuminated. Light is scattered as a result of illumination, creating an 'object wave' that contains the complete optical information of the object. The wave has both amplitude (brightness) and phase (the shape of the object), and the perception of spatial features depends on variations in image intensity. The structure of the eye balances sensitivity to light against the achievement of spatial resolution.[13]

Sighted humans, with two functional eyes, receive images projected onto different locations on the retinae, flat sheets of neural tissue. But these images are not seen. It is in the brain that the two flat images are translated into three-dimensional pictures, assisted by binocular registration, which enables stereo depth perception and the recognition of surfaces with specific shapes. However, because our eyes are offset horizontally, the differences are mostly horizontal, and vertical disparities play only a minor role in creating the impression of depth. Thus we see best (solving the correspondence problem) when the eyes are in the 'primary position', gazing straight forwards – effectively horizontal and with the head upright.[14] Students are encouraged to comprehend the idea of height in the visual field by assuming they are 'standing on a level surface outdoors (usually called the ground plane in the perceptual literature) and looking toward the distant horizon'. However, height in the visual field is a limited cue to distance, working best where objects exist on 'horizontal ground plane surfaces'. The problem is that the perception of visual space does not exactly follow the rules of Euclidean geometry, yet alternative models are also found wanting.[15]

The visual perception of scenes, including landscapes, is highly selective and abstract. The details of a pictorial image are quickly lost through 'inattentional blindness', whereas the more abstract properties are retained. Flat landscapes fare well in this system: picture an image divided into two equal horizontal planes, the bottom panel bare ground, the top clear, blue sky. No detail seems necessary, and the image is memorable. The same applies to the navigation of virtual environments, except that spatial memory is improved if the image is slanted by about 4°. This probably reflects the way oblique aerial views appear more natural than the vertical, and the role of up/down referents in language. Slant (the angle between the line of sight and the tangent to the plane) determines the perception of phenomenal data that change with the visual angle. For flat and many other surfaces, the perspective gradient decreases with distance whereas the density gradient increases – as can be imagined in raising one's eyes to look across a tiled piazza, the tiles seeming to become narrower and more closely packed, the uniformity of the grading signalling the degree of flatness.[16] These facts of physiology lay a firm foundation for the idea of flatness, as a concept with its roots in the senses and the very structure of the human body, and an explanation for the apparent naturalness of the concept.

An alternative origin for the concept of flatness can be sought in the topography of the natural world. Just as humans recognize the increased difficulty of standing upright on steeper slopes, so they might observe the increased instability of natural materials – sand, gravel, soil – and the capacity of even solid rock to fall from vertical cliffs. However, throughout prehistory, perfectly flat terrestrial surfaces were rare. Bodies of water – oceans, lakes and ponds – offered potential models, and still water might even provide a precise reflection, foreshadowing the mirror and the camera. However, perception of the horizontality of water surfaces is not strictly intuitive, and in any case liquids do not offer viable surfaces for the drawing of geometric figures.[17] Indeed, it has often been claimed that the straight line is an element of culture, in contrast to the chaotic jumble of the natural order; enigmatically embedded in ancient spiritual landscapes, but made more strikingly visible by modernity and imperialism. Human cultures create geometric topographies, whereas natural landscapes are essentially 'random'.[18]

A compelling experiential source of the three-dimensional model is found in human activity, especially the building of things by the addition of elements – using bricks or Lego – and by the cutting of elements through division, such as slicing an orange or guillotining a ream of paper. Other theories relate to perceptions of motion, direction, force and causality.[19] Every kind of measurement depends on the way we experience the material world, but does so by erecting a system of coordinates or assuming an absolute space – something we cannot, in fact, experience – derived from a real world of relative distance and motion.[20] As the mathematician James Franklin puts it,

> In *our* space, at the human scale, there is a continuous, straight path (that is, a path continuous and straight, down to the limits of measurement) joining any two points. The argument for the reality of *our* space does not depend on any claims about all possible geometries.[21]

More broadly, the spatial concept of flatness belongs to the large group of concepts based in generic generalization and hierarchical systems of classification that have unfolded dynamically. The concept of mass, for example, can be understood in terms of rank, from heavy to light, but also more abstractly in metric units: grams, kilograms, tonnes. The same applies to concepts of volume, distance and height, all of which can be measured, and not merely in relativist or conventional terms, however different the units of measurement may be. Flatness is a concept of slope, and in the real world degrees of slope can be measured and understood as deviations from the true plane, in much the same way that weightlessness occurs where gravity is very weak rather than in situations where gravity does not apply. We could say that in the strict two-dimensional sense of the word, 'flatness' lacks measurable variation, so possesses a condition of slopelessness. Thus the concept of flatness exists both in the abstract world of two-dimensional plane geometry and in the real world of measurable slope.

The fundamental universality of the three-dimensional model stands up across cultures, along with the plane and the concept of flatness. The model functions as a 'frame of reference', not only for the sighted but for the blind, by integrating diverse inputs, notably the sense of touch: this is put into practice in Braille and dimples at road crossings, for example, felt as deviations from flatness. It also fits very well with the pre-scientific experience that underlies phenomenology – including Heidegger's notion of 'being-in-the-world' that has more to do with the subjective experience of 'dwelling' than a Cartesian GPS – and the origins of fundamental geographical concepts, by exploring the parts to understand the whole.[22]

Only in the world of physics and the philosophy of science – and the world of the imagination – does the three-dimensional model appear inadequate. In physics, the dimensionality of the world is recognized as one of the most fundamental problems facing the discipline in the twenty-first century, and images of multidimensional

Overleaf: Murray Fredericks, *Icesheet #2426,* 2013, digital pigment print, 120 cm x 150 cm. Fredericks works with the photographic challenge posed by environments that offer minimal visual information, in this example Greenland.

spaces, hidden dimensions and parallel universes have popular appeal.[23] The fourth dimension is typically defined as time, but what exactly this might mean is far from clear, and the term has also been applied both to the related concept of motion and – immediately before Einstein – to non-Euclidean geometry. Particularly influential was the work of the mathematician Hermann Minkowski (1864–1909), who visualized the whole of (four-dimensional) space and its coordinate system stretched and squeezed by special relativity; and, rather than assuming a single space, developed the notion of an infinite number of spaces, in the same way three-dimensional space contains an infinite number of planes. This model has become known as Minkowski space-time.[24]

Just as difficult to imagine as the fourth dimension is a truly two-dimensional world, and in such a flatland, the unknown third dimension might as easily be predicated as time. Generally, although space and time are recognized as fundamental concepts in the construction of our universe, they are difficult to comprehend. We cannot see or touch them, but they are the absolute bedrock of our perception of the physical world. Of the two, space is the most essential. It seems possible to conceive space without time but not the reverse, just as it is easier to conceive space without matter or content than it is to have a concept of matter without space. Everything has to be *somewhere*, doesn't it? In this universe, the physical world has a separate existence and our perceptions capture exactly all of its elements. Alternatively, if the physical world does not really exist, our supposed perceptions may be a kind of virtual reality, fabricated in our minds from the neural spatial mapping system of the brain. These concepts are extremes. Each has its problems.

Only with Albert Einstein (1879–1955) was the Newtonian model of absolute space overturned. Much earlier, Immanuel Kant (1724–1804) had seen that perceived space is a creation of the understanding rather than of reality, but believed space could be experienced as an entity and that it serves as a container for all the objects we see within it. Kant gave priority to space in his *Critique of Pure Reason* (1781), arguing that 'the original representation of space is an *a priori* intuition, not a concept.'[25] Einstein showed not only that things look different to observers with different perspectives, but (in his theory of general relativity published in 1916) that gravity is due to the curvature of space-time. Thus he demonstrated that the shape of space is not absolute, and that objects of great mass can curve space in their vicinity – meaning not the trajectory of objects in space but the very stuff of space itself. It followed that the universe could not be static, but was either expanding or contracting. Among much else, these were ideas that transformed the meaning of flatness and its essential invariance.

The 'real' world, whether experienced intuitively or in science, is one in which time seems to flow forwards, the world is unambiguously three-dimensional, and 'numbers' – including the challenging 'zero' – appear to conform to a single system. This seems true to most, if not all, cultures.[26] It is this dimensional model that has valued measurement and given a vital role to abstract flatness.

Geometry and geodesy

The earliest establishment of geometry as an abstract science grew from the capacity to imagine a pure plane, a perfectly flat surface. Doing so had nothing to do with whether the Earth was or was not thought to be flat. Indeed, a primary challenge for people who recognized early that the Earth is round – yet clung to the idea that it is at the centre of the universe – was to establish the relationship between plane and sphere. The practical issue here was how to measure the Earth and project points from its surface onto a plane. It was a problem of mapping. Thus geometry declares in its name its origins in attempts to take the measure of the world, and to understand the unity and order of the cosmos through rational theoretical discourse. The related science of geodesy is concerned with the practical measurement and mapping of the Earth's (curved) surface, rather than the flatness of the abstract plane. In the long term, although geometry came to inhabit an abstract mathematical world, these concepts of mapping and measurement remained foundational and influential.

The development of theoretical or abstract geometry in the ancient world was a significant intellectual achievement, one which has stood the test of time. Geometry offered a further reason for admiration of the beauty of the universe, for reverence and wonder, but was also remarkable for its use of logic to attain formal proofs, through deductive demonstration and pure spatial reasoning. This achievement required the development of a theoretical geometry – understood as a system of universal spatial relationships – rather than varieties of knowledge that focused on unique qualities, quantities and locations. Certainly the development of Euclidean geometry grew out of the rules of dimensionality and spatial perception, but it seems wrong to say that it was simply 'an explication of the cognitive structures implicit in ordinary perception'.[27] It required a mathematical approach to observation of the universe and its elements, rather than anthropomorphic models, and it was necessary to pass from the practical and empirical to the philosophical and theoretical – a transition crucially important in the history of flatness.

The classical model of plane geometry established in Euclid's *Elements* (*c.* 300 BCE) was less concerned with numerical measurement than with spatial equalities. Euclid understood space as 'infinite in extent in all directions, infinitely divisible, and flat'. His geometry depended on spatial visualization or mental models, and idealization. Beginning with definitions of points and lines, Euclid moves forwards progressively to construct objects of higher dimensions. He conceives space as homogeneous and unbounded – demanding congruence – and creates the elementary flat figures of square, circle and triangle. This is a visual project, not one of measurement. Thus, rather than declaring that the internal angles of a triangle add up to 180°, Euclid famously said that they are equal to two right angles.[28]

Moving on to the three-dimensional world of solids, Euclid describes them with reference to known planar figures. For example, the sphere is defined by the rotation of a semi-circle around its diameter. More important for the concept of flatness, the five so-called Platonic solids or regular polyhedra not only possess pure symmetry

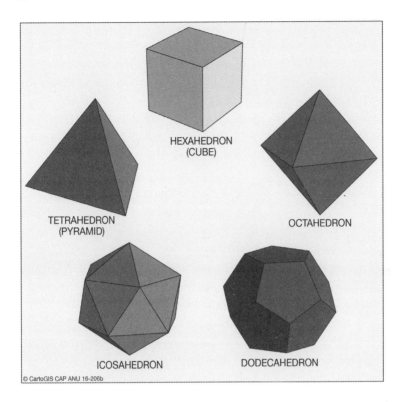

The five Platonic polyhedra.

but are made up of uniform plane faces, with straight edges and sharply defined vertices. The tetrahedron (pyramid), octahedron and icosahedron all have (plane) triangular faces. The hexahedron (cube) has square faces, and the (twelve-sided) dodecahedron pentagonal faces. Plato thought that the first four of these corresponded to the elements fire, air, water and earth respectively, and the dodecahedron to an Earth likened to a leather ball sewn together from twelve pentagonal pieces, representing quintessence.[29] In nature, crystals and organic cells represent the most efficient subdivision of three-dimensional space, following strict geometric rules determined by surface tension rather than gravity. Soap bubbles are spherical. On larger scales, the shape of the Earth's surface appears more chaotic, less pure in its geometry, less likely to exhibit the absolute symmetry of regular polyhedra, let alone flatness.

The geometry of solid figures had its most practical application in geodesy, the sister science devoted to the measurement of the Earth's surface. Geodesy is closely associated with the Greek polymath Eratosthenes (c. 275–194 BCE), who explained in his *Measurement of the Earth* how he found the circumference of the globe. While acknowledging some 'irregularities of surface', he worked with the assumption that the Earth is spherical and that the sun's rays are parallel. Eratosthenes also constructed a world map based on parallels and meridians, and this, together with his measurement of the circumference of the Earth, meant that, using geometry, the length of every parallel circle could be calculated. These achievements contributed to cartography as well as geodesy, but it is not surprising that for many centuries latitude continued to be measured more precisely than longitude. This remained true of geodesy in the Islamic tradition, which again built on the methods established in classical antiquity, and always accepted the sphericity of the Earth.[30]

Elsewhere, in societies all across the world, there developed quite complex knowledge of mathematical functions and spatial relationships, which can be identified in ancient architecture and structures constructed to chart the movement of heavenly bodies, and in navigational charts, for example. Elements of Euclid's system were clearly understood by Chinese thinkers at about the same time, but mathematics in China turned towards algebra. More broadly, geometric patterns – including fractals, unknown to Euclid – can be identified in textiles, pottery and other artefacts from many cultures.[31] Although the archaeological evidence is difficult to interpret and open to controversy, much of it points to the practical uses of geometrical knowledge, and the vital role of flatness as a quality in several areas of material culture, including the solution of problems of mensuration. However, it almost always lacks the systematic theoretical development found in Euclidean plane geometry.

Although abstract, Euclid's system accorded with the experiential physical world, reduced to two-dimensional planes and three-dimensional solid figures. Most important for the idea of flatness is Euclid's fifth postulate: 'given a straight line and a point not on the line, there exists only one straight line through the point parallel to the given line.' Often referred to as the 'parallel postulate', it was understood to derive from the nature of straight lines and the concept that space lacks curvature, and is therefore intrinsically flat.[32]

Euclidean geometry rules the way we picture and measure the world abstractly, and it has become the system taught in schools around the world. Its survival derives both from the apparent faithfulness of the system as an abstract structure and from the way it seems realized in the space we experience at our own scale. Its essential flatness works well for students sitting at desks with flat tops, drawing diagrams on flat slates or sheets of paper, transcribed from flat chalkboards, their feet planted on flat floors, and equally well for students looking at flat-screened electronic devices or making lines in the sand. In everyday life, similarly, the concept of the tangent plane is sufficient at small scales to enable our negotiation of the Earth's surface, using a flat street map as a close approximation to the real – spherical – world; and we rarely bother to wonder why it would cease to be functional when extended over a larger area. We think of curvature in terms of deviation from flatness or from the straight lines of Euclidean space – the plane curve.

These theoretical and practical assumptions were not effectively challenged until the end of the eighteenth century, when non-Euclidean geometries were discovered. This discovery was the work of several mathematicians, including Nikolai Lobachevsky (1792–1856), Johann Bolyai (1802–1860) and Bernhard Riemann (1826–1866), all of them associated with Carl Friedrich Gauss (1777–1855), who claimed and deserves precedence. Gauss's first enthusiasm was for number theory, and at the age of eighteen he famously constructed a regular seventeen-sided polygon using only a (Euclidean) compass and ruler. This interest in the problem of dividing the circle fed into Gauss's work in astronomy and theoretical geodesy, and his practical contributions to land surveying. In 1815 he was recruited to direct a great survey of the kingdom of Hanover, a project of triangulation that occupied Gauss for many years. The work was challenging, particularly because in some of the coastal areas the country was 'completely flat and practically on sea level' and elsewhere 'flat and covered by large forests', notably the Lüneburg Heath. Trigonometric survey requires long vistas from point to point, and Gauss had to negotiate with farmers for the removal of trees that obstructed the line of sight in order to complete the triangles. These challenges led Gauss to invent the heliotrope, an instrument that uses small mirrors to reflect sunlight that can be seen at great distances. He developed geodetic formulas for the calculation of coordinates and planned a major work but published little on geodesy.[33]

Although Gauss set little store by his contributions to the development of geodesy, they were, in fact, substantial and helped stimulate his revolutionary approach to geometry and the general theory of curved spaces. He contributed to work on the basic practical problem of cartography: how best to project a sphere (Earth) onto a plane. This fed into his theory of 'conformal' mapping – a term Gauss coined in 1843, in which complete similarity is preserved in the projection of points from one surface to another – and renewed interest in the status of Euclid's parallel postulate. As early as 1816 Gauss was convinced that an 'anti-Euclidean' geometry could exist – one in which the parallel postulate did not apply – and he set about developing a consistent model of what he called 'transcendental trigonometry' (which came to be known as hyperbolic geometry). In 1828 he established the fundamental theorem that 'in whatever way a flexible and inextensible surface may be deformed, the sum of the principal curvatures at each point will always be the same.'[34]

Essential to the Gaussian theory of surfaces is a distinction between intrinsic and extrinsic geometries. Thomas F. Banchoff claims that Gauss came to this idea by imagining 'the kind of geometry that would be discovered by an intelligent flatworm sliding about on the surface of a solid object'.[35] In 1870, fifteen years after the death of Gauss, the idea was explored further by Hermann von Helmholtz (1821–1894), a German scholar who was highly influential in studies of the physiology of visual space perception. Helmholtz argued that 'reasoning beings of only two dimensions' might be capable of working out a geometry, but only one of two dimensions.[36] They could study only the *intrinsic* geometry of the surface, because they were confined to using measurements of angle and length, made on the surface; but this geometry would vary according to the shape of the surface they inhabited, something they could not perceive directly.

If these beings (perhaps flatworms) inhabited a two-dimensional plane, they would develop a Euclidean geometry, in which the angles of a triangle would always add up to 180°, in accordance with the parallel postulate. On the other hand, if the flatworms inhabited a sphere – though the surface seemed to them flat – they would find that the angles of a large triangle would exceed 180°. In both cases, however, the geometric properties are intrinsic. Thus at a very

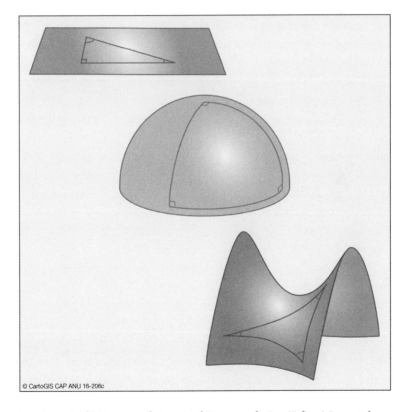

© CartoGIS CAP ANU 16-206c

A triangle on a plane (Euclidean geometry), a hemisphere (elliptic geometry) and a saddle (hyperbolic geometry).

local scale, such as the dimensions of a field or farm, the geometry appears precisely Euclidean, and measurements are entirely reliable for practical purposes, whereas, when it is seen from space, these principles fail. The view from space, looking down on the flatworm's world, exhibits the *extrinsic* geometry of the surface. The basis of this new approach lay in the rejection of the parallel postulate – while retaining the other axioms – and replacing it with its negation, the so-called 'hyperbolic axiom'.[37]

These ideas supported a new concept of geometry, in which the rules are different on different surfaces but not necessarily changed by the bending (without stretching) of the same surfaces. This new way of thinking connects directly with the notion that flatness is a question of scale and perspective – the curve of a small circle is vastly sharper than that of a huge circle. A barefooted man stepping painfully on a ball bearing will not think of it as flat, whereas the same man walking on a massive smooth cosmic sphere may easily be convinced of the flatness of the surface. In theory, a 'Flatlander' could identify what kind of surface he inhabited – plane, sphere or 'saddle' – simply by laying out a triangle and measuring its angles. Gauss, with a practical surveyor's interest in the curvature of the Earth, applied this experiment to the angles of the triangle joining three mountain peaks – Hohenhagen, Brocken and Inselsberg – but within the bounds of his measuring tools, he found they added to 180° and concluded that, intrinsically, space is flat.[38]

Surprisingly, however, the Gaussian 'measure of curvature' is zero not only on plane surfaces but on cylinders and cones. Gauss himself revealed the 'remarkable' theorem: 'If a curved surface, or a part of it, can be developed upon another surface, the measure of curvature at every point remains unchanged after the development.' Further, 'Upon a curved surface that can be developed upon a plane, the measure of curvature is everywhere equal to zero.'[39] Thus a flat sheet of paper can be formed into the shape of cylinder or cone without changing the dimensions of figures drawn on the surface of the sheet, or the distances between points. The same is true of a flat sheet rolled many times, like a roll of newsprint. On the other hand, a sphere always has positive curvature, while a 'pseudosphere' or saddle surface – such as an hourglass – is negative. Later mathematicians, notably Riemann and Poincaré, completed the emancipation of the notion of length and planar distances, but it was the work of Gauss that most captured the imagination with regard to flatness.

The non-Euclidean geometry of complex surfaces is difficult to visualize, just as it is difficult – probably impossible – to visualize a fourth dimension, or to think in terms of a two-dimensional world. But these ideas created possibilities for claims of metaphysical higher-dimensional vision and fantasies, some of them fanciful, others firmly rooted in the new geometry. One of the best known is Edwin Abbott Abbott's *Flatland: A Romance in Many Dimensions*. The book was first published in London in 1884, but Abbott had completed the manuscript ten years earlier, when the picture of a two-dimensional world and its geometries painted by Gauss and Helmholtz was current in popular science.[40]

Flatland contained the purported memoirs of 'A Square', who inhabits what Flatlanders (all of them two-dimensional figures) understand to be a giant plane (though they have no word for 'plane' and simply refer to Flatland). Most Flatlanders take their world for granted, but A Square is curious and discovers that if he walks due east for several weeks – along with his friends A Pentagon and A Hexagon – he comes back to his starting point. Further adventures lead to theories that, rather than a plane, Flatland is in fact a sphere ('hypercircle') or perhaps a torus (doughnut). More and more theories are advanced until it is decided to settle the matter by carrying out a comprehensive survey of the surface – reminiscent of Gauss's theoretical/practical interface – but when the surveyors return to their starting point, they find the world reversed to its mirror image. Abbott used the reversal puzzle to introduce the two-dimensional Möbius strip. Eventually, the Flatlanders understand that Flatland really has two regions, one resembling a torus and the other a Möbius strip, both of them definable as 'flat circle planes', a property shared with the cylinder and the sphere.[41]

This solution, along with all the suggested alternatives, belongs to the intrinsic geometry of the surface, as defined by Gauss. However,

A Square encounters A Sphere, visiting from Spaceland, a world of three dimensions, and is briefly taken aloft to look down on Flatland, so that he can view the astonishing extrinsic geometry of the entire flat world. A Square has to be told that he is living on a plane: 'What you style flatland is the vast level surface of what I may call a fluid, on, or in, the top of which you and your countrymen move about, without rising above it or falling below it.'[42] When A Square attempts to explain his vision to his fellow Flatlanders, they ridicule the concept of a three-dimensional world and he is imprisoned as a heretic.

As a clergyman and a headmaster, Abbott's intention in *Flatland* was to open minds to the existence of previously unknown higher dimensions in geometry, and hence the possibility of higher realms of spiritual existence. As for Gauss and Helmholtz, the objective was to show that, for inhabitants of a three-dimensional world, visualizing a four-dimensional universe was akin to the challenge facing A Square in his attempt to visualize three dimensions. Abbott emphasizes the problem by constructing images of the geometry possible in Lineland and Pointland, even the nightmare 'Abyss of No dimensions'.[43]

It is perhaps ironic that *Flatland* has sometimes been seen as a critique of the British class system, in the tradition of the seventeenth-century 'Levellers' who sought a return to the social equality that existed at the Creation. Rather than being a world of equality, Abbott's Flatland is inhabited by plane figures which take their places in a hierarchy determined by their shape. Status increases with the number of sides: women are Straight Lines, lacking angles and rationality, while males with sides so numerous that they can hardly be distinguished from a circle – rather like Gauss's seventeen-sided polygon – belong to the Circular or Priestly order. In between, work-men are Isosceles Triangles, middle-class men Equilateral Triangles, gentlemen Squares (as was the author of *Flatland*), the lower male nobility Hexagons, and so on. Thus Abbott suggested that this hierarchy of shape, as well as two-dimensional flatness, was not the only possible condition, and that the world could be reconceived in multiple dimensions.[44]

Abbott's principal objective, however, was to connect with the supernatural. He developed a natural history of faith in which science not only provided support to religious belief but was analogous to the progress of this knowledge. Abbott sought to promote the apprehension of mystery in God without the crutch of miracles. Although his religious ideas were largely undermined by their inherent relativism, the broader dimensional concept still found a place in modern Christian theology. *Flatland* proved highly influential, spawning numerous books, some of them mathematical – such as Dionys Burger's *Sphereland* (1965), A. K. Dewdney's two-dimensional *The Planiverse* (1983) and Ian Stewart's *Flatterland* (2001) – and several films, as well as comment from cosmologists and comedians.[45]

Non-Euclidean geometry required a return to the very definitions of 'point' and 'line', and a rethinking of the concept of the plane. It also led to the development of a more general theory of surfaces – understood as complex curves – and particularly minimal surfaces. In mathematics, a minimal surface locally minimizes its area, and has a 'mean curvature' of zero. Significant examples are found in highly attenuated soap films, created by the powerful physical force of surface tension, as in the plane or curved minimal surfaces formed when a wire loop is dipped in soapy water and withdrawn, their shapes determined by the shape of the loop. Down to about 1980, only three examples of minimal surfaces were known: plane, catenoid and helicoid. Recent work, dependent on massive computer power, has greatly increased the variety of topological shapes that satisfy the conditions required of minimal surfaces, though these are rarely visually flat and often appear contorted. The application of such forms has proved fruitful in areas such as architecture, just as ancient knowledge that in the plane the circle encloses the greatest surface area had great practical significance.[46]

All of these features of non-Euclidean geometry contribute to a malleable concept of flatness. Not only is it appropriate to see flatness in vertical and inclined planes, as well as in the horizontal, but it is equally valid to identify the quality of flatness in three-dimensional spaces, and to see flatness in seemingly contorted shapes.[47]

Statistical flatness

The fundamental principles underlying measures of flatness of all sorts are statistical. These measures apply not only to material surfaces, whether manufactured or natural, but to arrays of statistical data not necessarily distributed in space. Data collected from a human population, for example, can be displayed as a frequency distribution by means of a line graph or histogram, and its shape measured or compared with other curves or consistent surfaces, from earth movements and sound to urban profiles and manufactured materials such as saws and corrugated iron. Generally, a flat or straight line indicates invariance, the standard against which deviations can be measured.

The assumption is that any frequency distribution must be plotted against straight (flat) lines, the x and y axes of the graph. The measures applied are generally regarded as part of descriptive statistics, used together with measures of central tendency such as the mean and median, symmetry and skewness (whether the data are skewed to right or left, and the length of the 'tail'). Particularly in engineering, flatness, superflatness and hyperflatness are statistical measures of the shape of a frequency distribution, first applied to material surfaces such as concrete floors, and only later embraced by art and cultural critics. Another statistical measure, known as kurtosis, comes closer to concepts of perceived landscape flatness. Kurtosis was commonly employed throughout the twentieth century, understood as a measure of whether data are peaked or flat relative to a normal distribution. Its inventor Karl Pearson called this the degree of flat-toppedness, but the word 'platykurtosis' was sometimes employed, drawing on the more ancient usage that equated 'plat' and 'flat'. Although there are good reasons for abandoning the supposed statistical association between kurtosis and peakedness, the measure persists in texts for the earth sciences.[48]

One important application of these statistical concepts occurs in the analysis of sound. Here, the sound spectrum can be recorded in terms of the amount of vibration in each frequency (which will vary with loudness and pitch), as, for example, in samples of speech, birdsong or electronic music. The data are then compared with an expected pattern across the spectrum, and the degree of difference is measured. The most common measure is 'spectral flatness', which can be used to identify matches between sequences and to support audio fingerprinting. It is also applied to 'white noise', meaning a random acoustic signal of constant spectral density, typically heard as a hissing sound. Essentially, the spectral flatness measure quantifies how equal or random the data distribution is. When the magnitudes are uniform (as in a persistent drone) or are completely random (white noise), the measure equals one, whereas at the other extreme (when there is a single outstanding peak in the sequence), the value is zero.[49] The method follows both the best-fit theory of statistical flatness and the definition of flatness as invariance.

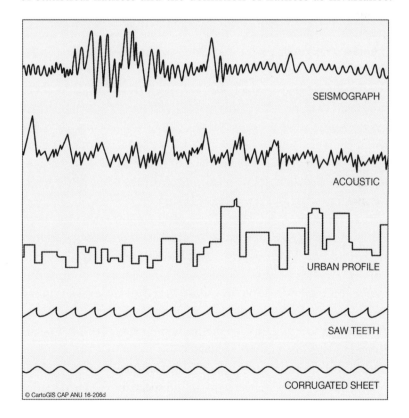

SEISMOGRAPH

ACOUSTIC

URBAN PROFILE

SAW TEETH

CORRUGATED SHEET

© CartoGIS CAP ANU 16-206d

Deviations from the flatline: seismograph, acoustic, urban profile, saw teeth, corrugated sheet.

Importantly, as in most measures of flatness, it gives topographic qualities to sound, opening the door for the concept 'soundscape'.

In the precision engineering of surfaces, it is assumed that absolute flatness cannot be achieved and does not exist in nature. Rather, flatness is always a matter of degrees of tolerance and of perception. In engineering, the measurement and monitoring of almost-perfect flatness or 'absolute planarity' is a major enterprise, vital to medicine, optics and construction. It is applied, for example, in the finishing of mirror glass for telescopes, synchrotrons and lenses; the electropolishing of steel plate, carbon panels, machine-tool tables and granite; and cast-iron surface plates. In medical technologies, tolerance of variation is small, and minor arbitrary variations can be life-threatening, whereas in the levelling of a field for irrigation, much more roughness is allowed. The tolerances acceptable in steel rolling mills fall somewhere between these extremes.[50] Regulations and standards can be established to control the allowable limits of variation within a 'tolerance zone'.[51]

The definition of what is flat and what is not flat depends on judgement as to allowable deformation, and remains open to debate and refinement. For these purposes, flatness is defined as 'the maximum distance between two perfect, parallel reference planes between which is placed the surface of interest'. Thus flatness can be calculated as an absolute maximum or as the mean deviation of the surface from the perfect plane (using the Gaussian method of least-squares, in which errors in multiple equations are limited to the sum of the squares of the errors). Most techniques depend on dividing the surface into a grid before measuring deviations from an ideal plane, or testing the tilt or slope at each point to find height differences relative to a designated zero elevation point, sometimes using triangulation.[52] Overall, there is substantial similarity in the fundamental methods and images applied to quite different materials, but typically referring back to the fundamental landscape model.

The roughness of a sheet of paper, for example, can be measured using profilometry – moving a stylus across the surface and recording vertical movements caused by irregularities – and calculating

The textured microtopography of a carpet presents measurement challenges similar to those found in the relative roughness of the surface of a sheet of paper.

indexes such as mean, minimum and maximum 'peak to valley height', the total 'peak count' and 'mean peak spacing'. The 'printability' of newsprint is determined in part by its surface roughness, measured by profilometry but alternatively by the so-called Bendtsen roughness test, which measures the amount of air that can flow through a sheet of paper clamped between a glass plate and a metal surface.[53]

In some applications – in common use until recent times – the techniques are more arbitrary. For example, in building construction, the straightedge method involves the surveyor laying a metal bar on the surface – a concrete floor or wall – measuring the maximum deviation under it, and then comparing it with allowable tolerances at selected points, but without clear rules guiding exactly where the straightedge should be placed. The time taken to make each measurement means that the distribution of points will be sparse. Further, in this method, the degree of deviation depends directly on the length of the straightedge: 2 or 3 metres for control of global flatness, and 0.2 or 0.3 metres for local flatness. Both measures are important: a floor might be quite level overall but contain pockets of irregularity, making walking across it uncomfortable or even hazardous. Similar techniques are applied to the measurement of flatness in steel plate, using standardized gauges first advocated by Joseph Whitworth in the 1840s. Here too concepts rooted in landscape analogies – such as peak-to-valley or uphill and downhill measurements – persist.[54]

Major innovations contributing to the more precise measurement of flatness, and doing it relatively cheaply, are the computer and the laser. However, computing power remained relatively limited until the 1980s, and the analysis of data time-consuming. It was necessary first to collect data for individual grid coordinates, using tools such as spirit levels and collimators (beam-focusing tools, first thought of by Gauss, who used them in astronomy), and then punching cards or tape to create input for analysis – using programs with names such as FLATEST, written for Fortran – in order to identify points of departure from the perfect plane.[55] Modern fast computers solve only some of these problems. More important for the measurement of flatness is the laser.

Terrestrial Laser Scanning has revolutionized surveying work and, particularly when automated, can deliver more reliable

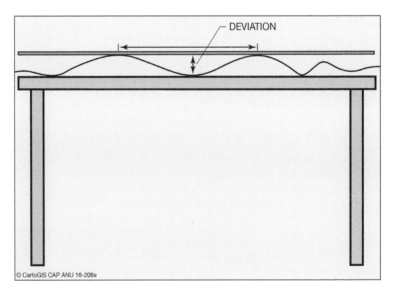

Measurement of flatness in steel products.

dimensional control than methods dependent on sampling points for the measurement of manifested flatness or 'surface regularity'. In this new method, a scanner sweeps the surrounding space with a laser light to collect three-dimensional data points at high density – collecting almost one million points per second – with the capacity to classify surfaces as not only 'flat' but 'super flat'. Even steel moved rapidly across roller tables, with severe vibration, can be measured this way, by recording variation between two parallel laser-projected lines. Terrestrial Laser Scanning is applied across a wide field of applications, particularly building and construction, which require accurate measurement to avoid structural failure and loss of life, but the tolerances are greater than those required in scientific or medical technologies.[56]

Other techniques of profile measurement – most of them still expensive when applied to large objects – include interferometry (an electromagnetic method of identifying surface irregularities, matched by holographic interferometry which uses lasers) and deflectometry (using a collimated optical beam and achieving a superior degree of certainty). Absolute measurements of flatness exploit the straightness of light propagation and the basic law of reflection, calibrated to national angle references. With the most sophisticated technologies, uncertainty can be reduced to less than a nanometre (one billionth of a metre). This, of course, refers to the ability to measure deviations, not to the actual flatness of a surface itself. Outside these super-refined conditions, however, problems arise when internal reference planes – dependent on laser beams, flat tables and mechanical rails, for example – prove themselves insufficiently flat.[57] Any flatness measure is, ultimately, a relative measure. The perfect plane is something for the imagination, rather than the hard reality of the bulky surfaces we commonly experience, whether natural or engineered.

Topographic flatness

As with so much else in the concept of flatness, the problem of scale is at the very core of topographic mapping. Global geodesy takes as

its model the perfect circularity of the sphere, whereas the measurement of small regions employs the (perfect) tangent plane. Both of
these models approximate nature but only at particular scales. Thus
global geodesy is concerned with the figure of the Earth (and its
gravity field), including the surface beneath the seas. Curvature and
gravity must also be taken into account in the geodetic survey of
large regions or nation states, in which the surface can be thought
of as an ellipsoid. On the other hand, although tied to reference
points established by such methods, in the plane survey of smaller
areas, the horizontal plane is generally an adequate standard, thus
depending on the assumption of local flatness in the midst of a
much larger curvature.

Although global geodesy might seem to have little to do with
landscape flatness, early attempts to measure the radius of the Earth,
and hence its curvature, did sometimes depend on observations
of distant horizons, seen from a high mountain. For example, in
the early eleventh century CE, the Islamic scholar al-Bīrūnī, best
known as a mathematician and astronomer, wrote that he found
in the Punjab 'a mountain peak facing toward a wide flat plain
whose flatness served as the smooth surface of the sea', enabling

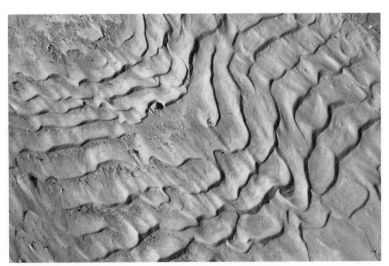

Mudflow, Mac Clarke Conservation Reserve, Simpson Desert, Northern Territory, Australia, 2015.

observations of the angle of dip to the horizon. Several kinds of measurement error crept into his calculations, including a failure to account for refraction. The basic principles depended not only on the visibility enabled by the flatness of the landscape but on the visualization of abstract geometric planes.[58] What al-Bīrūnī demonstrated is the advantage of applying abstract plane geometry on a flat earth surface.

A similar kind of spatial abstraction is essential to some of the earliest known maps, from Mesopotamia, which were little concerned with relief but served rather to establish the boundaries of agricultural units and monitor irrigation. These cadastral plans were needed because of the natural flooding of the flat riverine plains. These were regularly inundated by waters, which made their own natural level as well as upsetting markers on the land. The revolutionary idea essential to thinking this way was the concept of the abstract plane on which a model of the land could be conceived in terms of points and lines – which are themselves abstract concepts – and distances measured to scale.

Land surveying depends on the measurement of angles and distances in the vertical and the horizontal plane. The vertical at any point can be identified by a plumb-bob, its string pointing to the centre of the Earth. The horizontal is any line which is normal to the vertical, with an angle of 90°. Both the vertical and the horizontal are different at every point on the Earth's surface, but for small land units, as in cadastral mapping, these variations can be ignored. In practice, whereas the vertical is a true vector, it is impossible to measure the horizontal directly on the physical land surface, and typically it is measured at about 1 metre above.

From the seventeenth century, simple surveys were carried out using a plane table, a flat board mounted on a tripod, levelled using a spirit level. The survey was drawn directly on a sheet of paper stretched over the plane table, by sighting angles and making measurements in proportion. Every time the plane table was moved, up and down a slope, it was levelled in the same way, hence at a different horizontal. The fundamental assumption was that the land being surveyed was flat; differences in height above ground level

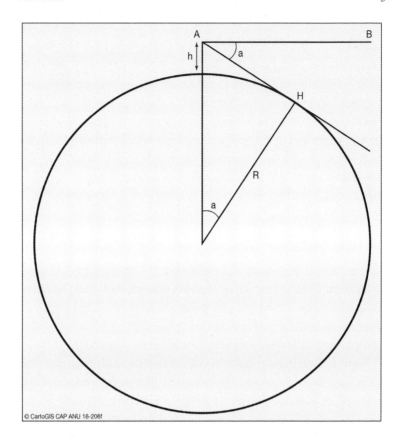

© CartoGIS CAP ANU 16-206f

Al-Bīrūnī's measurement of the radius of the Earth. The line AB is the tangent plane, touching the top of the mountain, and AH is the tangent plane touching the earth-circle at the horizon; where H is the horizon, *h* the height of the mountain and *a* the angle of dip to the horizon, equivalent to the angle at the centre of the Earth, and R is the radius. In addition to these two tangent planes, measurement of the height of the mountain *h* also depended on an imagined plane, passing through the base of the mountain and the point of observation, from which al-Bīrūnī took two altitudes.

could be read off graduated staffs and angles of elevation could be taken using instruments known generically as levels, but doing so was often seen as a separate operation. From the early nineteenth century, theodolites were used to make sightings, the readings booked and transformed into a flat map on paper in the surveyor's office. In setting up the theodolite, it was equally important that its axis of rotation should be normal to the plane of the horizontal circle. Whichever technology was employed, the 'levelling' of the instrument was essential. Electronic versions of theodolites and levels became common from the 1960s but the principles remained the same.[59]

The ability to view Earth from space opened up new ways of measuring surface elevations, using sensors carried by satellites. Employing the same basic principles as applied in aerial photography, digital stereo images can be created in bands from data generated by Advanced Spaceborne Thermal Emission and Reflection Radiometer (ASTER) satellite imagery to build up Digital Elevation Models (DEMs). These have great attractions, particularly because of their simplicity and the fact that many DEM products are available free of charge, but they often show poor resolution and spatial coverage, making them good for regional analysis but of limited application in small-scale studies. Further, although digital techniques have enabled massive advances in terrain analysis, they typically remain dependent on square-gridded or triangulated elevation data and exhibit errors of various magnitudes as well as uncertainty.[60]

One of the more important aspects of the problem is found in the analysis of topographic slope. Observation and smoothing error can have serious consequences for predictions of, for example, flooding and settlement planning. Fortunately for flatness, error in slope gradient measurement is least in flat areas (with values below 1°), which often have the most problematic hydrology, and greatest in mountainous zones (with slopes greater than 35°) and narrow valley floors. Less fortunately, valley bottoms are often quite flat but difficult to distinguish from surrounding hillslopes, particularly on maps where the contours are likely to be sparse, thus requiring a specific 'flatness index' when derived from DEMs.[61]

As with engineered surfaces, the measurement of land flatness typically begins with division of a territory or map into a grid of squares or data points. Erwin Raisz employed this method in 1948 to produce 'flatland ratio maps', by calculating the percentage of area in each square (or topographic map sheet) falling below an agreed slope, then plotting the values and creating isopleths. Raisz saw these maps as primarily of value to farmers, so distinguished only two categories: 'lands flat enough for plowing' and 'slope lands'. Alternative methods include counting the number of contour crossings around the edges of grid squares or quadrats, to produce 'isoclinal' maps; and counting contour crossings along straight lines drawn across a base map, to create 'average slope' maps. These calculations became increasingly popular when electronic computers made them easier – beginning in the 1960s, long before satellite images became available – and were used to produce primitive digital maps of terrain. Typically, such early terrain mapping left blank those areas in which most altitudes were identical, and slope and convexity could not be calculated. These were the 'flat' areas – marked by their emptiness and invariance.[62]

Geomorphologists have often been less precise, measuring relative relief rather than slope. Relative relief is the difference between the lowest and highest points in a land unit, sometimes referred to as 'local relief'. This measurement can be taken directly from contour maps. For example, in the 1940s one system attributed local relief of less than 15 metres to 'flat plains', 15–45 metres to 'undulating plains', 45–90 metres to 'rolling plains', and 90–150 metres to 'rough dissected plains'. Similarly, 'floodplains' have been defined as terrain rising less than 15 metres above the stream surface in a channel network. The geomorphologist Arthur N. Strahler combined slope and elevation but only in subjective terms, defining a plain simply as 'a land area whose surface is nearly flat or gently rolling and whose elevation is usually low'.[63]

For the geographer, the challenge is to construct maps of very large areas – continents or the whole world – that represent the topography objectively by means of a small number of types or classes. Here flatness is a relatively recent inclusion in the system of classification. When the cartographer Edwin H. Hammond attempted a solution in the 1950s, he found eight basic terrain types, the first of them labelled 'nearly flat plains'. In devising his system of classification, Hammond concluded that the most important characteristics are relative relief, profile and 'flatness'. He discovered that 'flatness' could be 'expressed in a surprisingly useful manner by the fraction of the given area which has an inclination less than some chosen boundary values'. For this purpose, Hammond equated 'near-level land' with a generous slope of less than 8 per cent, or 4.6°. On his map of North America, the category 'nearly flat plains', together with 'rolling and irregular plains', dominates the vast middle of the continent, and almost 90 per cent of Florida. Hammond also produced a map of South America, showing 'nearly flat plains' only in the great river valleys.[64]

In the 1960s Hammond contributed to a text on physical geography in which 'plains' were defined as 'having a predominance of gently sloping land, coupled with low relief' of less than 90 metres, whereas in the extreme category 'flat plains', more than 80 per cent of the area was defined as 'gentle slope', with local relief under 30 metres. Probably 'gently sloping' was intended to match the generous measure advanced by Hammond in this earlier work. A world map showing the various 'land-surface types' was offered, on which generalization makes Florida 100 per cent 'flat plains'. These measures of 'plains' and 'flat plains' remain in currency.[65]

Classification has also occupied pedologists, who believe that slope plays a significant role in the formation of soils. For example, K. M. Clayton has compiled a useful comparative sample in which both 'flat' and 'flat or almost flat' are slopes of less than 1°, which may also be described as 'almost level', whereas 'level' is below 0.5°. A more generous classification makes anything under 2° 'level to very gentle', corresponding to 'what are thought of as "flat" areas in typical erosional landscapes' and for practical purposes, including agriculture, said to fall into the 'no-limitation' category. These definitions have fairly general acceptance.[66]

Following in the tradition of the geomorphologist William Morris Davis, soil science has often focused on down-wearing or slope decline, assuming that 'normal' topography is undulating, neither flat nor steep. In this doctrine, flat sites are described as 'not normal' because they promote the overdevelopment of some 'horizons', as, for example, the clay of claypans, at the expense of a series of strata.[67] The same applies to level sites created from alluvium, loess or till, where the soil smooths over underlying relief, giving support to the association of flatness with uniformity of material and structure. On the other hand, soil struggles to form on slopes of more than 40°, so that mountainsides and cliffs are often as barren as are dessicated flat places.

The global distribution of slope angles is neither random nor normally distributed. Rather, there is a clustering at certain angles, including 45° and 40° at one extreme and 5° and 2° at the other, with angles greater than 50° called cliffs and those less than 2° flats. More broadly, surfaces with angles less than 5° have been classified as flat, 'as a reasonable boundary figure' but lacking objective criteria. The landscape also contains identifiable (measurable) discontinuities, at different levels of regional scale.[68]

In their statistical study of the relative flatness of the states of the u.s., the geographers Jerome E. Dobson and Joshua S. Campbell focus on the act of viewing the land, and point to the contrast between popular perceptions and measured topographies. In order to study the question, Dobson and Campbell sought 'a specific measure of flatness that would mimic human perception at close range'. They derive this measure from the visibility-at-sea model, in which it is established that an observer standing 1.83 metres tall can see the horizon at 5,310 metres. On land, they begin with 90-metre cells, projecting sixteen radians from the centre of each, continuing out 5,310 metres along the ray or measuring the angle if the ray intersects a higher cell on the terrain before reaching this distance. The results for the sixteen rays are then classified into 'flat or not-flat' categories, using the angle 0.32° as the cut-off point. The choice of this angle was based on 'personal experience with Great Plains landscapes'. From these measurements, Dobson and Campbell calculated a 'flat index' by classifying each ray as flat (1) or not-flat (0), and then adding to give each cell a score of zero to sixteen. Finally, they created four classes: 'not flat (0–4), flat (5–8), flatter (9–12), and flattest (13–16)'. A cell scoring sixteen was flat in every direction.[69]

As in Dobson and Campbell's model, the experience of crossing a flat plain has often been compared with voyaging on the ocean. Once again, the question of scale is vital to perception. Thus, although the sea's surface can vary from the flatness of the 'millpond'

to the 'mountainous' seas of the Roaring Forties, oceanic waves
rarely exceed 10 metres in height, measured from trough to crest.
Mountainous seas are temporary, and the mountains and valleys
of the seabed are hidden. Thus Earth's water surface is indeed very
smooth – locally flat – and accounts for 71 per cent of the total area.
Even the land mountains and valleys that appear so dramatic are
mere dimples on the surface of the globe. Whereas the equatorial
radius of the Earth is 6,378 kilometres, the highest land point reaches
a mere 8,848 metres and the hidden deepest ocean point only 11,040
metres, a difference of less than 20 kilometres. These basic metrics
are proof of the power of gravity to shape the overall form of the
Earth, and the relatively puny power of geological forces, however
cataclysmic. Gravity may appear weak in everyday life – we can
easily throw a ball into the air – but it has a cumulative effect and

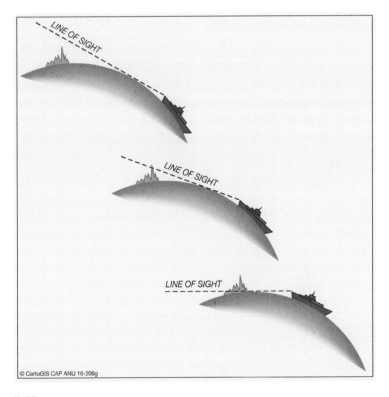

Visibility at sea.

determines the shape of any object with a diameter greater than about 500 kilometres.[70] The result is a universe of spherical bodies.

However true this may be, in everyday practical life on land – where almost all of us live – we still perceive certain local landscapes as flat, and extend the description to nation-states and even continents. The result is a conflict between our plastic perception of space and our capacity to establish absolute flatness. Further, flatness is a quality rather than a topographic feature that can be given a name, as in 'mountain' or 'valley'. Even such 'features' are difficult to identify and measure because mountains, valleys, cliffs, plains, rivers, waterfalls and seas all belong to a larger continuous surface, Earth, and its atmospheric envelope.[71]

Flatness presents a particular ontological problem. Whether or not we can say that plains and mountains really exist is unimportant so long we as we can agree that it is useful to name them as such. If flatness is understood as an absence or lack, it may seem to represent a mere blank, an emptiness, denied true existence. However, understood as an attribute, rather than an object, flatness has both a useful and measurable place in ways of perceiving the physical world and in living in that world. These perceptions also contribute substantially to human reflection on the meaning of life and the origins of the universe: does flatness need to be shaped or is it primordial?

THREE

FLATNESS IN EARTH HISTORY

'On the plains, the earth meets the sky in a sharp black line so regular that it seems as though drawn by a creator interested more in geometry than the hills and valleys of the Old Testament.'

Jill Ker Conway, 1989[1]

Throughout the universe, the most important factor in the geomorphology of any body is its surface gravity, which is a direct function of the body's mass. In the very long term, therefore, the overwhelming tendency is always towards sphericity, something we can see with the naked eye or telescope. Were we able to stand on the surfaces of the largest bodies (with the greatest mass), we would see them to possess an immense flatness. Up close, seen from space probes, their surfaces appear much more varied, pockmarked and roughened, the variations resulting from many local factors, temporarily defying the long drift to flatness and their inevitable sphericity. Viewed from space, Earth sits firmly in place, a solid detached object that is almost perfectly round and smooth. This is, however, a recent and uncommon perspective. For most of human history, we have looked to the heavens to try to make sense of our Earth.

Creation myths

When human beings first began to ponder the shape of their world, and to wonder about its origin, they seem most often to have assumed that it was flat. Although there is no direct evidence of this belief, it can be deduced from the many creation myths that have survived, together with ethnographic evidence, which in turn point to more ancient ideas. The earliest known sources for India – the Vedic texts, from the late second millennium BCE – see the cosmos as originally a tripartite unity, forced apart by divine power to form Earth, space and heaven. In ancient and early medieval India, however, Sanskrit texts compiled between the fifth and ninth centuries CE offered a different picture, representing the Earth as 'a flat circular disk' at the centre of an egg-shaped cosmos. In this model, the Earth's diameter is approximately 5 billion kilometres in extent, the whole teeming with beings of all sorts. Beside this image, Indian astronomers conceived a 'scientific' geocentric universe, but one that was never strictly separated from sacred mythology.[2]

Myths from Central Africa refer to earth being 'rolled out like a mat' or assume a simple flatness before the making of hills and valleys. Similarly, the psalmist said that Jahweh 'stretched out the earth above the waters' (Psalms 136:6). The Qur'an declares: 'And the earth We have spread out (Like a carpet); set thereon Mountains firm and immovable.' The image of the carpet is repeated, the eternal mountains serving as weights or pegs to hold it in place, and 'God it was Who levelled out the earth for you, that you may travel its diverse roads.'[3]

Genesis, some argue, sees the perfect landscape of the Garden of Eden as an oasis in a landscape of sand, a grassy carpet or lawn. Others find it closer to a plateau – closer to heaven – or a cosmic mountain, from which rivers could flow. Many scholars have pointed to continuity with the topography and mythology of ancient Sumer and the Elysian plain of Homer's *Odyssey*. Medieval writers found the mountain model more compelling: Alexander Neckam, in the thirteenth century, claimed that 'the earthly paradise had escaped the flood because it was on the top of a mountain that reached to the moon.' In the fourteenth century Dante's *Divine Comedy* placed it on the top of the mountain of Purgatory, the highest point of the Earth's surface. Cartographers had no difficulty finding a spot for paradise on their world maps, generally somewhere in the 'East' and sometimes sited on an island. In Christian theology, paradise drifted upwards – to a higher plane – closer and closer to the heavens, eventually settling in a Christian idea of heaven, towards which souls must climb or fly. Those who continued to believe in the earthly paradise as a real place, up until the eighteenth century, typically located it on the highest of high mountains, beyond reach of the Flood. It might even have been in Brazil, where God created Man, and the Flood was unknown.[4]

Understanding the surface of the Earth as flat raised difficult questions: how did the Earth remain stable and how could the rising and setting of the sun and the movement of the stars be explained? The heavens preoccupied mythmakers, partly because in clear conditions (as are now rare in most places) the stars shone brilliantly and seemed quite near, pressing down on the skywatcher, yet unreachable and unknowable. On the other hand, it took only a little terrestrial wandering to see that the apparent meeting of earth and sky at the horizon was an illusion. This raised the possibility that the apparent curvature of the heavenly canopy and the apparent fundamental flatness of Earth were equally illusory. An attractive solution, adopted by many cultures, was to imagine Earth as a disc, floating on a sea, covered by a solid dome. In this geocentric model, the flat earth is stable and stationary, the celestial bodies moving across the heavens. The principal purpose of this model was to explain the relationship between earth and sky, the real mystery. This was a mystery of the perceived universe, rather than the origins of God or of space. Matter requires an act of creation but space is just *there*, limitless. Space is taken as a given, not something that needs to be created: an understanding that contributes to the naturalness of concepts of flatness.[5]

Some theories of the origins of the universe assume the pre-existence of materials, in a state of chaos, in which the sky must first be separated from the earth, sometimes solid but often a watery surface completely covered by sea and swamps, and naturally flat; or heaven and earth may resemble a pair of enormous discs stretching to the horizon. Separation might also occur in multiples: upper earth (inhabited by human beings), middle earth and lower earth (the underworld), for example, found in Babylonian myth, and matched by equivalent levels in the heavens. Other creation myths are cosmic: supreme deities exist in an emptiness or void before creating the universe from nothing, *creatio ex nihilo*. Yet again, creation may begin with an initial separation or union of Father Sky and Mother Earth; or a being might dive from the sky to pull earth up out of the primordial waters, to float as an island.[6] Varieties of mythic models are sometimes combined; gods can be born or created during the process; and some societies have multiple creation myths, composed for different political or religious purposes.

The early Maya of Central America sacralized their entire universe, ascribing deities to many things ranging from geographical features to numbers and ancestors, driven by the calendar that controlled their 'conceptual cosmogram'. The Maya cosmogram had thirteen levels of heavens and nine levels of underworld, each of these levels personified in a deity and structured as a plane. The planes were schematic, often ascending a massive sacred tree, as was perhaps appropriate for a rainforest people, and inhabited by beings and forces that controlled time as well as space, through the 'spatialization' of the calendar. The 'great horizontal plane of the earth' was located between the upper heavens and the underworlds of death and night, the surface of Earth sometimes represented as a monster deity or turtle floating in an immense lake.[7]

Most people, everywhere, saw themselves as located at the centre of things. Most inhabited quite limited territories, small worlds. Even the peoples of large states – including the Chinese – long remained ethnocentric. Thus the horizon of the world was best represented by the circle, and the circle similarly charted the shape of the cosmos.[8] The seasonal circle lent itself to calendrical division and the identification of the cardinal directions, but even these were not essential at the local scale. Such understanding did not lead inevitably to the concept of sphericity, and the flat-earth model went unchallenged for a very long time.

The Greeks – credited as advanced thinkers – held on to this model until the sixth century BCE, and it survived the emergence of early abstract geometry. Thus Thales of Miletus (b. *c.* 625 BCE), who was acknowledged by the Greeks as the founder of physical

Ch'ŏnha Chegukto (Map of the Countries of the World), Korea, *c.* 1750.

science, believed that the earth both originates in and returns to water. According to Aristotle, Thales saw water as eternal (and therefore divine, full of gods) and thought that the earth rests on water rather like a log floating on a sea. However, pupils of Thales saw the Earth – and the moon and stars – as flat bodies, surrounded by air, which would naturally fall but were able to 'ride upon air on account of their flatness', rather like flat leaves. This was a potentially unstable cosmology in which the Earth did not even occupy the centre. Some of the ideas might have been borrowed from the Mesopotamians and the Jews, just as Thales may have drawn on Egyptian land measurement for the foundations of his geometry.[9]

There are good practical reasons for observing the fact that the Earth is spherical rather than flat. At sea, ships and islands disappear over the horizon, the tops of their masts and peaks disappearing last of all; and the flat surface of the sea and the steppe seem to curve at the horizon. The higher up a mountain, the wider the view. The solution proved no great challenge to creationist thought, which was always much more concerned with the thorny issue of explaining the emergence of life. Indeed, because the circle and the sphere were seen as the most perfect of all the geometric figures – surpassing the simple purity of the plane – it seemed justified to believe that creation had applied these to every element of the cosmos and its motion. After all, the sphere is not only absolutely the surface of minimum area to volume, but unusual in also itself enclosing space and in its impressive stability. It is the shape assumed not only by the Earth but by a raindrop or a unicellular organism.

By around 350 BCE Plato could talk of the Earth as a divinely created, intelligent entity made up of earth, water, air, fire and a soul, and with the most perfect and beautiful of all shapes, that of the sphere. The astronomical problem – how to explain the motion of celestial objects – was resolved, unsatisfactorily, by situating the spherical Earth motionless at the centre of the universe, surrounded by series of concentric spheres which carry all the celestial bodies and revolve daily around the axis of the heavens. To attempt to account for the observed facts, the number of these spheres was increased by the Aristotelians, to more than fifty. By the time of Eratosthenes (c. 275–194 BCE) – the librarian of Alexandria – the size of the Earth could be calculated to a high degree of accuracy, though the size and shape of the cosmos remained a mystery.[10]

In ancient China, three competing models coexisted, associated with different schools of cosmological thought. Probably the oldest was the Kai Thien theory, in which the Earth is understood to be 'a bowl turned upside down', covered by the heavens, making two concentric domes. The vault rotated, floating on the rim-ocean. Confusingly, this school 'asserted that the heavens are round in shape like an open umbrella, while the earth is square like a chessboard'. The Hun Thien (celestial sphere) school saw spherical motions in the heavens, centred on Earth, and pointed clearly to the notion of a spherical rather than square and flat earth, and the possibility that space is infinite. This theory, which resembled Greek ideas from the fifth century BCE, became dominant in China. The third theory emerged later, in the first and second centuries CE, visualizing space as infinite and empty, the celestial bodies not tied to concentric spheres of any kind but floating in space. It was an advanced conception but with a Taoist connection to the idea of a 'great emptiness'. The supposed centrality of Earth shrinks to nothing in the immensity of the universe.[11]

The flatness problem

Many models of the universe assume that spatial homogeneity extends beyond our visual horizon, forever. Today, the most widely accepted model of the universe, based on astronomical observation, sees it as 'flat or very close to flat'. In this context, however, flatness does not mean that the universe possesses a two-dimensional or planar surface but rather that the rules are the same throughout the universe. The fundamental principle of invariance is maintained, but it is necessary to think of it in a different way. Local, small variations due to gravitational inequalities exist – as Einstein showed – but in this model, it is possible to talk of a 'flat universe' with a 'flat geometry', a universe in which the rules of Euclidean geometry apply. Here the constant spatial curvature of the universe k has a value of zero, and the implication is that the universe is infinite because it must look the same from all points (and have no edge).[12]

Non-Euclidean geometries, however, indicate that k might be positive or negative, rather than the zero of the flat universe. A positive value of k would conform with a spherical geometry, in which the assumption of isotropy (looking the same from all points) applies and there are no edges, but a surface finite in extent. On this surface, we will always come back to where we started: triangles add up to more than 180°, and lines of longitude are straight and parallel at the equator but meet at the poles. Such a finite system is known as a 'closed universe'. This model was first advanced by the French mathematician Henri Poincaré, who argued that a universe may be conceived in which 'straight lines' would not be rectilinear, and non-Euclidean 'planes' could intersect. Data derived from microwave space probes has recently given support to such a 'Poincaré dodecahedral space', but things look different at different scales, and it remains a question whether we inhabit a 'small closed universe' or occupy just one expanding bubble in the midst of innumerable others. Alternatively, where k is negative, a hyperbolic (saddle-like) geometry applies, in which space can be 'negatively curved', parallel lines diverge rather than converge, and triangles add up to less than 180°, creating an 'open universe'.[13]

Beyond the values of k is the question of their stability over time. Whereas the current energy density of the universe is observed to be 'flat' – corresponding to a model of the universe dominated by matter – the Big Bang theory requires an increasing deviation from the flat model of the evolution of the universe, suggesting that its geometry is unstable. Thus the 'flatness problem' in cosmology asks: why should the initial energy density of the universe be so finely tuned that it is equal, or almost equal, to the critical value $k = 0$? One solution could be that the universe was created with precisely the flat geometry known from observation, and that this would persist throughout time. An alternative solution is offered by the theory of 'inflation', first advanced in the 1980s. In this model, the early universe experiences a period of massively accelerated expansion, which comes to an end only when the geometry comes very close to flatness, with k approaching zero. The flatness problem remains.[14]

The question of time also concerns the cosmological theories of many ancient societies, in which 'the horizontal universe' and indeed life itself can be understood only as part of the 'unceasing flow of time'. The Maya, for example, says the anthropologist Miguel León-Portilla, constituted space and time as 'a homogeneous entity' or at least believed that 'Isolated from time, space becomes inconceivable.' Without time, nothing would have meaning and there would be a return to 'primeval darkness'. In these models, time is marked out in space by the movement of the celestial bodies and changes projected onto the flat earth. It is the flow of time that imbues the landscape with sacred or supernatural features.[15] Such models were not much disturbed by the concept of a heliocentric solar system, developed in the West in the sixteenth and seventeenth centuries, or by Isaac Newton's discovery of force vectors which seemed absolute even when projected into the heavens. What proved more unsettling was the idea that time and space might be the same thing.

In physics, Einstein gave birth to the idea of the block universe, in which there exists only a unitary four-dimensional space-time or 'block' of events that represents all places and all times. In this universe, there is no past or future, no up or down: everything happens at once. It is a world drastically different from the one we perceive. Thus it is not surprising that physicists cannot agree on the reality of this four-dimensional world or what it looks like. In physics, both three-dimensional and four-dimensional descriptions of the material world are consistent with the science and can be used interchangeably. This is because the observable world is not a 'flat 3D space' but contains light from the past. When we look into the distance, we look into the past. This is our observable universe. For example, we see the sun as it was about eight minutes ago; if it suddenly exploded, it would not even exist, but we would observe it in our present. Here lies the absolute present of Newtonian physics, in which the 'light cone' within which we can observe the world as three-dimensional forms a 'flat hypersurface' where time is zero, and the world is 'intrinsically flat'. However, if we abandon this 'flat geometry' and allow Gaussian curvature, the hypersurface of the light cone curves into four dimensions and the observable world is 'extrinsically curved'.[16]

It is striking that – within the observable universe – most galaxies belong to just two essential types: discs and spheres, matching the leading models found in creation myths and ancient science. The first kind of galaxy is shaped like a flattened disc, composed of spiral arms. More numerous are elliptical galaxies, many of them close to spherical. Knowledge of these shapes was first established in the late eighteenth century, through astronomical observation, but it was not proved until 1952 that our own galaxy, the Milky Way, is typical rather than unique, and that the solar system is not at its centre. We now know it to be just one in the immense number of galaxies in the visible universe, a 'galactic plane' marked by its character as a flat disc, about 100,000 light years in diameter but a mere 1,000 light years thick. Its flatness is shared with the shape of the solar system.[17]

In thinking about the 'flatness' of the universe, it is useful to return to the question of scale. From a local perspective, the world immediately around us can appear uniform or chaotic, smooth or rough. The 'cosmological principle' declares that on a very large scale, everywhere looks much the same throughout the universe – that the universe is remarkably homogeneous and isotropic.[18] This principle fits neatly with the solution of the flatness problem offered by inflationary cosmology. It fits equally well with the concept that the universe we can observe appears flat, in much the same way in which the surface of the ocean looks flat provided you can see only a small, calm region of it, rather than the local chaos of crashing waves or the great curve of the Earth. The same principle applies to the terrestrial surface, depending on the scale of observation.

Flat earth theories

The discovery that the Earth is not the centre of the universe but merely one of the many spherical bodies that make it up did not prevent the persistence of flat earth theories. Some of these theories were rooted in religious ideas and creation myths, but typically they sought their evidence in science and objective observation. Modern creationist thought, in opposition to the model of evolution, continues to focus on the problem of explaining life, with only minor concern for the shape of the land, and almost never adopts a flat earth theory of the world. Similarly, contemporary climate change sceptics do not claim that the world is flat. In spite of the lack of association, creationists and climate change sceptics have often been referred to as metaphorical 'flat-earthers', for their stubborn unwillingness to accept the obvious. The symbolism depends not only on the primitivity of the belief, but on the power of the fundamental concept of space to identify the depths of ignorance and the vacuity inherent in flatness.

It has sometimes been argued that the notion that the Earth is flat persisted among 'educated' Mediterranean people long after the ancient recognition of its sphericity. It proved hard for 'vulgar' opinion to deny 'the obvious truths of a flat earth, vaulted over by the arch of heaven', while occasionally it was argued that the inhabited world might not be spherical but merely the top half of a globe sliced in two with a flat base. Some historians also identify a retreat from the classical solution in the period from about 300 CE to 1300 CE, associating it with the rise of Christian ignorance. Central to this myth is Christopher Columbus, said to have set out to disprove the flat earth theory. It is now accepted that this is not an accurate picture of medieval geographical knowledge – at least among the knowledgeable, by the seventh century – and that the myth was an invention of nineteenth-century historians who overemphasized the writings of a handful of eccentrics.[19] Long-distance European, Chinese and Pacific Islander voyagers did not know what they might meet when they set out towards the horizon – how much might be water and how much land – but they must rarely have been persuaded by theories that saw them falling off the edge of the earth-disc or sailing across infinite expanses of flat ocean.

At the same time, throughout the medieval period, Latin and Greek cosmological literature was largely limited to European scholars and churchmen, and theoretical debate – including the idea that the Earth is square – persisted to the thirteenth century. Those who were able to read vernacular texts – romances and chronicles – probably visualized the world as a flat circle, divided in three in the manner of a T-O map, showing Asia, Africa and Europe occupying the three segments created by a T set in an O, and the outer band of the circle as an ocean. Those who could only listen mostly imagined the world as flat.[20] It can also be argued that, throughout the world, the many peoples who were not voyagers empirically thought of the world as flat. Even when the evidence that the Earth is a sphere was crystal clear, doubters remained.

Religious ideas were vital to the survival of flat earth theories. The debate experienced a revival in the nineteenth century as part of a broader debate over the validity of scientific knowledge, particularly where it seemed to contradict the Bible, and a challenge to the standing of science as an increasingly specialized and professionalized activity. In England, the modern movement began with Samuel Rowbotham (1816–1884), who engaged scientists in debate over literal interpretations of biblical texts. Taking the pseudonym Parallax, he argued in his book *Zetetic Astronomy: Earth not a Globe!* (1865) that the Earth is an immobile flat disc, with the North Pole at the centre, and surrounded by a never-ending wall of ice. His model of the universe was based on mathematical calculations, together with experiments designed to prove that the surface of the sea is flat and observations made along a 10-kilometre stretch of the Old Bedford Canal, in the flat landscape of the Fens, to deny convexity (the Bedford Level experiment). He also accepted a literal reading of Genesis, believing that the Earth was created in six days, was less than six thousand years old and would soon be consumed by fire.[21]

Parallax toured England giving public lectures. Often he was ridiculed and chased out of town. However, he also acquired disciples and notoriety, and by the 1870s concerned members of the scientific community – notably Alfred Russel Wallace – entered public debate and even took up wagers on the convexity of water surfaces. The flat-earthers were defeated, but they had no interest in accepting the 'science' and soldiered on. They understood zetetics as 'free enquiry' and emphasized the importance of questioning the authority of elite science. Fundamentally, their objective was to defend the literal truth of the Bible against the new knowledge of science, notably astronomy, geology and biology. They embraced flat earth theory in order to carry this attack to an extreme, even when they did not themselves truly believe. Organized flat-earthism began with the establishment of the Universal Zetetic Society in England in 1893, directed at the 'blasphemy' of science in its rejection of the truth of the Holy Scriptures. This was the same intellectual milieu that generated Abbott's *Flatland* of 1884, a work that challenged dimensional understanding while accepting the science behind the new mathematics.

Twentieth-century advocates of the case for a flat earth increasingly shifted their argument from the certainty of creationist readings of the Bible to a questioning of science. More experiments were

Prof. Orlando Ferguson, *Map of the Square and Stationary Earth*, Hot Springs, South Dakota, 1893:
'Four Hundred Passages in the Bible that Condemn the Globe Theory, or the Flying Earth, and None Sustain It.
This Map is the Bible Map of the World'.

conducted by the Zetetics, who typically claimed fraud and conspiracy when contradicted. Many rejected the reality of gravity, referring to Einstein as well as Newton. Some argued that space has four dimensions, but identified these as 'length, breadth, depth and height', rather than entering the world of non-Euclidean geometry. In the 1920s flat-earthers could still claim, 'The curve of the earth has never been seen, and celebrated airmen have declared it is non-existent.'[22]

By the 1930s flat-earth advocacy had shifted from England to the u.s., where Christian fundamentalism flourished. Belief in the reality of hell as well as heaven went together with the rejection of theories of gravity, evolution and modern astronomy and a (futile) search for explicit mention of flatness in the Bible. The model of the universe remained much the same as that described by Parallax. Experiments were once again carried out on large lakes, and the apparently new fact that Australians could stand upright without falling off the earth was introduced.[23]

Space exploration provided the ultimate challenge to flat earth theory, but also fuel for a new conspiracy theory. The founding of the International Flat Earth Research Society (IFERS), based in London, in 1956, was followed a year later by the orbiting of Earth by the Russian satellite Sputnik. The approach adopted was simply to dismiss the entire space programme, including the moon landings, as a hoax, and insist that the Earth is a plane disc of infinite dimensions, with the North Pole at its centre. Orbital space flight was no more than circling over a flat surface. Willingness to believe that the moon landing was indeed a fake encouraged interest in flat earth theory, and reconnected with a critique of science as blasphemy, but membership of IFERS, always tiny, plummeted. The Society was reincorporated in the U.S. in the 1970s, and then returned to London in 2009. In the U.S., the Bedford Level experiments were repeated on Lake Tahoe, where once again no curvature could be seen. The results were published in the *Flat Earth News*. Into the twenty-first century, advocates maintained that the world-disc has an edge that one could indeed fall off, surrounded by Antarctica in the form of a vast ring of mountains. To see the truth that the Earth is flat, it is necessary only to look at it.[24] This was an attitude fundamental to the zetetic approach, a democratic definition of realist common sense, in opposition to elite intellectualism and the professionalization of science, but finally liberated from religious fanaticism.

As late as the space programmes of the 1950s and '60s, fundamentalist Christians in the U.S. – including Billy Graham – persisted in seeing heaven as a 'place', part of the traditional up/down relationship between God and Man, and sometimes considered the desire to explore space as profane or even blasphemous. As an important symbolic element of the Cold War, the race was also used by the Soviet Union, whose astronauts found no evidence of a heavenly paradise out there. By the 1970s neopagan religions and secular environmentalism had found a new (though ancient) divinity in Mother Earth, or Gaia, who needed to be rescued from pollution and from being turned into a desert. The ecological sacralization of Earth was buttressed by the failure of the space programmes to find attractive sites for human colonization. The moon seemed desolate, Mars inhospitable and Venus, once thought of as an Edenic partner to Earth, even more hostile. All of these heavenly bodies were effectively dead places. Earth looked even better viewed from space.[25]

By the end of the twentieth century, flat earth theory was liberated from its association with fanatics, eccentric utopians and geophysical outcasts, but offered opportunities for the free expression of light-hearted whimsy. Short-lived Australian and Canadian Flat Earth Societies happily played a comic role. In the 1990s a Flat Venus Society was called for, with the ironic though serious objective of countering the impression that the planet was marked by soaring mountains and deep canyons, as promoted by NASA video images derived from large vertical multipliers.[26]

In spite of science, it remains true that the sphericity of Earth – together with its motion and the idea of gravity – is a complex and counterintuitive concept, understanding of which cannot be acquired by simple direct observation. Infants begin with a naive small-world model in which they discover the physics of falling down and its relationship to the flatness of the surface on which they crawl or toddle. Young children, when told that the Earth is round, sometimes stubbornly prefer to see it as a flat disc or propose compromised models not unlike those suggested by flat-earthers ancient and modern, such as a bowl-shaped world with a vast flat platform inside on which people can stand and move about securely. Slightly older children worry why people on the underside of the globe do not fall off. However, resistance to scientific interpretation is weak, and today most children seem willing to acknowledge their secure footing and begin to accept the spherical argument by the age of five. Acceptance appears early among Australian children, followed by Europeans, and then Americans, but is apparently delayed in India and the Pacific, for example, where indigenous spiritual cosmologies prove more persistent – notably the image of the world as a flat disc, supported by water.[27] In the formation of these models, the recent ability to see Earth as pictured from space gives everyone a clear advantage and – unless dissenters resort to conspiracy theories – removes the possibility of arguing for alternatives, however intuitive.

The face of the Earth

A more grounded problem is confronted in thinking about the origins of the Earth's surface features, and the distribution of different types of landform, including the problem of flat places. Creation myths are generally less interested in this question than in the relationship of Earth and the heavens, and the origins of human beings, but some attribute the shaping of landscapes to the work of supernatural animals or beings, and most of these myths assume a flat starting point. A myth from Central Africa says that 'mountains and valleys came into being from the flat surface of the earth when the first (giant) forefathers started to till the land with a hoe'. In Aboriginal Australia, the idea persisted that an originally flat and formless world existed until mythic heroes emerged from

Blue Marble, composite image of Earth's western hemisphere, 2000.

below to create the diverse landscapes – mountain ranges, sandhills, swamps, springs and soakages – that we see today.[28]

Enuma Elish, or the *Epic of Creation*, one of the earliest known Babylonian myths, written about 1200 BCE, sees the origins of the universe as the product of conflict between gods (often equivalent to the five cosmic elements of ancient polyhedral geometry), and the ascendancy of Marduk (the city god of Babylon) over Ti'amat (the sea). In an act of creative destruction, Marduk kills and dismembers Ti'amat, and from her fillets makes the constellations and the seasons; then makes clouds, rain and streams; piles up mountains from her breasts; and finally establishes the Earth on Ti'amat's lower half.[29] This seemingly backwards account forms a mirror-image to the story of the heavens, and emphasizes the importance of the making of mountains from an implicitly level surface.

The Torah – God's revelation to Moses at Sinai, commonly understood as the first five books of the Hebrew Scriptures – suggests a flat earth, probably a disc, resting on pillars and solid heavens, like a tent.[30] According to Genesis 1:9, on the third day of Creation God commanded, 'Let the waters under the heaven be gathered together unto one place, and let the dry land appear.' Nothing further is offered about the shaping of the surface of the Earth. How the 'hills and valleys' came to be is left open to interpretation. Rabbinical exegesis sometimes suggested that at the beginning of the third day the surface of the Earth was a plain covered by water but by its end mountains and hills had appeared all over the world. Other versions imagined an original level surface, made mountainous only as punishment for the sin of Adam and Eve or for Cain's murder of his brother Abel, and declared that the Earth would not become level again until the time of the Messiah. Alternatively, some held that before the Deluge, the Earth was plain and smooth, lacking both mountains and rain.[31]

In the Bible, the words 'hill' and 'valley' are more common than 'plain', and 'mountain' is used much more frequently. The environment the Israelites occupied was, after all, hill country, contrasting strongly with the coastal and maritime ecology of the geometric Greeks. High hills and mountains are first mentioned in Genesis when covered by the waters of the Flood (7:19–20), and a plain provides an appropriate setting for the building of the Tower of Babel (11:2), but the only biblical use of 'flat' to describe landscape occurs in Joshua 6:5 and 6:20, when the walls of Jericho fall down. Christian readers of the Bible – and the masses who had the Word interpreted for them – could not help but notice the relative prominence of mountains in the sacred texts. Believing that the world in which they lived was much like the landscape created by God, and that the Earth was young, there seemed little need to search for alternative explanations of the form of the land. At the same time, the constant repetition by the church fathers that the original Earth was 'plain' contributed to the persistent notion that even learned Christians long believed the Earth was flat. In the Christian West, salvation history forgot some of the lessons of Aristotle and reduced the age of the Earth to a mere six or seven thousand years, giving little time for earth-changing processes to remake the landscape. Until the Reformation of the early sixteenth century, Christians regularly not only thought of the Flood as punishment for sin, but saw chastisement in the mountains that emerged when the waters retreated, replacing formerly fruitful plains.[32]

Although catastrophist geology did not lend itself to the creation of flat surfaces, models that allowed time for the slow development of landscapes did not necessarily imply a primordial flatness. More often, the created surface of Earth was imagined as smooth, like an egg. The concept meshed with the idea of the Circle of Perfection, the most perfect design God could create, reflected in everything from the human head to the round world and the spheres of Ptolemy's universe.[33] This model was challenged by Nicolaus Copernicus (1473–1543), who conceived the model of a heliocentric universe, but it remained heretical – against scripture – in Christian Europe until the early seventeenth century, when the idea of infinity opened the door to evolutionary thought, by conceiving vast reaches of time and space in which innumerable alternative universes might be created and destroyed, and there is time for even the slowest incremental changes in form and structure.

In spite of these advances, the idea of the original perfect circle and the primordial Mundane Egg remained influential. Thus Thomas Burnet's *Sacred Theory of the Earth*, first published in Latin in 1681, struggled to reconcile current scientific knowledge with scripture, asserting that the Earth before the Flood was 'smooth, regular, and uniform, without mountains, and without a sea'. In the bloom of youth, it was as 'plain as the Elysian Fields', displaying no wrinkles, scars or fractures, but fertile and fruitful, and 'even and uniform' all over. There was no tilt to the Earth's axis, and the seasons too were uniform in this paradise. It was the Deluge – both the rain and the rupturing of the Earth's crust to unleash the waters of the abyss – that changed all this and produced the confused, ruined Earth we know today, disfigured by mountains and subterranean cavities; and, said Burnet, it was the coming Conflagration that would restore the original perfection of form.[34]

The emergence of modern geological thought in the West depended on an acceptance of the concept of uniformitarianism – meaning that the shaping of the world can be understood as a product of forces identifiable in our present – and an understanding that the world is indeed very old. This became possible with Isaac Newton's formulation in the 1680s of the general principle of gravity, 'according to which every two particles of matter in the universe attract each other with equal forces, whose magnitude is directly proportional to the quantities of matter (masses) of these particles and inversely proportional to the square of their distance'. It operated throughout the universe, which Newton saw as an absolute space, a container that exists even if empty. Gravity marked the completion of the mechanization of the world-picture and heralded the general mathematization of science. It enabled Newton to assert that the Earth is an oblate spheroid and, inter alia, provided an explanation for the fundamental smoothness of the Earth's surface.[35]

At about the same time, in Western Europe, mountains began to be perceived as sublime – even beautiful – landscapes, while flatness gradually came to be disparaged. The original meaning of 'sublime' had indeed been 'elevated', so it was well suited to the worship of mountains. Sublimity came to indicate the vastness of the natural

landscape and universe, God's creation, perhaps a 'dreadful' or a
higher form of beauty. Beauty had to be balanced against practicality.
Thus John Ray (1627–1705), who saw the hand of God in all creation,
paid great attention to the many benefits of mountains in order to
declare,

> the present face of the earth, with all its mountains and
> hills, its promontories and rocks, as rude and deformed
> as they appear, seems to me a very beautiful and pleasant
> object, and with all that variety of hills, and valleys, and
> inequalities, far more grateful to behold, than a perfectly
> level country, without any rising or protuberancy, to
> terminate the sight.

But this was an unnatural state, said Ray; the world's surface was
ineluctably being reduced to 'a perfect roundness' and would 'be
one day overflown by the sea, and rendred uninhabitable'.[36]

Altitude seems to have gained an increased value and veneration,
particularly in Western Europe, during the eighteenth century. There
emerged a secularized view of height, an 'adoration of height for
height's sake', which found delight in altitude and verticality.[37] Thus
the English critic John Ruskin (1819–1900) devoted an entire volume
to 'mountain beauty', arguing that wild mountain beauty was not
only consistent with 'the service of man' but indeed 'more necessary
to his happy existence than all the level and easily subdued land
which he rejoices to possess'. Scholars have dated this transition
to the eighteenth century, when there occurred a radical shift in
(lowlander, English) ideas about 'Nature', played out in philosophy,
theology, astronomy and geology, and represented in literature.[38]
Attitudes appear more ambiguous on a global scale, however, and
it is not easy to find praise for very flat places in any period, in spite
of the obvious functionality of flatness in everyday life. Most often,
mountains were compared to valleys, not flat landscapes.

A large part of Ruskin's volume on mountain beauty is devoted
to an almost-encyclopaedic introduction to geology and geomorphology, derived from scientific knowledge but driven by 'the stages

of Creation' set out in Genesis. Ruskin devotes a whole chapter to 'The Dry Land', noting that up to this point 'the earth had been *void*, for it had been *without form*,' and arguing, 'The command that the waters should be gathered was the command that the earth should be *sculptured*.' Without pretending to know precisely how this was achieved or over what time, Ruskin felt assured in claiming that God did not waste time with flatness but gave priority to spectacular mountain-building. Without mountains, Earth 'must have become for the most part desert plain, or stagnant marsh'. Although the finger of God could be seen in every detail of the making of the world landscape, God's greatest goodness could be found in the mountain tops, Earth's 'natural cathedrals', from which vantage point the surrounding landscape could be commanded and visually flattened.[39]

A very different understanding was achieved in China as early as the twelfth century CE, when the Neo-Confucian Chinese philosopher Chu Hsi saw the world going through a series of very long cycles of creation and destruction, with the earth emerging from a watery chaos. As a result, he said, 'Even today, when we stand on a high elevation and look far and wide, the company of the hills looks like the waves of the sea.' Importantly, he observed conchs and oyster shells embedded in high mountains and believed that these had been raised up from the primordial sea. Such understanding was far in advance of the idea that the sea must once have stood at the level of the mountain tops and indeed that the mountains had been raised up. The Chinese held mountains in awe – as places of pilgrimage – but were advanced in their ideas about erosion and the concept of geological time, the time required to flatten the highest peaks. Even the present universe was calculated to be 97 million years old. It was not necessary to defer to a creator 'Master of Heaven'; matter possesses its own spontaneous energy or intelligence; the universe is a continuous process of development, constantly reorganizing space. These were ideas that exasperated the Jesuit missionaries when they first came to China.[40]

Buddhist cosmography similarly venerated mountains, and had little concern for flatness. In its earliest forms, beginning in the sixth century BCE, the universe was believed to contain countless world-systems – each with its own sun, moon, nine planets and many stars – and each of them centred on the sacred mountain Meru. From the summit of the mountain to its base were 31 levels of existence, with humans towards the bottom and at the top infinite space, infinite consciousness and nothingness.[41]

Modern geomorphology

Modern geomorphology assumes that the present landscape of the Earth is almost all youthful – no older than the Pleistocene – and the product of generally gradual and orderly processes that have operated in the same way throughout geological time. The Pleistocene, commencing 2.6 million years ago, experienced many cycles of glaciation, but the tectonic plates moved relatively little, and from the beginning of the epoch the continents were placed more or less where they are today.

Geomorphologists study the development of flat landforms, but typically express this interest in terms of the evolution of slopes, the subject of some controversy. Indeed, some look to departures from flatness for clues to the origins of slope formation, declaring that a 'perfectly plane and horizontal erosion surface would reveal little of its manner of formation'. One of the most influential theories is that advanced by the American geomorphologist William Morris Davis (1850–1934), who emphasized the role of denudation and degradation, in the gradual wearing down of 'youthful' slopes and the generation of flattened landforms associated with 'old age'. Often, it has been argued, degradation and flattening go together with a certain pessimism, rooted in the decay of nature – think of the Slough of Despond in John Bunyan's allegorical *Pilgrim's Progress* of 1678.[42]

An alternative to Davis's model was proposed by the German geomorphologist Walther Penck (1888–1923), who focused on the wearing back of slopes, and declared it a law that 'Flattening of slopes always takes place from below upwards.' The debate between Davis and Penck preoccupied geomorphology for decades, but the

Claypan, Witjira National Park (Simpson Desert), South Australia, 2015.

two were at one in accepting the fundamental role of flattening in mass movement. As Penck expressed it,

> No part of any surface of the earth, no matter how denudation works upon it, can ever thereby become as a whole steeper. It can only become flatter. The most important law obeyed during the development of denudational forms is this principle of flattening.[43]

Recent theories tend to be more eclectic and quantitative in approach, recognizing differences in process between environments, such as sandy deserts versus humid tropical regions. However, they persist in seeing the final stage of the landscape cycle as marked by scarp retreat, the deepening of alluvial fill, the gradual flattening of slopes and the coalescence of pediments, resulting in extensive plains or 'imperfect planation surfaces'. Also known as peneplains, pediplains, exhumed plains, etchplains and palaeoplains, such planation surfaces include 'the broader, flatter, and more

Overleaf: Diamantina National Park, Queensland, Australia, 2014.

time-dependent surfaces'.[44] These are common in some of the world's flattest places – the ancient desert landscapes of Australia, for example.

Another world exists beneath the oceans, but the relative flatness of the ocean floor is poorly understood. Deep-sea exploration is recent but by the beginning of the twentieth century the geographer William Morris Davis could declare it was marked by the 'monotony' of its vast plains.[45] In fact, in addition to chains of seamounts, the sea floor consists of mid-ocean ridges rising to 3 kilometres above the surrounding surface, and plateaux. To measure the shape of seamounts, marine geologists have developed a flatness index, calculated as the ratio of minimum summit diameter to minimum basal diameter. This shows the largest seamounts, in the region surrounding Easter Island, to be 'pointy cones' (flatness 0.2 or less), whereas the smaller ones exhibit much greater variability (down to 0.6).[46]

It is the presence of free water, together with Earth's unusual plate tectonic cycle, that distinguishes it from the other planets of the inner solar system, smoothing the surface. As a result, unlike the typically basaltic crusts of the other planets, Earth's continental crust is constantly recycling and re-melting to create a rich geological diversity of elements. Indeed, the evolution of Earth's continents appears to have depended on the availability of sufficient water for the creation of granites, and the balance between water and land has changed relatively little in spite of movement, thus enabling a smooth (flat) surface. The continental crust is 35–40 kilometres thick, six times thicker and less dense than the oceanic crust, thus explaining the higher elevation of the continental surfaces, which float higher because of their relative buoyancy. If the waters of the oceans are removed from the globe, it becomes clear that the continents are not merely the features that protrude through the ocean surface, but rather the dominant topographic features of the Earth's solid surface. The continents are remarkably flat plateaux, very close to sea level with the exception of some substantial mountain ranges, and surrounded by relatively steep continental slopes.[47]

Other bodies in the solar system – such as Mars and the moon – have evolved geomorphologically much more slowly than Earth.

Probably the tallest volcano in the solar system is Olympus Mons, on Mars, which towers 26 kilometres above the surface (three times the height of Mount Everest). Olympus Mons is perhaps 400 million years old, whereas volcanoes in the humid climates of Earth rarely remain recognizable features for more than one million years. Overall, the topography of Mars is markedly asymmetric, in strong contrast to Earth, which has twice the diameter. On Mars, most of the southern hemisphere is above the mean elevation and most of the northern hemisphere below. In spite of this contrast, Mars has a vast region of flatness, as smooth as the abyssal plains of Earth's oceans, and described as 'the flattest surface in the solar system for which we have data'.[48]

FOUR

VERY FLAT PLACES

'The boundless, flat country, in which straw-thatched,
wooden hamlets closely huddle together, has a poisonous
quality which devastates a man, and empties him of desire.
When a peasant goes beyond the limits of his hamlet and
looks at the emptiness around him, after a time he feels that
this emptiness has filled his heart.'

Maxim Gorky, 1922[1]

These sombre sentiments attributed by Gorky to the Russian peasantry have many parallels. According to John Ruskin, writing from a very different class perspective in the middle of the nineteenth century: 'If the scenery be resolutely level, insisting upon the declaration of its own flatness in all the detail of it, as in Holland, or Lincolnshire, or Central Lombardy, it appears to me like a prison, and I cannot long endure it.' Ruskin declared mountains 'the beginning and the end of all natural scenery'.[2] These preferences appear to persist. Mountains came to be understood as wilderness, places deserving conservation and official protection, and peoples inhabiting mountain ecosystems came to be shown respect, with the establishment in 1995 of a global Mountain Forum, and the United Nations' declaration of 2002 as the International Year of Mountains.[3] Flat landscapes struggle to achieve a similar profile.

Flatness is routinely regarded as boring and depressing. If the entire surface of the Earth is considered – the water and ice as well as the land – this negative assessment is certainly true. But the great oceans are not merely boring or depressing, they are also unstable, lack varied resources and are not practical sites for human activity without the use of enabling technologies. When human beings think about landscape preferences, they think almost exclusively about terra firma. On the other hand, the early history of global migration saw many people clinging close to coastlines, and the modern world has seen a demographic push back towards the oceans. More than half of the world's population now lives within 200 kilometres of a coast – 10 per cent of the land area – and more than half live in cities. These proportions are increasing rapidly.[4] However, although many cities are coastal, these urban populations rarely think of themselves as people of the sea. When modern people travel overseas, they fly high above the waters rather than voyaging across the surface. Increasingly, we undertake such travel through corridors of non-places that convey us through flattened architectures tenuously connected with natural landscapes. We benefit by the flatness of these artificial architectures but rarely attribute aesthetic values to very flat places.

Theory

The definition of 'landscape' and the history of the word is a contested area. It is understood almost entirely as a terrestrial feature, only occasionally opposed to the concept of a seascape. Landscape has been associated with the emergence of capitalism and national identity, as well as ideas about social justice and the body politic, law and property, and labour. It also competes with concepts of place and region. Theories about landscape preferences, however, generally adopt less weighted concepts, and choose definitions akin to that advanced by the geographer Jay Appleton, who called landscape 'the environment visually perceived', our image of reality. Leaving aside what this means for the unsighted person, and the problematic notion of beauty, the aesthetic viewing of landscape can mean simply the 'pleasure associated with or deriving from perception'.[5]

More broadly, there is a strong relationship between place attachment and landscape preference, meaning that we prefer places that resemble those we know and regard as our own. It follows that people tend to prefer landscapes that possess qualities associated with places experienced in childhood. This is a model in which preferences are culturally driven and related to the idea of a 'sense of place', a complex and hard-to-measure concept reflecting work, family and social relations rather than simply an attitude to the physical environment. An alternative theory contends that landscape preferences are innate, rooted in our evolutionary biology, and shared by people with different cultural and ethnic backgrounds, independent of the specific environments of their youth. The conclusion to this debate is that people do value their childhood landscapes but particularly appreciate places that possess qualities thought to be shared universally and innate. These qualities are found in landscapes which are open and natural, with water present. Concrete evidence of the value placed on such sites is found in the premium paid for houses with panoramic water views, with prices highest at the shoreline and decreasing with distance.[6]

Studies of landscape preferences often depend on surveys, requiring subjects to rank a sample of (still) photographs of 'typical' scenes. This may seem an indirect approach, but it reflects the two different though related meanings attached to the word 'landscape'. These were expressed clearly, for example, by Samuel Johnson in his *Dictionary* of 1755: (1) 'A region; the prospect of a country', and (2) 'A picture, representing an extent of space, with the various objects in it.'[7] In each of these definitions, landscape is understood as something to be viewed, either directly by the eye or as an image constructed by an artist. Thus the study of landscape preferences through images is not as indirect as it might first appear. Johnson, in eighteenth-century England, had in mind a person standing on a rise, perhaps, looking out over a stretch of country, sketching it on a pad, or walking or riding through it at a leisurely pace. This notion of the viewer was soon to change, and with it the perception of space and flatness.

How we view the physical world depends very much on motion and hence scale. The same piece of ground appears very different to a farmer ploughing a paddock behind a team of horses, compared to a passenger in a train speeding through the countryside, let alone a person seeing the world from the porthole of a space station. What seems to the farmer level and linear may become for the commuter a smudge in a more diversified landscape, while from outer space what appeared flat to the farmer is indubitably proven to be, in fact, curved. A trekker may have eyes more for the next safe foothold than for the vista, and the speeding motorist as much for the smooth wide surface of the road as for the distant prospect. The passive passenger in a jetliner, feeling no friction, barely notices the landscape or even the cloudscape.

These contrasting pictures are products of dramatic differences in speed and distance. Again, the effects are tempered by scale. Rapid motion depends on movement across a smooth/flat surface. If the surface is irregular or rough, motion is impeded by friction, and the bumpiness of the passage will discomfort the traveller, just as will happen if the passage bounces erratically from side to side by deviating from a forward-moving straight-line route. For most of human history, people have moved slowly across land and sea, and rarely had access to an aerial or elevated view, though sitting astride a horse was often a way of imposing authority. Although great speed is now possible in some contexts, farmers continue to move slowly across their fields, elevated somewhat and encapsulated in air-conditioned cabins, and very much conscious of minor aberrations in linearity and furrow height, colour and spacing, however sophisticated and powerful their machines.[8] Very rapid motion has become available only in recent times, enabling new scales of observation. Most of this rapid transit is done sitting in a chair, sometimes elevated but in the common case of the motor car with the traveller's eyes nearer the ground than those of a standing person.

Attempts to account for landscape preferences in terms of human evolutionary experience have no place for rapid motion through space. Rather, such aesthetic preferences are understood to be artefacts of ancient environments, which no longer determine survival yet continue to be influential in everyday perception and behaviour. The broadest version of this argument – generally referred to as 'habitat theory' – contends that humans respond positively to visual signs, including shapes, colours and patterns, because these draw on primal forces that indicate a species-diverse environment, in which the presence of living things can provide food and other materials. Human beings, and other organisms, select habitats in which to live and reproduce, but their choices are neither ideal nor free, because mobility and knowledge are always limited. On the other hand, idealized aesthetic preferences may be expressed for landscapes (habitats) that appear to enhance survival, even if they do not, in fact, contain needed resources.[9]

A more specific argument, often called the 'savannah hypothesis', posits a preference for landscapes reflecting the open – and perhaps flat – grassland environments, spotted with large trees, in which hunters evolved. Gordon H. Orians, for example, argues that

> we enjoy being in savannah vegetation, prefer to avoid both closed forests and open plains, will pay more for land giving us the impression of being a savannah, mold recreational environments to be more like savannahs, and develop varieties of ornamental plants that converge on the shapes typical of tropical savannahs of Africa, the probable site of our evolutionary origins.

Those who suffer from agoraphobia – first named as a disease in 1871 – can, however, find reasons to fear empty spaces or 'infinite vastness' just as much in modern architecture and city planning as in wild, open landscapes.[10]

Related to the savannah hypothesis is 'prospect-refuge theory', developed by Jay Appleton, who claimed that preferences derive from a desire to see without being seen. Hunters required both the security of a safe haven and clear vistas (prospects) to observe their prey. Few human beings now live as hunters but the contention is that all of us share innate reactions formed in the distant past that we are unable to shake off in viewing the landscapes of the modern world. Yet another hypothesis, known as 'information-processing theory' – essentially an extension of prospect-refuge theory, and hence a variant of habitat theory – proposes that people prefer environments that facilitate and stimulate the acquisition of knowledge conducive to survival.[11]

Although these theories or hypotheses are quite distinct, all of them point to the significance of complexity in the forming of aesthetic landscape preferences. It is argued that human beings react positively to physical environments that are made up of two or more contrasting elements and offer the possibility of resource-richness because of a visible diversity of life forms that might be exploited directly or because the simple existence of complexity suggests that other life forms (humans) could also expect to find succour. This leaves little room for flat places, seen as two-dimensional, open and empty – effectively devoid of complexity. It must be emphasized, however, that the theories outlined here all see landscape in terms of the definition adopted by Johnson in the eighteenth century – as a region (an extent of land) that might be viewed by a person standing on a hill, observing the scene, or by an artist recording it on canvas – as the immediate exploitable environment.

At smaller scales – as in the example of the wheat farmer viewing his fields or the child crawling across a carpet – things look different, and open up possibilities for flatness to enjoy a degree of aesthetic preference. For the wheat farmer, in particular, the landscape of the farm is not fixed but changes seasonally with the cropping cycle, each stage marked by contrasting versions of linearity and flatness. Outside broadacre farming, it is possible that none of this will make sense. For example, farmers of tropical food forests live in the very heart of organic complexity organized in both horizontal and vertical layers with relatively little value placed on flatness and linearity; and rice farmers may look across a deep valley of levelled terraces. This suggests that the desirability of flatness depends very much on scale, as well as the speed at which it is surveyed and the distance of the viewer from the scene; and that it might vary with modes of economic exploitation and with the seasons, which may in turn be defined by the resources they offer rather than by the calendar.[12]

In addition to the theories of landscape preference discussed thus far, it is useful to notice briefly another variety of theory, that linking landscape with behaviour. Put together, these two strands of theory create a loop in which the landscape is both an object of human choice and a preference, and at the same time a causative factor determining human behaviour. The latter variety of theory – sometimes termed 'environmental determinism' – has a long history. It survived and prospered into the twentieth century, when many Western (imperial) commentators felt comfortable in advocating the view that elements of culture and 'civilization' were derivatives of topography, soil and climate. This argument put a heavy emphasis on climate but also saw altitude and slope as central variables. A basic dichotomy was plain/mountain.

Flat landscapes – plains – fared well in these comparisons, seen as the homes of the world's great agricultural regions, and accounting for most of the world's population and economic development and urbanization, with easy access and communications. Thus Ellen Churchill Semple argued, in her *Influences of Geographic Environment* of 1911, that plains had the power to 'facilitate every phase of historical movement', whereas mountains tended to 'retard, arrest, or deflect it'. However, Semple also argued that 'A flat, monotonous relief produces a monotonous existence, necessarily one-sided, needing a complement in upland or mountain.'[13] Although much of this theory is now discredited, it is hard to deny the role of the physical environment – including flatness – in setting the parameters for human development and exploitation, and thus influencing landscape preference.

Low, flat places

The truly great low, flat place is the world-ocean. The waters of the world have a connected unity that is global rather than local, though the perception of flatness is, of course, always local, limited to the horizon and its curvature. Thus some regions of the ocean are notorious for their roughness – where the Roaring Forties blow, for example – and almost everywhere short-term roughness is a function of changing winds. At the other extreme, the sailor on a becalmed vessel on the open ocean was the one most likely to be surrounded by a flat sea, the most likely to go mad. Unlike the terrestrial experience, at sea there is always the expectation that conditions will change in the short term and that equilibrium is represented by flatness. In geological time, the level of the oceans has varied significantly and present coastlines were established only around 6,000 years ago. This change saw sea levels rise more than 100 metres, sweeping across flat coastal shelves and bulldozing loose materials inshore. On a daily basis, tidal difference is significant in some regions, but the waters are held in place by gravity to a temporary overall flatness.[14]

Local terrestrial flatness takes a number of forms and occurs at quite different scales. Small islands and archipelagos can be almost completely flat and low, yet form the homes of nation-states: the Maldives, for example, or Tuvalu, well known because of their great vulnerability to sea-level rise, tsunamis and cyclones. Most obviously in the case of the Pacific, such small islands extend their terrestrial flatness into a vast surrounding sea surface. On the continental land masses, whole small nations can similarly be known as characteristically flat: the Netherlands, for example, one of the flattest of the Low Countries, where sea-dykes protect reclaimed land from the incursion of saltwater and river-dykes control flow through low-lying polders. The same processes of erosion and sedimentation, together with changes in sea level, also operate at smaller scales, creating coastal sandflats and mudflats, and also river flats, which consist of small areas of flat land alongside streams, generally fertile and well watered in the midst of more barren land types.

In Australia, the quintessential flat place is the Nullarbor Plain. Here flatness blends most perfectly with ideas of emptiness, nothingness and absence, as intended by its very name, and by the abstractly straight lines imposed on it by European people. The defining artefact is the railway, built in the 1920s, that connects the Indian and Pacific Oceans. At one point on the Nullarbor, the rail travels 530 kilometres in an 'absolutely straight line', and 'almost dead level'. Here

You look back on the shining rails which run on towards infinity. You look forward and see the same twin threads drawn out until they melt into one another. Elsewhere there is nothing but the plain and the sky. The plain rolls away to just such a circular horizon as the voyager by water sees when out of sight of land.

In recent advertising, the Nullarbor is likened to an ocean, the train ploughing through the shallow waves of sand in the style of a cruise ship.[15]

Most of Australia's deserts are 'exceedingly level', and the salt flats of Lake Eyre (when dry) have proved an ideal surface to set land speed records. The same is true of the Bonneville Salt Flats in Utah, covering little more than 100 square kilometres but elevated at 1,286 metres above sea level.

Elevated flat places

One hundred times larger than Bonneville is the desert playa Salar de Uyuni in Bolivia, sitting at an altitude of almost 4 kilometres on the southern Altiplano, or high plateau, of the Andes. Sometimes called the world's 'largest salt flat' and sometimes 'the official flattest place in the world', Salar de Uyuni covers more than 9,000 square kilometres. A GPS survey made in 2002 measured relative relief across the surface of only 80 centimetres, even though the region is tectonically active, so that it is 'remarkably flat'. Elsewhere

Table Mountain, Cape Town, South Africa, 2004.

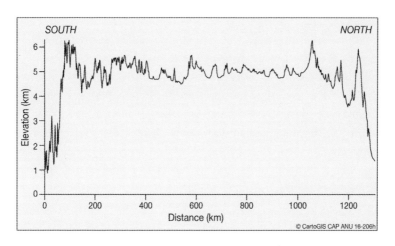

North–South profile of the Tibetan Plateau.

in the Americas, playas with as much a 1-metre local relief have been termed 'extremely flat'. The Salar de Uyuni was wet until about 15,000 years ago, when the level of the lake began to fall and desiccation commenced, but its flatness is sustained by the shallow water that flows across the surface, grading the salt in solution, leaving the rest to gravity. However, the surface salt often forms natural hexagons, an efficient solution to the overlapping of circles that occurs elsewhere in nature. The Salar de Uyuni is popular with tourists and photographers for the 'sense of sublimity' evoked by the 'flat, arid terrain that extends with no seeming variation into a vast distance across 360 degrees of horizon'.[16]

Vastly larger again, the Tibetan Plateau contains 82 per cent of Earth's land more than 4 kilometres above sea level and spreads over an area almost 3,500 by 1,500 kilometres. It is the world's highest plateau. More surprising, the Tibetan Plateau is relatively flat. High-resolution digital elevation modelling was first applied to Tibet in the 1990s, finding a mean elevation of 5,023 metres above sea level. Whereas relief is as much as 6 kilometres along the abrupt edges of the plateau, it is about 1 kilometre or less for most of Tibet. The boundaries are most abrupt to the north and south, falling away rapidly in steep slopes, whereas the western edge of the plateau merges with mountains and the eastern slopes downward more gradually. In central Tibet – a region of internal drainage – slopes average only about 5°. This morphology excites geologists because the 'flatness' of Tibet suggests that it has not experienced major compressional deformation in recent geological time and that instead crustal flow has levelled the surface, perhaps related to ancient basins and the evidence of remnant elevated terraces. The origins of the plateau are much debated: how can low relief exist within the active collision zone of the Indian and Eurasian plates? The debate also illustrates clearly the relative measure of 'flatness', the plateau appearing level to the eyes of a geologist whereas through the goggles of a car driver, the land is uninviting for a world land speed record trial.[17] Smaller plateaux often have much flatter tops, created by differential erosion of softer and harder geological strata, sometimes jutting out of larger smooth expanses. Here, the table offers a common analogy, as in South Africa's Table Mountain and the Spanish mesa.

From Florida to the Great Plains

In the U.S., debate has long existed over the relative flatness of the states. The question was taken seriously in 2014 by Jerome E. Dobson and Joshua S. Campbell, who developed a visibility-at-sea measure of flatness derived from digital observations, in order to assess 'personal perception of topographic landforms at fine scale'. Contrary to popular perceptions, Kansas is not the flattest state. Proof of this status had seemed to be given in 2003 when a group of geographers, publishing in the *Annals of Improbable Research*, showed that 'Kansas is flatter than a pancake'; but every state in the U.S. is, in fact, flatter than a pancake.[18] The real title, according to the measurements of Dobson and Campbell, goes to Florida, with 52 per cent of its land falling in the 'flat, flatter and flattest' categories (compared to 44 per cent for Kansas, which ranked seventh). The least flat state was West Virginia, with just 12 per cent in these classes.

Florida's flatness is often watery and leaks into the state's long sea coast. Thus Dobson and Campbell speculate that the popular

'The Great Plains', from William Morris Davis, *Elementary Physical Geography* (1902).

failure to recognize the state's flatness may be influenced by the density of its woods and the presence of standing water, whereas in other regions of the u.s. false perceptions of flatness may derive from 'the preference of interstate highway planners for long, level stretches of interfluve compared to the general topography spanned by smaller roads'.[19]

Charles Dickens, crossing the prairie by coach in 1842, visualized the landscape as 'a tranquil sea or lake without water, if such a simile be admissible'. The 'very flatness and extent' of the picture impressed, but 'left nothing to the imagination', and proved 'oppressive in its barren monotony'. Other travellers remarked on the loneliness, desolation and interminable monotony of the plains, and many invoked the metaphor of the ocean. What Dickens found most disturbing in the landscape was not so much the open spaces of the prairie as the marshy tributaries of the Mississippi, where – in direct reference to *Pilgrim's Progress* – the monotony of the scene suggested that 'the grim domains of Giant Despair' might be nearby, in a 'flat morass'.[20] Early European explorers of the American West often had strong positive responses to open savannah environments with scattered trees and lots of grass, whereas they reacted negatively to flat, treeless plains.[21]

At the beginning of the twentieth century, William Morris Davis illustrated his discussion of the Great Plains with an iconic image, without comment. These plains, he said, were formed of 'many layers of sands, clays, and gravels, washed from the mountains and now lying one over the other, many hundred feet in total thickness and nearly horizontal'. Uplift had begun the process of dissection, but in some regions 'vast areas stretching farther than the eye can reach are monotonously even and almost as uniform in soil as in surface'. Davis found the landscape similar to the plains of western Siberia. Thus by 1931, when Walter Prescott Webb's sentimental *The Great Plains* was published, it had become easy to identify as a primary distinguishing characteristic of the region the fact that it formed 'a comparatively level surface of great extent'. Webb believed the Westerner's 'vision had been enlarged by a distant and monotonous horizon', endowing 'him' with a certain independence or unconventionality.[22]

Modern American writers helped mythologize the Great Plains, coming to see the region as the nation's sentimental 'dreamland', where a lost agrarian life somehow survived. Definitions of the region's boundaries varied from writer to writer, and shifted over time, with new names attached – from Great American Desert to Heartland – but its topography was relentlessly 'flat-lying' or 'flat and spare', with only rare 'vertical punctuations to the omnipresence of horizontal space' and few 'aesthetic or conceptual signposts' amid the emptiness to direct its interpretation. Increasingly, however, the image was seen to contrast with the reality, only a small proportion of the region being judged truly flat. Part of the fault, it was said, lay with the railroads, which followed the flattest possible routes through the landscape. Jay Appleton observed, 'The Great Plains of North America are rarely absolutely flat, but their vastness is such that small undulations can't destroy the sense of distance which is the overwhelming feature of the prairies.' And Marilynne Robinson, in her novel *Gilead* (2004), associated a spiritual love for the prairies with the fact that here there was 'nothing to distract attention from the evening and the morning, nothing on the horizon to abbreviate or delay', a place where mountains would represent 'an impertinence'.[23]

On the Canadian prairies, Appleton observed that the land was 'trenched by shallow valleys which carry the larger rivers, like the North and South Saskatchewan, a hundred feet or so beneath what is really a low plateau rather than a plain'. They spread from the Red River towards the Rocky Mountains and the Arctic, occupying the provinces of Alberta, Saskatchewan and Manitoba, and are almost as large as Western Europe. From Winnipeg to the foot of the Rockies is a distance of more than 1,200 kilometres. Modern motorists travelling across this vast expanse describe the region as 'flat and boring', but, as Gerald Friesen contends, the long stretches of rolling plains are interrupted by post-glacial hills and valleys, 'sometimes as low blue ranges on the horizon, sometimes as winding slashes cut deep into the surface of the land'. Covered by grass, the southern prairies were the home of the buffalo (bison), and the openness of the landscape was shaped by these great herds. But the prairies have a complementary relationship with the surrounding landscapes of parkland and boreal forest, and they were traditionally linked by the seasonal exploitation of more than one of the three niches: prairie, parkland and forest. Nineteenth-century expeditioners into this 'empty' land compared the prairies

The vast, flat landscape of the Mongolian Plateau, 2014.

with the Russian steppes, recognizing that the region was composed of 'three great planes' or 'prairie levels', separated by gentle scarps, 'rather like three steps on a stair'.[24]

Russia

Yi-Fu Tuan contends that a sense of spaciousness is associated with the idea of freedom, that freedom implies the power to act in an open and unfettered manner. Citing Gorky's anguish, expressed in the epigraph beginning this chapter, Tuan argues that for the Russian peasantry, 'boundless space' meant only despair and 'spoke of man's paltriness as against the immensity and indifference of nature'. Gorky, writing in 1922, believed that the many centuries over which enserfed Russians had been denied freedom had created a people with little attachment to place, because 'There is always somewhere to go; the empty plain unrolls on every side and the distance calls seductively'.[25]

The flattest region of Russia is generally thought to be found in the steppes, but the great Siberian marshland is equally level and bleak in the imagination. Even much nearer to Moscow, in the seventeenth century, writes Valerie A. Kivelson, 'the lofty presence of church steeples' proved prominent 'on the otherwise flat landscape of central Russia'. Fields might be labelled *ploskoe* (flat). Russia's vast forests were also described as 'terrifying, wild and impassible', not simply because they were thick but because they stretched unbroken across the vast expanse of the flat Russian plain.[26]

Kivelson, in her study of the cartography of seventeenth-century Russian land settlement, observes that empty, unmarked territory created uncertainty and fears of litigation. Seeing emptiness as a problem contrasted with the way it was used to justify European conquest in North America and elsewhere, where an empty map was testimony to the supposed absence of an existing people and culture. In Russia, the expansion of settlement was a long, slow process. Muscovite property holders were challenged by the task of 'defining and delimiting pieces of that wide, flat, homogeneous land' and faced 'the overwhelming, haunting problem of emptiness'. They built up an extensive vocabulary to express different varieties of emptiness, attaching the term to openness, remoteness, lowness and marginality. Much of the land consisted of plots which had been ploughed but not inhabited or formerly ploughed and abandoned, known as *pustosh* (meaning 'empty' or 'empty spaces').[27]

Images of the Russian landscape failed to engage painters in the great era of settlement expansion, and their aristocratic patrons could see nothing in the monotonous terrain of the steppes that could compare with the scenic beauty of France and Italy. Not until the late nineteenth century did there begin to emerge a school of Russian painters who could begin to find majesty in the flat, wide expanses and big skies of their own land.[28] This newfound appreciation reached an evocative climax in *Vladimirka Road*, painted in 1892 by Isaak Levitan, born in a Jewish community in Lithuania. Here Levitan depicted the dismal route taken by numberless prisoners on their shackled march to Siberia, long established as a place of penal servitude.

Siberia played a role as an iconic site of severe exile – the land of the dead – through a long line of literature. In these literary landscapes, Siberia is portrayed as perpetually trapped in cold winter and the dark of night – ignoring the reality of its hot summer months – and as uninhabited infinite cosmic space, an endless plain where 'mountains vanish'. Thus Anton Chekhov (1860–1904), who thought the Siberian highway 'the longest and . . . the ugliest road in the whole world' and found inspiration in Levitan's landscape art, said in 1890, 'The fascination of the taiga lies not in giant trees or in silence, but in the fact that perhaps the migratory birds alone know where it ends'.[29] Arkhip Kuindzhi's painting *Landscape, The Steppe* from 1890 perfectly evoked the misty vagueness of the flat horizon. Although regarded as a maverick, Kuindzhi proved highly influential, contributing to the emerging modernism and to Russian minimalist art in the early twentieth century.

Continental flatness

Attempts to estimate the relative significance of different land types at a continental and global scale became popular in the 1960s. Early estimates defined 'flat plains' as areas with more than 80 per cent 'gentle slope' and local relief of less than 90 metres, whereas 'plains' did not have to satisfy the slope rule. Globally, 34 per cent of all land consisted of plains (though only 4 per cent of these were 'flat plains') and a further 15 per cent 'plains with hills or mountains', accounting together for half the terrestrial surface. 'Flat plains' were most common in South America (15 per cent of the continent's land area), North America (8 per cent) and Australia with New Zealand (4 per cent), whereas plains of all sorts were most common in Australia with New Zealand (55 per cent), followed by South America and Africa. Separating New Zealand (and Tasmania) from the Australian continent serves only to confirm its place as the flattest, on this calculation. Although containing vast flat lowlands, Eurasia is the 'roughest' of the continents.[30]

The earliest known exact use of the phrase 'flattest continent' was applied to Australia in 1954, in discussion of the scarcity of water for power generation.[31] This claim had no obvious basis in comparative measurement but stemmed from the concept of absence – the lack of water and of mountains. The first complete definition and measurement of Australia's flatness occurred in 1977, when the geographers J. N. Jennings and J. A. Mabbutt noticed the 'absence of lofty young fold ranges' that made Australia 'the lowest of the continents' both in terms of the highest point (at 2,225 metres compared to its nearest rival, Antarctica, at 5,140 metres) and mean altitude (330 metres compared to 650 metres for South America). The difference was, however, less obvious if Europe was separated from Asia. Jennings and Mabbutt found a mean altitude of 290 metres for Europe (compared to 860 metres for Asia, including

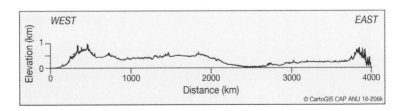

West–East profile, across Australia, from Exmouth to Byron Bay.

Russell Drysdale, *The Drover's Wife*, c. 1945, oil on canvas, 51.5 cm x 61.5 cm.

Europe), less than for Australia. They argued that this similarity concealed a significant difference and that other indexes showed it was 'the *flatness* of Australia which must be stressed rather than the extent of lowland'. They found Australia contained only 2 per cent of plateaux above 1,000 metres, and concluded it was not a continent of low, coastal plains, but of elevated plains. In this way, Jennings and Mabbutt created a new vision of the landscape, noting the general lowness of the land but emphasizing flatness at whatever elevation. The continent's flat landscapes exhibited a unique monotony: 'to travel hundreds of kilometres without significant change in landform is commonplace.'[32]

This statement by Jennings and Mabbutt in 1977 provided the strongest basis for future claims to the flatness of Australia. Writers were quick to identify Australia as the flattest of the continents, and photographic collections, travel books and general descriptions eagerly accepted this new perception of the land. In 1986 the declaration found its way into the official *Year Book of Australia*, stating, 'Australia is the lowest, flattest, and (apart from Antarctica) the driest of the continents.'[33] No measures of flatness were offered, and flatness and lowness continued to be confused, but this founding statement proved influential and was frequently copied in one shape or another. With the entire continent declared flat, the notion of 'lowness' was sidelined, and specific sites soon became 'awesomely flat' or 'very flat'.

In spite of a growing subtlety, recent references to Australia as the 'flattest continent' persist in using absolute lowness as its measure, with statements that as much as 40 per cent of its area rises less than 200 metres above sea level or that as little as 6 per cent is above 610 metres.[34] In 2012, however, Geoscience Australia not only declared the continent 'the flattest on Earth' but also calculated average slope across the continent at only 1.4°. This satisfies quite well the definitions of 'flat' topography advanced by geographers. That it applies across the continent is remarkable. More positively, writers found compensation in Australia's 'landscape variety' and argued that it is 'hardly dull', with 'the monotonous flatness of the Nullarbor Plain' and the lowness of Lake Eyre simply two among many types.[35] This relatively recent positive perception of Australian flatness emerged in parallel with a growing scientific understanding of the deep history of humanity on the continent, dated to 50,000 years ago or even earlier. The latter finding came as no surprise to Aboriginal people, who had long come to live within the nuances of flatness.

Emptiness, monotony, boredom

Having identified invariance as central to the concept, it is also no surprise that the repetitive character of flatness is closely associated with ideas of predictability, monotony, absence, emptiness and bore-dom. However, the significance of these ideas can be quite different for different social groups, and can change over time. In Europe, the beauty of the flatlands of North Groningen, in the Netherlands, began to be appreciated only in the late twentieth century, after landscape artists revealed the region as a worthy subject. Early Europeans in Australia often complained of the monotony of the bush – every tree unique yet always a tree and a eucalypt – and even when they climbed above the canopy, the surface stretched to the horizon like a great green sea. Australian settler society saw empty landscapes – particularly the desert – as places that could drive you mad, the 'psychological void' or 'dead heart' of the continent. Painters began to take it seriously in the 1930s, and now the 'red centre' is seen as vibrant and colourful, good for the soul, with a rich indigenous culture.[36]

In her memoir *The Road from Coorain* (1989), the Australian academic Jill Ker Conway charts her progress from 'the empty earth' of western New South Wales to the leafy colleges of Massachusetts. On the plains, she recalls, 'the horizon is always with us and there is no retreating from it. Its blankness travels with our every step and waits for us at every point of the compass . . . Because of the flatness, contrasts are in a strange scale.' The sparsely populated landscape was marked by a silence 'so profound that it pressed upon the eardrums', but for those born into it, the 'annihilation of the self, subsumed into the vast emptiness of nature, is akin to a religious experience'. In 1945, when sent to Sydney to attend school, she learns literature through the eyes of English writers: 'As for landscape, we learned by implication that ours was ugly, because it deviated totally from the landscape of the Cotswolds and the Lake Country, or the romantic hills and valleys of Constable.' Travelling with her mother in the 1950s, Ker Conway reconfigures her attitude to the land, appreciating the beauty of Australia only after seeing the real, rather than imaginary, landscapes of England and Europe. But, finding an emptiness in her personal and intellectual life, she heads for Harvard.[37]

The monotony and boredom associated with flat landscapes is not confined to arid places, and recent interpretations sometimes trace the psychological impact of flatness through boredom to depression and mental illness. Wetlands too can induce such feelings. Thus Graham Swift's *Waterland*, published in 1983, tells of his

growing up on the English Fens, where his father was a lock-keeper
on the River Leem and 'the world is flat . . . with an unrelieved and
monotonous flatness, enough of itself, some might say, to drive a
man to unquiet and self-defeating thoughts.' Viewed from the river
bank, raised to contain the waters, the land

> stretched away to the horizon, its uniform colour, peat-black,
> varied only by the crops that grew upon it – grey-green
> potato leaves, blue-green beet leaves, yellow-green wheat;
> its uniform levelness broken only by the furrowed and dead-
> straight lines of ditches and drains, which, depending on
> the state of the sky and the angle of the sun, ran like silver,
> copper or golden wires across the fields and which, when
> you stood and looked at them, made you shut one eye and
> fall prey to fruitless meditations on the laws of perspective.

Murray Fredericks, *Salt 305*, 2007, digital pigment print, 95 cm x 250 cm. At Lake Eyre, South Australia, the red hue of the lake bed appears when it dries following flooding. Fredericks's photograph evokes a notion of infinite space, not simple flatness.

In this environment, pondering the significance of human history, Swift finds that, 'Reality is uneventfulness, vacancy, flatness.' Thus most of us struggle to find a role on the stage of historical events. We are anxious to feature above the flatness of our 'unsung existence' but typically remain stuck in the emptiness of our humdrum lives.[38]

Jay Appleton, in a memoir centred on his creation of prospect-refuge theory, recalled a turning point when 'a sense of exhilaration eventually triumphed over one of monotony and boredom which in childhood I had come to associate with the Fens.' As a child, he had found the Fens 'not only dull, not only alien, but almost hostile', representing the 'melancholy which easily attaches itself to flat places'. His newfound view of the Fens came, said Appleton, through the eye working 'in collaboration with the imagination', something to be experienced 'never more so than in flat country where the level horizon invites the assumption that the land must go on and on and on'. It encouraged an 'expansive feeling of liberty'. His feelings were similar on approaching the Low Countries by sea, where the dunes carried his mind beyond, across the marshes, polders and heathlands, unseen but vivid. These imagined excursions led Appleton to reflect, 'Some people have been attracted by the simplistic argument that, because mountains are widely acclaimed as beautiful, therefore flat country must be intrinsically devoid of beauty.' In addition to the lack of logic in this argument, Appleton noted the paradox that the Low Countries had spawned great landscape art, and therefore 'any theory of landscape aesthetics which dismisses the attractive powers of flat country would have to take this into account.' All of this fitted into his idea of landscape as a 'warning system', providing clues about what lay ahead, towards the horizon.[39]

FIVE

FLATTENING THE WORLD

'The methods of transforming the topography have become monstrous . . . Today any developer can erase the irregularities of a site in a few days and at little expense. We are thus present at the birth of the "bulldozer landscape".'

Pierre von Meiss, 1990[1]

It is an apparent paradox that in our efforts to reshape the surface of the Earth, human beings have frequently sought to create an artificial flatness or smoothness – in spite of the purported aesthetic attractions of diversified, elevated landscapes. Level surfaces – whether floors, platforms or pathways – have many practical advantages over uneven surfaces, and flat things can have both practical and aesthetic attributes. Thus the flattening of the physical world takes many forms and occurs at a wide variety of scales. Railways follow routes as flat and straight as possible, crossing viaducts and passing through tunnels, constructed at great cost. Aircraft take off from vast flattened tarmacs. Sport is played on levelled playing fields. Cloth is placed on an ironing board and ironed flat with a flatiron or a smoothing iron, the ironing board set on a level floor. However, even the most mundane efforts to flatten things are short-lived: a shirt will soon need to be ironed again, and a lawn mown. Human action directed at changing the face of the Earth and imposing spatial order, on a grand scale, always displays a certain hubris when placed in geological and cosmological contexts.

Earth-moving

The earliest human earth-moving activity was directed at mining and the digging of pits rather than levelling. This began to change with the development of agriculture, particularly irrigated agriculture, around 10,000 years ago, and the invention of the wheel, around 5,000 years ago. In relatively broad, flat fertile plains, irrigation was achieved by means of canals and dykes bringing water from rivers. In some cases, as in the early modern Venetian Republic and Dutch Republic – described as 'amphibious states' – irrigation, drainage and land reclamation occurred in parallel. Where the land was steep, terraces were cut into hillsides, using simple hand tools, to create intricately engineered step-like sequences of flat fields, fronted by stone walls where possible. Rainwater spilled down to fill these terraces, creating a more perfectly level surface in each unit and a broad landscape-image of fragmented flatness in the face of

Terraced hillsides, Longsheng county, Guilin, China, 2009.

natural steepness. Terracing was widespread across the world from ancient times, including among the Inca of southern Peru around 1200 CE and particularly in China, where wet-field rice began to dominate the agricultural system from the same time.[2]

Wheeled carts significantly increased the capacity to haul earth and rock, as well as creating a demand for levelled, graded, smooth surfaces on which to move these carts efficiently. On the other hand, agriculture roughened the earth's surface where raised fields were made to assist drainage and ploughing created ridges, or by unintended erosion. Early cultivators sometimes created great middens of domestic waste, manure, animal bone and organic matter, but equally they sometimes flattened these mounds to create rich and deep soils. Water was sometimes moved in elevated aqueducts, creating a linear level running through the landscape with a small gradient. The growth of cities resulted in construction that drew materials – stone and mud – from pits or exposed slopes, but in turn used these materials to build with flat surfaces.[3]

The mechanization of earth-moving entered a new era with the Industrial Revolution. By the middle of the nineteenth century, mobile steam shovels were shifting unheard-of amounts of material in a single scoop, setting the foundations for the enormous earthmovers of the twenty-first century. In mining, this work was dominated by excavation, and the consequent piling up of spoil heaps. In contrast, hills and steep slopes within city limits were sometimes levelled to enable growth and supply materials for construction. For example, steep-sided hills in the heart of Rio de Janeiro were removed in the 1920s – the city's modernist moment – and their earth used as infill to create level sites for housing.

Human beings now move more earth than any other geomorphic agent, a striking feature of the Anthropocene. Roger LeB. Hooke estimates that today an average 6 tonnes of earth and rock is moved per capita annually, with the quantity reaching 31 tonnes in the U.S., for a global total of about 37 billion tonnes. In earlier periods, the quantity was much less.[4] In the long term, agriculture and deforestation accounted for the largest part of this earth movement, most of it unintentional and localized but induced by the clearing of soil cover, cultivation and the trampling of domesticated animals, resulting in accelerated erosion and sedimentation. The local roughness or 'ruggedness' of eroded 'badlands' seems emblematic, but in the longer term human action has contributed indirectly to a broad levelling, by loosening materials for gravity to do its geomorphic work.[5]

Heroic projects continue to play a role. For example, in Mao's China, productivity was increased by the rationalization of practices and the creation of plains, formed by moving mountains (or at least hills), lopping off ridges and filling gullies. By these means, new land was brought under cultivation, and yields increased through the mechanization and irrigation that was facilitated by the flatness of the fields. In some places, the process also expunged older terracing, more simply cut into the natural slopes. Particularly during the Cultural Revolution, the creation of plains was understood as part of the idea of continuous revolution towards socialism and communism, symbolizing revolutionary ardour. Existing landscapes were often completely transformed, resulting in new field patterns and boundaries.[6] Although lacking an ideological justification rooted in social levelling, capitalist economies made equivalent landscape transformations in both agricultural and urban settings. Only occasionally was the process labelled shameful 'degradation'.

An increasing proportion of this movement is now consciously directed at precise levelling on the horizontal plane. The vital tool in this process is the rotating laser, sending out a beam to a target on a bulldozer, for example, and directing its operator to raise or lower the blade.[7] With the world's rapid urbanization, much of this activity has been directed at the preparation of sites for building and access. Small hills and ridges are reduced or removed completely, the overburden used to fill up existing depressions. By the 1960s, the emerging environmentalist movement in America was decrying the clearing of open land for the making of an insatiable suburbia, seeing it as creating 'a vast expanse of dirt crisscrossed by bulldozer tracks, with no topographical features, no vegetation – indeed, no visible life of any kind'.[8] In the twenty-first century, such flattening has come to be called the creation of 'ground zero', a term derived from the first atom-bomb blasts of 1945. At the other end of the cycle, the vast amounts of waste produced by modern urban consumerist societies typically goes to 'landfill', tipped and bulldozed into existing holes in the ground until level with the surface.

Draining

Before the age of urban dominance, levelling on a grand scale was mostly performed with agriculture in mind. Some of the easiest projects were the draining of wetlands, typically areas that were already relatively flat. Thus the product of drainage is essentially dry flat land, rather than new areas of flatness. The flatness of the land revealed by draining effectively matches the flatness of the prior watery surface, linking the concept of flat land with the broader perception of the sea, noted many times. Indeed, draining has often gone hand in hand with the construction of defences to keep out the sea, and 'reclamation' typically means the creation of barriers in the sea behind which – landward – the saltwater is pumped out to reveal the pre-existing flat sea floor and enable its occupation and tillage.

River flats consist of small areas of flat land alongside streams, created by erosion and aggradation of sediment. They are generally fertile and well watered in the midst of more barren land types. The same processes of erosion and sedimentation, together with changes in sea level, also operate at larger scales, as, for example, in the notoriously flat landscape of the Low Countries – the Netherlands and Belgium – where the sea made net gains on the land until the early fourteenth century. Sea-dykes protect reclaimed land from the incursion of saltwater, and river-dykes control flow through the low-lying polders, which vary in size from tiny patches to major projects, often well below sea level. Techniques developed in the Netherlands played a major role in the flattening by drainage of the Fens of southeastern England, on the other side of the North Sea but part of the same geological region.

The Fens are particularly interesting because they include the expansive southern area known as the Bedford Level, the site of nineteenth-century experiments designed to prove the Earth was flat. The Fens had long been flat, marshy and regularly inundated, the region's rivers struggling to drain into the Wash, but large-scale drainage projects were not considered until the seventeenth century. In 1630 the Earl of Bedford, a large landowner, contracted to drain the expanse known as the Great Level, and later called (beginning in the 1660s) the Bedford Level. He employed the Dutch engineer Vermuyden to build a system of drains and dykes, roads and bridges, initially to create 'summer lands', free from water during summer but still exposed to winter inundations. Problems remained, however, notably a lack of gradient in the rivers to ensure their efficient out-flow. The rivers were, in fact, too flat, and hence wide and shallow, winding in their course and confronted by powerful tides. Another problem resulted from a lowering of the surface of the fens following drainage, caused by the shrinkage of the peat level once the moisture was removed. Technological improvements over the following cen-turies, particularly the use of windmills and steam engines, led to the adoption of artificial interior drainage systems. The result was mathematical regularity in the landscape. By the twentieth century, the scene was dominated by straight lines, crossing at right angles, paralleling the flatness of the 'vast plain'.[9] In the twenty-first century, residents complained of wind turbines towering over the flatness, ruining the vista.

Clearing and cultivating

The great project of earth-moving occurred in tandem with the onslaught on the forests of the world. Globally, between 1950 and 2000, approximately 12 million hectares was cleared each year, compared to just 0.6 million hectares per year in the 1920s and '30s. Probably the peak occurred in the 1980s, but these rates substantially exceeded those of the Industrial Revolution, and pre-modern rates were in turn a lot less. Much of the recent clearing has occurred in the tropics, where the forests have been mined for timber for the developed world, often to make flat products such as sawn timbers, plywood, veneers, chipboard, fibreboard, and pulp and paper. Most of the cleared land is planted with crops or grasses to produce food for the West, the land levelled, with low standing plants presenting a flat surface to the gaze.[10]

Agriculture is the major contributor to earth movement, and typically results in local flattening. Agriculture also accounts for the largest proportion of forest clearing, creating openings in the landscape where the cover has been flattened as a preliminary to further levelling. The world in which agriculture first emerged, along with the domestication of plants and animals, and urbanization – beginning about 10,000 years ago – was thickly forested. The use of fire also served to destroy forest cover and replace it with open grassland, as an aid to the hunting of kangaroo and buffalo, for example. In some places, as on the prairies, this occurred on a grand scale, yet rarely affected the shape of the land surface. After 1700, global cropland expanded dramatically – by more than five times – at the expense of both forest and woodland, and grassland and pasture, though cropland remains only one-tenth of this total. In the long term, the clearing of the forest for crop farming was the most significant factor in creating new landscapes around the world, making possible the use of ploughs and earth-moving machines which grew substantially in scale and in their ability to create level lands. Deforestation was rarely reversed.[11]

In agriculture, the individual field possesses its own micro-topography, in which 'hills' and 'valleys' reflect and create variation in soil and dampness, with consequences for crop yields and the costs of cultivation and harvesting. Generally, farmers have always sought to reduce these inequalities, by levelling (or at least smoothing) the surface as much as possible or, where the natural slope was steep, creating stepped levels by terracing. However, ploughing a narrow furrow with a single mouldboard sometimes had the reverse effect, as in the 'ridge and furrow' pattern created when the plough was made to follow around a strip for many seasons. Modern mechanical technologies, such as multiple disc ploughs, subsoilers, scarifiers and harrows, particularly when applied to temperate cereal crop production, have all had a levelling effect, and required larger and larger fields. Farmers apply a variety of surveying techniques to perform the analysis of field slope but, because the cost of survey increases rapidly along with improved accuracy, they are most willing to spend more in situations where relative flatness is essential, as in irrigated agriculture.

In general, modern capital-intensive agriculture prefers flat lands, and large farms and fields, because these conditions enable the most profitable deployment of large, expensive machines in cultivation and harvesting. For example, some of the world's best coffee grows on steep slopes, but there it is impossible to use mechanical harvesters, because they would topple over. The consequence is that where machines are seen as a substitute for costly labour, coffee is grown in inferior environments that have the advantage of being relatively flat. In this way, it is the economics of agriculture that creates both a preference for flat sites – especially when the flatness is extensive – and an incentive to make lands level in order to create sites viable for megamachines. In grain farming, the broad, straightedged combs of modern harvesters demand predictable and continuous conditions – the invariance of flatness. When powered by steam, around 1900, a heavy roller was sometimes attached to the front of the machine to help smooth the ground and keep the engine level.[12] These actions all depend on an understanding of the earth's surface as a commodity, to be moulded to produce maximum profits in mature capitalism.

Lawns

Whereas the levelling of agricultural lands can be seen as a product of strictly economic decision-making, the desire for similarly flattened lawns has often been understood as a luxury. Thus Thorstein Veblen, in *The Theory of the Leisure Class*, first published in 1899, singled out the lawn as an example of 'pecuniary beauty', in which the capacity to allocate resources to an imitation pasture matched the lawn's 'sensuous beauty'.[13] In the twentieth century, increased wealth spread the lawn more broadly across classes and it lost some of its social cachet. In contemporary domestic living spaces, the lawn has become the most monocultural and uniformly flat cultivated landscape: a carefully tended geometric area of mown grass.

This is a recent cultural phenomenon, however, and the lawn is a feature not universally appreciated. Geographically, the modern lawn appears concentrated in Western Europe and countries colonized by Europeans. In Africa and Asia, on the other hand, it is common to maintain a bare swept plot around the house, a different kind of flatness and emptiness. Chinese gardens lack lawn, the ground being either paved – sometimes in a carpet-like flower pattern where the ground is level – or simply left rocky. The traditional Zen garden can consist of raked stones, very level, with small islands of rock jutting out from a plane surface, without rivers and valleys. As in Chinese painting, the 'blanks' are not negative absences but rather the emptiness that makes it possible to move freely and maintain an active mindful energy, with the potential for spiritual animation.[14] The gravel garden adopted in Renaissance Italy and other water-poor environments was, however, an environmental compromise, retaining the green of the lawn in tiny patches.

Historically, the lawn was rare everywhere. Its antecedents were open pastures or meadows, cropped by grazing animals such as cows and sheep. It matched the notion of Eden as a heavenly garden, or at least an open landscape, and the pastoral image of Arcadia. However, in the medieval West images of the Garden of Eden as an enclosure, from which Adam and Eve had been expelled, were common. The walled garden became a place of refuge, shut off from the ugliness of the sinful world. This was not an idea confined to Christianity. The gardens of Islam were similarly sheltered by walls, containing an idealized orchard separated from the desert.[15]

In early modern Europe, garden design employed a variety of symmetrically arranged geometric figures, enclosed within a wall: concentric circles, triangles and rays that mirrored architectural orders and made most sense viewed from above, cartographically. Generally only a few of these flat, geometric spaces were horticulturally lawn-like. Beyond the walls of the garden, in most of Europe, a more extensive lawn might be created by planting a turf of wild grasses, but rarely involved earth movement or levelling, and typically provided grazing for useful domesticated animals. Such distinct open spaces were viable only on large estates, in the same way that woods were maintained for hunting. The most vaunted example is the parkland at Versailles, created for Louis XIV after assuming the French throne in 1661. It took more than twenty years to complete and employed almost 40,000 workers, who levelled mounds, drained marshes and imposed symmetry on the landscape – so that, viewed from elevated spots, the king's domain seemed to stretch to the horizon.[16]

By the later nineteenth century, both the rich and the growing middle classes of the U.S. and parts of Western Europe began to appreciate the levelled lawn as a thing of beauty, integrated into garden design. For centuries, the concentration of housing into congested spaces, surrounded by walls, had meant security for city-dwellers. Now, detached houses came to be preferred, surrounded by an idealized version of gardened wilderness, and increasingly including a large, weed-free lawn, as homogeneous and flat as possible. Not merely an aesthetic pleasure, the lawn served as a barrier or transition space – almost a moat – between street and front door, an open prospect that might be monitored through the refuge of a curtain or crack. The flatter and emptier the lawn, the more effective it was. This appreciation of the lawn went together with a growing enthusiasm for open green spaces in the industrialized city. Here the best example is Central Park in New York City, commenced in 1858 and intended to transform the marshy site, full of ravines and rocky outcrops, into an undulating greensward. The result was a varied yet egalitarian landscape, specifically designed not to be flat and sterile, yet made rectangular so that it could slot into the city grid, overlooked by taller and taller buildings.[17]

In the twentieth century, suburbanized America was taught to see the front yard not as a site for the cultivation of food crops or a tangle of flowering shrubs, but as the place to create a standardized surface of clipped grass, as level as possible.[18] In Australia, the suburban front lawn was sometimes called 'the outside carpet', or the idealized 'billiard-table surfaced lawn'. Smoothness was highly valued, but flatness was not always desired. In gardens and parkland, the lawn might be allowed to follow the natural contours or be landscaped to create slopes. Pegs could be set out in a grid across the surface, and then knocked down to a chosen level or slope by placing a timber plank along the pegs. Absolute flatness required a spirit level. Where a truly flat lawn – 'as smooth as shining glass' – was desired, as in a bowling green, attention had to be paid to drainage at the construction stage. Here a sub-base could be created shaped like a low pyramid, sloping away from the centre in four directions to facilitate runoff; this was covered with gravel, then soil to make a level surface for the turf. If the entire surface was not carefully levelled, water might collect in pockets, resulting in a lack of uniform growth. The surface had to be maintained by occasional top dressing to remove inequalities.[19]

A flat or smooth surface was also preferred in mowing the grass of the lawn, especially when using a scythe. Reel mowers were more forgiving but still preferred flatness. Motor mowers became cheap in the 1950s, making suburban lawn care relatively easy – though noisy and dangerous. Homeowners were told that it was not enough to mow 'a collection of poor grasses and flat weeds'. The turf needed to

Turf (lawn grass), cut and rolled for delivery, Austria, 2005.

be renewed, because 'An uneven surface is not desirable for a lawn, and any bumps or depressions should be smoothed out.' In the richer countries, specialized farms were established for the propagation of lawn, using preferred grasses, to be cut out in strips and rolled up like carpets to be installed wherever wanted. Sometimes the garden was conceived as possessing a number of 'rooms', repeating the specialization of domestic interior decoration, the lawn replicating the carpet and the floor. Early reel lawnmowers imitated carpet nappers; and bowls could be played on a carpet (indoors) as well as a grassy (outdoor) rink. However small the patch, the lawn brought 'a little dignity and spaciousness to the home'.[20]

Environmentalists in the later twentieth century criticized the heavy ecological cost of the lawn care industry, which entails massive consumption of fertilizers, herbicides and water. Cultural and aesthetic criticism throughout much of the twentieth century saw the front lawn as representative of the uniformity and conformity found in suburbia, from the sameness of the houses – 'little boxes' – to the uniformity of the asphalted streets and the people. The constructed flatness of the lawn stood out as the central symbol, its monotonous monochrome creating a 'green desert' of boredom.[21] The flatness of the lawn, the concrete driveway, the walls and the windows of the house, proved ideal subjects for the 'flat' painting of the suburbs, however colourful, diverse and creative the inner life of the dwelling.

Lawn cemeteries were an American creation, beginning with Hubert Eaton's plan for a memorial park at Forest Lawn, California, in 1917: 'devoid of misshapen monuments and other customary signs of earthly Death, but filled with towering trees, sweeping lawns.'[22] The lawn cemetery erased the pyramids and burial mounds of the past, with no more than a flat plaque flush to the surface marking the place of an individual's interment. It mixed kitsch with modernist minimalism in much the same way as the suburban lawn. Subsidence was avoided by using steel caskets placed in concrete bunkers. Forest Lawn became a popular site for visitors, and the model spread.[23] The plan was always to achieve a sweeping undulating landscape, with groves of trees and a scattering of statues, more like a golf course than a football field.

In public spaces, 'Keep Off the Grass' signs tutored the ignorant to understand that the carefully tended lawn was a thing of beauty to be looked upon, a work of perfection too fragile to sustain even a footprint. At home, the lawn satisfied the desire for 'prospect' of even the smallest household, ideally to be viewed from the 'refuge' of the porch or perhaps peeping through curtains.

Roads and railways

Roads come in many shapes and surfaces but modern transport technologies have placed a premium on smoothness and straightness. Thus the general mission of road-building and surfacing is definitively towards flattening, by cutting and filling. In practice, the cost of creating a completely level road system is generally so great that most roads follow the contours of the land. Modern passenger cars can travel up slopes of about 7 per cent without reducing speed, but anything greater than 20 per cent is challenging. There is also a lower limit, required to enable drainage in most lands, of about 0.3 per cent. So long as the drainage can be handled, in flat country the road pavement itself can be level.[24] On very flat land, a flyover or interchange may be the most prominent feature in the landscape.

Slow-moving foot traffic, whether human or animal, could cope with relatively bumpy paths and uneven road surfaces. Wheeled transport, on the other hand, demands smoother and harder surfaces, for comfort and speed. Paradoxically, as the wheel replaced the foot, walkers benefited from these engineering improvements, by default. By the middle of the twentieth century, tennis shoes or sneakers were no longer restricted to the smooth surfaces of tennis and basketball courts, and high heels could be worn while shopping as well as at a courtly ball. The less people walked and carried loads, as part of everyday existence, the less specialized their footwear became, thanks to flatness.[25] The more the motor vehicle became a kind of prosthetic, the more people demanded flatness wherever they roamed.

Among the more famous of the ancient road systems was that of the vast Roman Empire, designed primarily to facilitate the movement of troops and reaching a total length close to 300,000 kilometres. However, it is wrong to imagine the typical Roman road as 'wide, straight and flat'. Rather, the builders paid close attention to variations in terrain, and the empire stretched across much mountainous country. The earliest roads consisted of gravel or flint on a clay foundation, leading to the development of paving, using blocks of flint or basalt, and multiple layers of compacted clay, sand, crushed stone and gravel, with a thin mortar, creating a rudimentary form of concrete.[26] Improvements took a long time to emerge, with little innovation in transport technologies. Not until the early nineteenth century did 'macadamized' surfaces build on these ancient foundations by laying broken stone of similar size in successively compacted layers, bound together with tar or asphalt (bitumen).

The advent of the motor vehicle – and the almost contemporary invention of the bicycle – radically changed requirements. Fast-moving wheels required relatively flat surfaces to ensure a comfortable and safe journey. Further, whereas slow-moving horse-drawn

Sandy road, Simpson Desert Conservation Park, South Australia, 2015.

traffic packed down gravel and macadam, the weight and speed of motors broke up the surfaces and swept gravel into windrows. Nowhere were road systems prepared for this onslaught. In the u.s. until 1909 there was not a single section of paved road in the rural regions. The demand quickly led to the construction of roads using concrete, and to a lesser extent brick, but the costliness of these materials meant that macadam or asphalt concrete remained predominant in spite of the need for constant repair. The network of paved roads became extensive only in the 1930s, and the building of interstate highways began in the u.s. only in 1956.[27]

Global estimates suggest that there was a total of more than 50 million kilometres of roads in 2010, with an additional 25 million kilometres to be built by 2050. Regions most lacking roads are typically low-density remote places, such as the Amazon, the deserts of North Africa and Australia, and the sub-Arctic. This prediction means not simply a substantial flattening of the spaces immediately affected but further impact through the reduction of biodiversity, environmental damage and the spread of connected flatness into

Concrete paving, laid *c.* 1955, Stuyvesant Avenue, Ewing, New Jersey, 2014.

Global road network density, 2013. Density is least in the blank zones.

driveways and car parks. Roads cut through the Amazon, for example, typically generate secondary and tertiary routes, spreading out in a swathe, flattening the landscape through deforestation and agricultural exploitation.[28]

In these ways, there can be a disjunction between the road itself and the surrounding countryside, the road sometimes the only relatively flat surface in the landscape. The motor car, particularly because of its speed, requires a smooth, level surface for comfortable operation, quickly giving birth to parkway and autobahn in the interwar period. Whereas these systems sought to blend the road surface into the contours of the landscape, after 1945, particularly in the U.S., the emphasis shifted to efficiency and the brutal carving out of straight, flat freeways and expressways. Wherever possible, the road followed the flatness, 'along a grade of least resistance', leaving low hills, dunes, bluffs and knobs off in the distant view, while the dips and hollows are invisible. Interstate motorists saw only the flatness. It was left to locals to 'sense a slight unevenness' and enjoy the view from an overpass.[29]

The penetration of the flatness of the road surface into other environments is most obvious in the development of car parks and parking stations, extensions of the road system but specialized in removing parked vehicles from the roadside. The soft shoulder and verge often merge into the roughness of the surrounding landscape, sometimes with hazardous semi-concealed gullies and gutters. The

car park too began as a natural area of grass or grit, but grew in time
to be a much more perfect flat surface, made with ideal, homogeneous, flat materials such as asphalt and concrete, a place where the
motorist might search for an empty space. In contemporary America,
the area occupied by parking space is vast, equal to the area covered
by roads. But whereas the 'open' road suggests freedom and motion,
and flattens the perception of the surrounding landscape, the car
park brings to mind only unromantic congestion and closure,
piecemeal flat places. However, in the period before the development
of multistorey car parks (parking garages) – from the 1920s to the
'60s – buildings were demolished and entire city blocks levelled in
order to create parking lots in the centres of big cities. In 1960 as
much as 28 per cent of the land of downtown Los Angeles was
occupied by streets and a further 38 per cent by off-street parking.
The intrusion was even greater in Detroit, where in 1972 a total of
74 per cent of the downtown area was dedicated to the motor
vehicle. The result was a landscape of skyscrapers jutting out from
a surface eroded and flattened, asphalted and concreted, in which
roadways, pavements and car parks created a continuous level.[30]

Ironically, the car park shares only the most abstract features of
the traditional verdant park rooted in nature. Particularly in the
modern American urban landscape, the parking lot is the most
utilitarian and predictable element, thus contributing to the sameness that characterizes such cities. It is this invariance that the
parking lot shares with the essence of flatness. Inevitably, therefore,
parking lots are rarely considered an aesthetic contribution to the
urban landscape. As the geographer John A. Jakle and the historian
Keith A. Sculle comment, 'When empty of cars they were particularly vacuous to the eye, but even when they were filled with cars a
certain vacuousness remained. Row on row, lot to lot, and block to
block, a sea of parked cars flattened to the gaze.'[31] In its flatness, the
parking lot emphasizes the practicalities of negotiating a vehicle in
and out, but its very uniformity removes the spatial landmarks
needed for wayfinding and replaces it with a void. Returning motorists, disorientated by this lack, wander about, as on an open plain,
searching for their vehicles.

Locomotives, even more than motor vehicles, love flat lands. Whereas motor vehicles are capable of tackling short, sharp corners and steep slopes, the relative bulk and heaviness of trains makes them much less tolerant of roughness and steepness. Thus the shift from road travel with soft-hooved animals to the iron wheels of the locomotive running on iron rails, beginning in the 1830s, was revolutionary. It enabled for the first time the building of the 'mechanically perfect road'. As Wolfgang Schivelbusch argues in his classic work *The Railway Journey*, 'The railroad did this first and foremost by means of the rail, which was harder, smoother, more level, and straighter than any road before it.'[32] Excavation and embankment, levelling up and levelling down, were used to make the path flat and straight; and where the mountains were too high and the valleys too low, tunnels and viaducts were built at great cost. Vaclav Smil estimates the movement of earth, gravel and fill required at an average 3,000 cubic metres per kilometre, a massive quantity on the global scale. Vast networks spread around the world, with 775,000 kilometres by 1900. In spite of reductions in some countries, this almost doubled by 2010.[33]

Early rail travel was often described as visually fatiguing, impressions constantly changing. What used to be in close-up was lost in the rush of speed. Some attributed this directly to the fact that they moved on a flat surface, inducing monotony and inevitable boredom. Other travellers, however, developed a fresh mode of perception, embracing the elevated vistas offered by embankments, and the variety of mountain and ravine engineered by cuttings. As Schivelbusch says, the railway created a new panoramic landscape, one in which 'an intrinsically monotonous landscape' was 'brought into an esthetically pleasing perspective'.[34]

The rail journey became a relatively isolated business, with much in common with the sea voyage, and particularly suited to travel across vast, open – naturally flat – surfaces. However, the development of high-speed rail, beginning in the 1960s, meant trains could travel much faster than one typically could on sea or in a motor vehicle, and for certain distances, it competed with air travel. Such high speeds – approaching 500 kilometres an hour – required continuously welded track and large turning circles, placing a premium on flatness and straightness. Even maglev – magnetic levitation – systems need track that is reliably invariant.

Dams and canals

The engineered capture and confinement of water takes many forms and varies considerably in scale, from swimming pools to massive reservoirs. In every case, however, the outcome is an artificial flat surface. These watery surfaces conceal and replace pre-existing natural and cultural landscapes, many of them occupying narrow valleys because these sites were the most efficient places to contain large volumes of water. They create extensive flat surfaces in the midst of rugged topography.

Some ambitious projects were completed in ancient times, probably beginning in the Middle East but also in India, China, the Roman Empire and Central America. The greatest surge of activity occurred in the twentieth century, when mechanized earth-moving machines became available. The total number of dams, ponds and reservoirs is difficult to establish, and depends on definition. In the U.S., for example, there are about 75,000 dams greater than 2 metres high, with more than 61,700 cubic metres of storage. Total storage climbed rapidly between 1930 and 1970, and then levelled off. Most of these dams in the U.S. are small, and the largest part of the storage is accounted for by a few really big reservoirs.[35] The relationship between storage and surface area is not simple, and some of the most extensive reservoirs are relatively shallow. Further, some reservoirs expand existing lakes rather than interrupting natural streamflow. Lake Victoria on the White Nile is dammed at Owen Falls, covering 66,400 square kilometres, whereas the Hoover Dam on the Colorado River has a surface area of just 659 square kilometres. Globally, large dams cover a surface greater than the total land area of Italy. The result is a significant local flattening of the landscape.

Canals create linear flatness, but where possible they follow the contours of the land, with the occasional lock to change the level. The Suez Canal, opened in 1869, was a flat sea-level channel, but the more challenging Panama Canal (1914) had six double locks to make a stair-stepped water bridge. Around the world, wherever channels were required for irrigation or the delivery of water power, surveying instruments were developed to ensure excavated channels followed the contours, always heading downslope but at controlled velocity and force. The spirit level was just one such instrument, and many simpler devices took advantage of the natural level-finding characteristic of water in order to project towards the horizon.[36]

Architectural platforms

What is the relationship between the built environment and the land on which it has its being? Why seek to engineer the surface before building? The simple answer is that gravity denies the practicality of anything other than a level starting point. Architecture demands a platform. This does not mean that all cultures choose or prefer flat sites for settlement but that each dwelling unit requires a level base, even if cut into the side of a steep, rocky hillside. A horizontal plane is essential to any formal arrangement of space intended for human activity. Uneven surfaces and ramps have their place but generally link lived-in levels rather than disrupting the fundamentals of layered horizontal spatiality. On a ship rolling in heavy seas, things have to be secured, and the Leaning Tower of Pisa is easily seen to be hazardous. Only level surfaces are capable of providing visual stability. Thus the creation of a level plane is not only useful but has a wider visual and visceral architectural significance.[37]

Architecture is a constant struggle with gravity. The construction of shelter is therefore a hazardous business, the more so the taller a building stands above the ground. Traditional vernacular architecture – the buildings that housed people through most of history – worked closely with the immediate environment, modifying the topography only marginally and drawing materials from what could be found nearby. Gravity was in control but the hazards were limited. Houses took many shapes, in their walls and roofs, and in their internal structure, often growing organically, in an additive fashion through clustering and/or subdivision. Large, tall buildings, however, demanded quite precise measurement and accurate specification, and the close definition of spatial terms. Thus a point indicates a position in space; a line is a point extended, gaining the properties of length and direction; and 'A line extended in a direction other than its intrinsic direction becomes a *plane*,' with properties of width, shape, surface and orientation, but, conceptually, lacking depth. The flatness of the plane does not always depend on horizontality. In a building, a floor is a base plane, a wall a wall plane and a ceiling an overhead plane. In surveying a site, however, the horizontal plane provides a fixed point of reference, sometimes literally, as in the plan drawn on a plane table, and sometimes abstractly, in a positional geometry justified to match a horizon, as level as a seascape.[38]

The grandness of the idea of the base plane or platform can be admired in everything from classical Greek architecture to ancient Mesoamerica, India and China, and the modernism of Frank Lloyd Wright, who tried to think outside the box. For example, the house known as Fallingwater, built over a natural waterfall in the hills of Pennsylvania in the late 1930s, demonstrated Wright's 'insistence on horizontal continuity at the expense of all else', denying even ramps and spirals.[39] In ancient Mexico, the top of a mountain might be sliced off to create a flat surface, to provide the foundation for stone temples and palaces. In the case of the Maya, the building of their temples on vast platforms above the horizon of the surrounding forest offered the possibility of a new perspective that resembled more the openness of the ocean than the claustrophobia of the jungle. The platform and its ceremonial buildings seemed to float on a green sea. Architects in the West have drawn on this notion of 'transcendent detachment from the immediate surroundings and engagement with distant horizons' and borrowed the platform to site structures as iconic as Jørn Utzon's Sydney Opera House, which seems to float above the harbour. The abstraction of the platform is 'radically modern', its design 'eliminating the need for any deviation from the ideal of an absolutely level, horizontal plane'.[40]

Utzon had travelled to the Yucatán in 1949, following a visit to Wright's Taliesin East, and published a reflective essay on 'Platforms and Plateaus' in 1962. He said the Mayan platforms converted 'the jungle roof' into a 'great open plain', and observed that with this 'architectural trick', the people had 'completely changed the land-scape and supplied their visual life with a greatness corresponding to the greatness of their Gods'. Other architects have maintained an enthusiasm for the platform, and the abstract evocation of land and sky, as in, for example, some of the schemes of Tadao Ando, working in a reductionist, raw style, using concrete, glass and steel.[41]

In all of this architectural history, it is striking that the funda-mental plane – the floor – remains defiantly flat, however topological and contorted the rest of the building's surfaces might be. Geodesic domes, derived from polyhedra, always appear as truncated spheres, their floor area determined by the point at which a horizontal datum plane is passed through the dome, whether at the equator or nearer the poles, or following a great circle.[42] The result is an archi-tectural form reminiscent of ancient cosmologies in which a flat earth is covered by the dome of heaven. The compromise is a tribute to the overwhelming practicality of flatness for the upright human

Frank den Oudsten, exterior of the Schröder House, Utrecht, by Gerrit Rietveld, 1924.

being walking about. Ramps may be functional, but sloping, undulating, bumpy floors are hazardous and exhausting, fit only for funfairs. The same rules apply to fixtures and furniture, with flat surfaces used to keep things secure and efficient – in everything from tables and benchtops to sleeping mats and beds. Inside a perfect sphere, everything would slide down into a central heap. Even in a bubble-tent, there is nothing worse than rolling downhill in the night or feeling a rock under your hip.

A vital feature of twentieth-century Western architecture is 'the use of horizontal planes to define spatial settings without recourse to enclosing uprights'. Rather than the confinement created by walls, the visual field of a building could be opened up, through the use of 'open plan' internal design and the ability to look out through large plate-glass windows, drawing the eye to the horizontal. The architect Pierre von Meiss, while bemoaning the evils of 'bulldozer landscape', admitted the virtues of some large-scale examples, such as the creation of the Dutch polders, but overall could find few good reasons for 'the radical transformation of a topography'. At the level of the house itself, however, he saw the necessity of regularity, symmetry and repetition, in all of which flatness can be seen to be implicit.[43]

Flattening interpreted as symbolic of Westernization/globalization sometimes reaches to the very heart of holy places. In the contemporary world, the transformation of Mecca is a striking example. Beginning in the 1970s, the city surrounding the Kaaba – the ultimate destination and focal point of the Hajj – began to be levelled, the old buildings and historic sites bulldozed and replaced by 'modern' architectural forms and highways, and rectangular steel and concrete structures (most of them hotels for pilgrims) built as close as possible around wide, empty, flat and open spaces. Even the surrounding mountains were levelled, while the giant Makkah Royal Clock Tower, completed in 2012, towered above. Once again, the world's tallest buildings were rising up in the Middle East, though matched by competitors in East Asia, easily exceeding 500 metres and expected to go beyond 1 kilometre. From an engineering point of view, buildings with heights of up to 3 kilometres are feasible, but there are economic and environmental costs, and health issues linked to increased heart rate variability.[44]

Planning flatness

The flatness of Tiananmen Square in Beijing is matched by its great extent. Designed in the seventeenth century, it was expanded in the 1950s to reach the present size of 44 hectares, 500 metres east–west and 860 metres north–south, on the order of Mao Zedong, making it the central point of the nation. Tiananmen's scale was intended not only to provide a stage for parades and rallies but to 'demonstrate its openness and magnificence', though some critics complained that if made too big, 'it would be so vast that it looks like a desert and it falls out of proportion to man'. The urban spread of Beijing was compared to 'the making of a pancake' – recalling images of Texas – but from the 1980s was transformed by large-scale demolition and rebuilding. The great 'expanse of green' and the 'vast expanses of flatland beyond' that had surrounded Old Beijing became 'a sea of tall, concrete buildings'. Critics pointed to the environmental and aesthetic costs, preferring a 'horizontal' city. Tokyo similarly is said to have expanded like the making of a type of pancake resembling a pizza.[45] New York City, by contrast, developed in the twentieth century along with the skyscraper, its profile resembling a histogram.

The relationship between topography and rectangular survey has a long and complex history. Whereas the grid has much in common with the two-dimensional concept of flatness, it loses its advantage when applied rigidly to landscapes with diverse elements and varied slope. City planning in the u.s. offers prime examples of the disjunction between rectangularity and topography. San Francisco is held up as a prime case of this failure, some of the streets so steep that it is exhausting to walk or cycle up them, while out-of-control cable cars rocket downhill to disaster.

Spatial planning of the modern city, argues Bernd Hüppauf, had as its main objective 'the eradication of the crooked anatomy of old towns and its replacement with clear and geometrical arrangements'. In Western Europe, from the end of the seventeenth century, absolutist rationality was directed at achieving symmetry and order, and towards the removal of anarchic relics 'where lanes wriggled like worms, where no façade was regular and everything seemed warped'. Urban reconstruction was applied aggressively in metropolitan centres – notably in the case of nineteenth-century Paris – but smaller settlements often escaped, retaining their geometrical disorder long enough to be eventually regarded as worthy of preservation as proof of a nostalgic vernacular truth performed in their contorted streets and architectural roughness.[46]

The early American Republic sought to apply rectangularity at almost every level in its expansion westwards, from the boundaries of the states down to the boundaries of the individual farm. Major rivers disrupted the regularity of the state boundaries, but variations in slope were generally not allowed to affect the laying out of the grid as though on a flat sheet in the office of the cartographer and surveyor. In New York the city's commissioners ordained the imposition of a rectilinear street plan with uniform blocks in 1811. In spite of some notable deviations, the plan proved a 'great leveller'. Millions of cubic metres of rock and soil were moved to create flat lots, equal in area, encouraging rapid economic development and enabling travellers to find their way easily through the landscape. Although criticized by Alexis de Tocqueville for its 'relentless monotony', condemned by Henry James as a 'primal topographic curse' and labelled more recently as an exercise in plane geometry, devoid of aesthetic value, the city's map became a well-known and resilient part of its character.[47]

By 1924 Le Corbusier could declare the straight line and the right angle essential to spatial order: 'We must have the courage to view the rectilinear cities of America with admiration.' For Paris, he advocated 'a *vertical* city', in which skyscrapers – built solely with steel and glass – rose freely from extensive open spaces and avenues, thus replacing the 'flattened-out and jumbled city such as *the airplane reveals to us for the first time*, terrifying in its confusion'. However, he also saw moral value in vastness, which conferred dignity, declaring that 'the eye of man who sees wide horizons is prouder.' By the 1950s

Architectural circles within an imposed plane rectangular grid: Ouagadougou, Upper Volta (Burkina Faso), c. 1930.

many town planners saw the need to choose between cities in which height zoning was applied rigidly to buildings or cities of towers set in wide-open spaces, along the lines advocated by Le Corbusier.[48]

In planning for both town and country, flatness does not always demand rectangularity. Indeed, it is interesting that theoretical attempts to explain the spatial distribution of (unplanned) human economic activity and settlement typically begin with a uniform surface but hardly ever find rectilinear patterns. This is very clearly the case in the concentric land-use rings discovered by Johann Heinrich von Thünen (1783–1850) in his study *The Ideal State* (1826), one of the earliest attempts to explain the spatial pattern of land use according to a simplified model of the movement-minimization problem in economics on a flat uniform plain. As a practical farmer, working in Mecklenberg, northern Germany – a region regarded as mostly flat and low – von Thünen recognized the importance of transport costs when everything else was equal. Another German scholar, Alfred Weber (1868–1958), built on these concepts to develop a theory of industrial location, assuming all transport was by rail, on 'a mathematically flat plain where the mountains are razed, the valleys filled, and the swamps covered'.[49]

Central place theory, which seeks to explain the spatial distribution of human settlement and its hierarchical ordering, was first
outlined in 1933 by Walter Christaller (1893–1969). Once again,
Christaller found a pattern of concentric circles marking the cost
of movement to services, similar to the models of von Thünen and
Weber but hierarchical. Since these circles would necessarily overlap,
Christaller found the hexagon to be the most efficient straight-sided
geometric shape to divide the space equally. The only alternative
regular tessellations are provided by the square and the equilateral triangle. The hexagonal solution was already known from the
natural world, where it is seen surprisingly often, as for example
in crystals, saltpans, body-plans and honeycombs, especially where
it can generate horizontally.[50]

It is interesting that the closely related concept of 'least-effort',
developed in the u.s. in the 1940s by George Kingsley Zipf, was
applied to the cost of moving people to a particular location, specifically the front line of battle in a war to repel invasion by an enemy.
Zipf said, 'The path will be a straight line only when that is the
easiest path; otherwise the paths will go around swamps and over
and around mountains – whatever is the easiest.' Generalizing, he
argued that 'as the traffic between two points increases, it will be
economical to straighten the route between them, and to make it
more nearly level, as soon as the (probable) amount of work that is
saved by the shorter and more level route is sufficient to offset the
work of straightening and levelling.'[51]

Whereas the theories of von Thünen, Weber and most of their
successors were little known to social and economic planners,
Christaller joined the Nazi Party in 1940 and went to work on the
proposed transformation of the settlement landscape of Poland and
beyond. Indeed, the formal geometry of Christaller's theory was
co-opted to create a spatial vacuum, directed at removing people
(mostly Jews and Slavs) from conquered lands in order to create an
'empty space', to be reoccupied by Germans. This was represented
not only by depopulation but in the shape of the landscape, which
was 'literally bulldozed'.[52]

Ground Zero

The original ground zero was defined by the dropping of atomic bombs on Hiroshima and Nagasaki in August 1945, marking the place on the ground immediately below the point of detonation. The initial effect of these attacks was the dramatic flattening of the built environment through the impact of the blast and the associated fire storm, which reduced the cities to rubble, more so at Hiroshima where the site was flatter. There were precedents in the firebombing of Dresden in February of the same year, in the 'carpet bombing' of cities (first named in 1943) that comprehensively covered the surface in the same way a carpet covers and levels a floor, and also in the barren wastes of the no-man's-land of the First World War, but the atomic attacks were vastly more total.

In the longer term, wars typically focused on the destruction of the enemy's architectural mass, particularly the knocking down of protective city walls and the burning of buildings, but only in the twentieth century did powerful tools – such as tanks and bulldozers – become available to enable large-scale earth-moving and hence flattening. Battlefields were long limited in size and, where pitched battles were the preferred contest, open, level surfaces were often chosen and even agreed on. Little was done to engineer these surfaces. Guerrilla warfare, which also had a long history, took advantage of landscape diversity and roughness, and prospered in prospect-refuge habitats rather than on open plains. On the Western Front of the First World War, trench warfare was designed to reduce vulnerability on exposed, level fields.

In general, the immediate effects of warfare were towards a flattening of the landscape, but the continuing impact of military activity was limited. Only after 1900 was this process truly transformative, particularly as a result of the way action shifted from land and sea to war in and from the air. Even in this recent period, many elements – such as the use of camouflage, which responded to aerial visualization by creating deceptive spatial patterns that blended with the homogeneity of the desert, for example, flattening out the pictorial field – were temporary in their impact on topography. At sea, the aircraft carrier quickly became a necessity to support fighter planes. This resulted in a new type of vessel with a severely flattened deck, beginning with the uss *Langley*, transformed in 1922 to carry a massive wooden 'flat-top' across the length of the ship. Modern 'militarized' landscapes share the flatness resulting from the building of roads, car parks and airfields that characterizes the contemporary world. The same is true of virtual military landscapes in video gaming.[53]

When the towers of the World Trade Center in New York were reduced to rubble by aerial terrorist attack on 11 September 2001, the site quickly became known as Ground Zero. The destruction of the Twin Towers, built in 1972 to a height of 417 metres, was memorialized in many visual and graphic forms across the u.s.; matched by terrorist slogans on high-rise buildings in Tehran, declaring 'Down with the usa.'[54] By 2014 a single defiant tower, One World Trade Center, had been built on the site, rising to 541 metres – the tallest building in the u.s. Ironically, u.s. military action in Iraq, in response to 9/11, saw the establishment of a base on the ancient archaeological site of the city of Babylon, where an extensive area was 'flattened' for a helipad and other purposes, covered with gravel and compacted.[55]

Broadly, it seems that although human beings have done more to flatten the world than to elevate it, this flattening is rarely seen as something deserving celebration, whereas building up gives status and instils pride. Attacking the Twin Towers, which stood so tall, represented an assault on the hubris of elevation, something which can be traced back to the Tower of Babel, and equally the rebuilding represented defiance. Similar attitudes can be seen in attempts to defy Nature by the building of mountains to transform the environmental regime.

Eccentric over-reaching is not a thing of the past. In Australia, there was a call in 1979 for a 'man-made mountain' to benefit climate, industry and environment. It was to stretch 1,780 kilometres across Australia at longitude 130° (along the eastern border of Western Australia), and rise 4 kilometres, with a base 10 kilometres wide and a 2-kilometre plateau on top. The primary objective was to create rainfall, but the mountain was also meant to serve as a store for produce to stabilize global markets, a hedge against nuclear war and much more. In the Netherlands, a project was announced in 2011 to build a 2-kilometre-tall mountain that would offer ski slopes and hiking trails to the people of this 'billiard-table flat' country, to counter its 'boring' flatness.[56] The amount of rock and soil to be shifted in these projects is immense, and they are hard to take seriously. Very tall towers are easier to accept, as affordable symbols of human ambition and the denial of flatness.

In the ancient world, the burial mounds of rulers sometimes rose above the landscape, built of earth or stone. In China, the best-known imperial burial mound is that at Xi'an, built of earth at the beginning of the Qin Dynasty (221–207 BCE), but its height was only about 45 metres. Towers and pagodas, generally built of wood, occasionally reached above 100 metres, but they became less favoured during the Han Dynasty (206 BCE–220 CE), when the Confucian understanding that tall buildings disrupt the harmony of heaven and earth came to hold sway.[57] The biblical story of the Tower of Babel, found in the book of Genesis (11:1–9), said only that the tower was built of brick, intended to 'reach unto heaven', and that when God scattered the people to 'confound their language', they stopped building the city. The story had parallels in other traditions, with sources putting the height of the tower at anything from 200 metres to more than 10 kilometres. Many narratives described God sending a great wind to destroy the tower, seeing it as a symbol of man's over-reaching desire to test the limits of stone and brick, and the patience of the Almighty. The spires of European cathedrals – built of stone or wood – did not exceed the height of the Great Pyramid until the fourteenth century, and long remained the most prominent features in flat landscapes. Buildings more than 300 metres high did not exist until the late nineteenth century, and they had to await the arrival of strong, modern and flat materials.

The biggest ancient structures were pyramidal and built of stone. Massive stone blocks, carefully squared, created the Great Pyramid of Egypt, constructed for the Pharaoh Khufu and completed around 2674 BCE, reaching 147 metres. Its sides had an angle of 52°, and the square base was oriented precisely to the cardinal directions. In spite of its colossal size, the Great Pyramid withstood erosion and today remains as high as 139 metres. For almost four thousand years, it was the tallest structure in the world, and it remains the largest building, sitting firmly on the Giza Plateau and built with extraordinary geometrical precision on a levelled base.[58]

SIX

LEVEL PLAYING FIELDS

'It is the flatness of the stage that makes choreography probable, just as it is the flatness of the stadium that increases the probability of athletics.'

Bernard Cache, 1995[1]

The 'level playing field' is a recent phrase, used first in the U.S. in the 1970s to indicate fair dealing. The analogy needed no explanation. By the 1970s the modernization of sports was already far advanced, symbolized by its topographic standardization but marked also by a broader process of regulation controlling the rules, tools and behaviour of games. The sites of sport were typically separated from the natural landscape and regarded as perhaps the most extreme examples of the reduction of space to geometry associated with the image of modernity. Times and distances were measured with great precision, and the spatiality of sport assumed an isotropic surface – in which physical properties have the same measure in every direction – much like the conditions required of a 'flat' universe.[2] Modern sports are also highly repetitive in their elements, taking the spectator to the edge of monotony by requiring that the fundamental conditions be the same in each iteration. Think of the performance of the serve in tennis.

Venues for pre-modern games lacked almost all of the regulatory and standardizing features that characterize modern sport. The most obvious exceptions were the ceremonial plazas of the Pre-Columbian Americas used for the ball game and the carefully designed arenas and stadiums of the geometry-obsessed ancient Greeks and their Roman imitators. Even these lacked the standardization of surfaces and compliance codes found in the modern era. Most often, before the nineteenth century, sports were played on agricultural fields or pastures, existing tracks or the streets of towns, without clear spatial boundaries and without a clear distinction between players and spectators. Little was done to ensure the playing surface was level. This shift is sometimes explained as part of modernization and globalization, but it had also to do with concepts of time and the idea of 'leisure' and with the commercial opportunities that came to be seen in this new area of discretionary spending.

On an international scale, the process of spatial and temporal quantification in sport began to become intense only in the late nineteenth century. It occurred in a period of high imperialism, when European colonialism brought 'modern sports' to many parts of the world and used them to teach doctrines of fair play and hence equality, parallel to the doctrine that all peoples were equal in God's sight – ideas which ultimately helped undermine claims of Western superiority and justifications of empire. Colonized peoples embraced these new sports enthusiastically, whenever given the chance, and quickly began to appear in international competitions, delighting in defeating their imperial masters even before decolonization.[3]

Standardization stemmed both from a political desire for social control and from a growing impulse to measure and compare. World records could only be taken seriously if contests were equal. Sport became a source of national as well as individual pride and identity, and a significant element in the global economy. Increasingly sophisticated technologies were applied to improving the performance of sportspeople and the surfaces on which they performed, not least the level playing field. Ironically, the levelling and standardization of sport facilitated the ranking of performers and their allocation to subsets of skill and achievement. Increasingly such rankings served to focus attention on the very small number of individuals or teams that made it to the top. The rankings were used in turn to determine pay scales, with international stars earning immense prizes and the vast majority missing out. Thus the precision applied to the levelling of playing fields and the measurement of performance enabled the construction of new forms of inequality. It was the conquest of celebrity over the rough democracy of sport played on a beach or in a cow paddock.

The competitive aspect of sport in its modern form made it an ideal subject for economic analysis. Beginning around the time games became modernized and commercialized, in the 1970s economists began to consider the implications of sport for the understanding of markets, competition and optimality. The 'received theory' was that 'the perfect game is a symbiotic contest between equal opponents'. It was also assumed that sports fans preferred to see balanced competition, to conform to the 'uncertainty of outcome hypothesis'. A close finish indicated perfect competition. In fact, it has been shown that the audience for sport enjoys dominance, in which differences in market power – to buy players for teams – lead to imperfect competition.

Particularly in the contemporary market for media rights, in which revenue is not closely tied to place or 'home team loyalties', equality between teams in a league is not necessary to achieving optimal returns.[4] The vast amounts of money involved often prove tempting to officials and players, upsetting equity in the location of competitions and the fixing of matches. Thus in 2015 when FIFA (the International Federation of Association Football) officials were arrested in New York under charges of bribery and corruption, the director of the FBI declared that by their actions 'That field that is so famously flat was made tilted in favour of those looking to gain.'[5] Occasionally tampering with the actual playing surface is used to advantage one team or player over another, when money or glory is at stake.

Running, walking, swimming

It is striking that some of the first known efforts to ensure equality in sports performances came from the Greeks, with their intense concern for measurement and relatively advanced understanding of cosmology, notably the relationship between line and circle. Their democratic impulse might also seem to parallel the notion of sporting fairness, though paradoxically – Greek democracy was revolutionary but incomplete and flourished within the heart of a slave society, which helped create the leisure time essential to the development of games.

For the Greeks, standardization seems chiefly to have meant the measurement of length and control of the start in running races. The stadia they constructed were often located in natural valleys, so that the zone of competition could be on level land surrounded by banked terraces. They mirrored amphitheatres created for the performance of drama. Originally a religious structure, dating to the sixth century BCE, the ancient Greek stadium was the stage for athletic contests: foot races of varying lengths, wrestling and boxing, and the pentathlon (discus, javelin, long jump, wrestling and a foot race one length of the stadium). In its earliest form, the ancient stadium was typically a flat, rectangular space 163 metres long and 15 to 30 metres wide, bordered by earth embankments for spectators to stand or sit on.

The evidence is limited, but archaeological excavations show that tracks were made of hard-packed clay or a composition of clay and sand, and were fairly smooth, with a gentle slope of around 0.5 per cent. The terraces dug out of the bordering ground for standing spectators – up to 50,000 of them – were also quite flat. Standardization was applied to the lengths of the ancient Greek stadia: they were by definition 600 feet (183 metres) long but the ancient foot was not itself standardized, varying from place to place and over time. With a range of perhaps 0.278 to 0.32 metres for the foot, the stadium could stretch from 166.8 to 192 metres. These variations mattered little, however, because it was the winning of the race that was celebrated, not the time.

What the Greeks took most seriously was ensuring that runners covered the same distance and started at the same time. The start was controlled by the use of gates, opened (almost) simultaneously by the starter. The distance covered was standardized in the shortest race – the *stadion*, one length of the field – simply by having the runners compete in marked lanes. The longer foot races all required turns around a pillar, and thus the distance covered by a runner varied with his position at the starting line. Here the Greeks applied their understanding of geometry, making the starting line a curve with marked starting positions, from which the runners converged. The archaeological evidence of these curved lines from about 500 BCE represents the earliest proof of this geometric knowledge, specifically π, the relationship between the diameter of a circle and its circumference.[6] Together, these features appear very modern, but runners remained firmly placed in their environments and were determined only to defeat their immediate competitors; they did not challenge time or what could be achieved at other sites. International competition came much later, demanding specially designed level surfaces.

Walking and running are normal forms of movement, made easier or harder by the slopes on which they are performed. Engineered surfaces – made flatter and smoother – are designed to reduce the amount of energy expended and increase speeds and/or distances. The benefits are clearly apparent in everyday life but significantly increased when these activities are 'sportized'. Athletes run and walk faster the straighter their lanes; sharp turns slow them down. Downslope tracks produce faster times and steep ascents slower. Although cross-country and marathon races are run almost entirely on existing everyday routes, up and down, the shortest sprints are on the straightest, flattest and smoothest surfaces which still enable traction. It is the surfaces used for short races that have become the most 'placeless' and geometrically abstract.

Modern running tracks are frequently coated with polymers, as are the soles of running shoes, to act as shock absorbers and reduce injury. Free-flowing liquid polyurethane mixes can be laid on substrate in situ, or prefabricated, creating synthetic surfaces perceptibly flatter than tracks of grass or cinders. Grass remained a favoured running surface into the 1960s but had by then largely been replaced by cinders (variously composed from mixtures of ashes, slag, concrete, sand, mortar and marl, and differing from place to place), and by the end of the twentieth century synthetic surfaces were the only form permitted in international competition. The running track became uniformly flat and empty, placeless, indeed approaching 'the theoretical isotropic plane/plain'.[7]

It is the contact between foot and ground that determines speed in running and walking. For walkers, speed depends on both stride length and rate; for runners, stride length is most important. Stress on the body, and the possibility of injury, is greater downhill than on level tracks.[8] Studies of the factors leading to long-term improved performance in sport typically identify demographic change, drugs and new technologies. The flatness of the track is not considered significant; it is simply taken for granted for all distances except the marathon, the running event which has demonstrated the greatest improvement in recent times and is most affected by environmental factors (such as altitude and temperature), but is the least standardized with little ambition to be run on flat, synthetic surfaces.

Swimming in a pool offers the natural flatness of the water level but is severely constrained in scale so that long races are swum in straight lanes with many abrupt turns. The same applies to rowing, though generally without turns. In surfing, however, a flat sea is inimical to the achievement of high scores. What is wanted is a well-proportioned wave, with enough continuous height and shape to enable a smooth descent down its face. Similarly, skiing on snow is typically downhill, the skier taking a mechanized chairlift back to the top of the run, whereas the skater on a frozen pond or rink enjoys the natural flatness of the ice, and increasingly performs indoors.[9]

Riding and driving

Competitive racing on horse and camel developed early in Europe's history and dominated large regions of Asia. Initially the natural landscape provided the stage, but prepared race tracks and circular forms developed in urban settings and provided models for races between wheeled vehicles, pulled at first by horses, and then much later powered by motors. In 'flat' races, horses are ridden on grassy surfaces – making 'turf' a general term for horse racing. The tracks are sometimes straight with a distant turning post, but in modern times are most often circular, or have one or two sides flattened to create a 'straight' for the finish. Sometimes the straight section comes off as a tangent. Where grass is hard to grow, the racing surface may be sand or natural dirt, but levelled wherever possible. Unlike running tracks and playing fields, horse racing has only reluctantly shifted to artificial surfaces, partly because of failures in early experiments – beginning in the 1960s – and partly because of the idealized natural setting of the racecourse, with its large and generally open and empty centre.

Early races using wheeled vehicles – the chariots of the ancient Middle East and the imperial contests of the Roman Coliseum – used the same tracks as riders in such venues, with a similar desire for smoothness for speed, and hard rather than grassy surfaces. Motor vehicles raced at high speed on grassy tracks that were quickly churned up, creating roughness and ruts, or became slippery mud when wet. Flat concrete surfaces were soon developed, thus creating the model for the German autobahn.[10] Full-throttle F1 motor racing combines flat straights with hazardous banked curves, but the preferred sites for land speed records have always been the flattest extensive natural surfaces, found on salt lakes such as Bonneville.

In cycling, although the earliest velodromes (built in the late nineteenth century) had flat tracks throughout their two straight sides and semicircular ends, recent versions are steeply banked. BMX (Bicycle Motocross), invented in the 1970s, draws on the thrills and spills of constructed roller-coaster tracks. Established in 1903, the Tour de France quickly introduced 'mountain stages', which are run in addition to 'flat' and 'hilly' stages, all now aided by gears and support teams, and offering spectacular landscapes, seen (on television) from a helicopter. Flatness does not always produce the most interesting sport for the spectator.

Ball games

In a few ball games – volleyball, for example – the objective is to prevent the ball touching the ground, but for most of them, it is the behaviour of the ball when rebounding from a plane surface that is crucial. These games are some of the most popular of all world sports, and they provide the ideal model for the concept of the level playing field. It is here that unpredictability of surface can most influence the outcome of a contest. In modern versions of these games, the desire for uniformity and flatness in the playing surface is a given, whereas the shape and microtopography of the ball used in each of these sports can vary significantly, as can the use of different parts of the body and different tools. Players are rarely permitted to interfere with the playing surface or the ball. Exceptions occur in some more 'gentlemanly' sports: in cricket, a batter may tamp down the pitch, gently, with the toe of the bat, and in golf it is regarded as good form to replace divots, to make the surface equal for all players. In some ball games, teams change ends each quarter or at half time – or after a number of games, as in tennis – to equalize conditions.

Mathematical analysis of the physics of ball games typically assumes a flat, horizontal surface, and concerns itself with matters such as the frictional forces created by differences in the shape of balls and the shape of bat or club with which they are hit. The velocity of a ball is generally reduced on meeting a flat surface, though with the application of spin it may gain speed. Similarly, the angle of trajectory after hitting a pitch is generally reduced, but depends on its spin, friction between ball and surface, and the 'coefficient of restitution' or 'degree of bounce' (the ratio of the velocity of separation to the velocity of approach, determined by the elasticity of the ball). Where the surface is sufficiently rough, any spin will be moderated by friction. Where the surface is flat enough, the ball may skid on impact and retain its spin, so that a golf ball with bottom spin may come to a sudden halt on its second bounce on a green. A tennis ball hitting a smooth boundary line may shoot through unexpectedly low; a cricket ball striking a bare spot may fly under the batter's guard; and on the perfectly flat cloth of a billiards or snooker table, a ball can be made to swerve by creating an initial skidding motion. Deformation in the playing surface is more difficult to study outside the simple assumption of flatness and rigidity, even though deformation of the ball – notably in squash and tennis – can be considerable at the moment of impact.[11]

Cobbled street, Edinburgh, 2008.

The world's most popular sport is football (soccer), played with a round ball of predictable bounce. Other codes of football use an oval-shaped ball, with less predictable bounce, and permit the use of the hands as well as the foot: Rugby League, Rugby Union, American football, Gaelic football, Australian Rules and International Rules. All versions are affected by the flatness of the ground, so efforts to ensure evenly fought contests are directed particularly at the playing surface. Smoothness is essential to the predictability of the ball's rolling trajectory and bounce. It is also vital to the way a player may slide along the surface to kick a ball or score a goal, or to inhibit another player. The unregulated progenitors of football, played on cobbled streets and open fields, lacked these features. Similarly, in many of the poorer modern communities where the game has become popular since 1945 – particularly in Latin America, Africa and Asia – games are played wherever a space can be found, typically without demarcated boundaries and on a rough surface, where only courageous players willingly fall or bravely attempt a slide. Beach soccer lacks these hazards but is accessible only to some.

Codified in the late nineteenth century, in Europe and North America, football was regarded by the ruling classes as an exemplar of courage and obedience, ideal for the training of manliness and the inculcation of the idea of 'fair play', on the relatively manicured fields of private schools. In the twentieth century, professionalization and commercialization – and the performance of national as well as local identities – changed the character of football, in all its forms, by bringing money to construct stadiums with perfect pitches, carpeted with friendly, grassy smoothness. However, even the most expensive modern pitches are a compromise between efficient drainage and absolute flatness.

In soccer, growing demand slowly led to the adoption of artificial playing surfaces in countries that could afford them. In 2004 they were approved by FIFA for professional international contests. These artificial surfaces have generally been designed to mimic the biomechanical characteristics of natural grass, with the turf 'carpet' including 'grass' filaments of standard lengths to match different mowing styles. Player safety is central to choosing between alternative surfaces, but cost is always vital. In American football, an elevated 'crown' runs down the centre of the playing field with a slight curved slope to the sides, to assist draining and avoid ponding. A small area at the end of the field is known as the 'flat', and the 'flat route' is a passing play in the game. Thus the seeming homogeneity of the level playing field is shown to have its own internal variations, subjected to scientific analysis through the mapping of their microtopography, and subtle differences in mechanical properties, in much the same way that precision agriculture entails the mapping of cropland field by field.[12]

Jumping and throwing make more complex demands on the body, but the desire for a level surface remains strong. Players prefer natural grass surfaces in American football, though often use artificial surfaces in off-season practice. When the women's games of the 2015 FIFA World Cup, held in Canada, were played on an artificial surface, rather than on the grass used for the men's tournament, the players complained. On the other hand, games similar to basketball have almost always been played on prepared surfaces, stretching back to the ancient Americas, when the centrality of the plaza was matched by symmetrical and geometric playing grounds, with specially created smooth surfaces, for various kinds of contests using balls.[13]

The ball games discussed thus far all involve kicking or throwing. Another important variety is hitting a ball (or disc) with a stick. Once again, the preferred surfaces are flat and smooth. The billiard table was sometimes taken as the example of a perfectly level surface, on which the balls were expected to behave consistently anywhere on the surface. Its green felt surface mirrored the lawn. Table tennis depends on a hard, flat surface but one that is similarly always painted green. The principles were easily applied to outdoor variants, such as croquet, hockey (which originated in India) and Asian games played on horseback or camelback. Polo, for example, originated in Persia, found its way to China by the seventh century CE and became popular with high society, along with other violent sports such as riding and hunting. However, by the tenth century CE, Chinese society had shifted away from popular amusements and the traditions of the – open, flat – steppe. The ruling classes developed a contempt for physical activity and left athletic competitions to the lower classes. Modern sports were reintroduced to China only in recent times, under European influence.[14]

Perhaps the game with the greatest claim to fairness is cricket: to say 'It's not cricket' is to suggest a particular action is not even-handed or gentlemanly. This expression is a product of Victorian England, to be placed alongside 'British justice' and 'playing by the rules', and the Christian version of the golden rule that one should do unto others as one would wish to be done unto – the fairness of the level playing field. In spite of these equalitarian ideals, English cricket possessed the same ambiguities as the class system and imperialism. In England, players were divided between 'gentlemen' and 'players', the latter professionals lacking social status. Cricket had been exported to the empire much earlier than this, first to the Americas in the eighteenth century, and then to Africa and Asia.

In the West Indies, black men were sometimes expected to bowl and fetch, while white men batted. In South Africa, race ordered many aspects of the game until the end of Apartheid. The social and political inequalities spilled out onto the field.

In cricket, a grassed field of up to 2 hectares in area surrounds a pitch. The area of the field is allowed to vary from ground to ground, but in England the length of the pitch was set – at 22 yards or 20.12 metres – as early as 1744, thus beginning the process of standardization and the creation of 'placelessness'.[15] Bowlers look for variation in bounce and direction when the ball hits the pitch; fielders hope for predictable smooth running of the ball across the outfield. Only a brave fielder might dive for a one-handed catch when the ground is rough and rocky. Most attention has always been given to the preparation of the surface of the pitch. Traditionally, the pitch was always mowed grass or turf, its condition varying with moisture and growth, and typically becoming 'flatter' and less predictable as the grass was worn down through a match.

A 'flat wicket' lacks bounce, disliked by fast bowlers but loved by batters and slow (spin) bowlers. Batters fear tracks with erratic 'deformations', such as bare patches and crevices, that create un-expected variations in pace and bounce; and dry, abrasive surfaces. Once again, sports scientists have mapped the topography of pitches in precise quantitative detail, in the same way that football field surfaces have been analysed spatially.[16] Spectators generally prefer some sort of balance that makes the sport exciting. Historically, matches sometimes lasted for many days until a result was finally achieved, played at such a slow pace that the boredom of repetition fundamental to flatness affected all but the most dedicated.

A carefully laid cricket pitch with a neatly mowed outfield is an expensive thing. At a local level, cricket is frequently played on surfaces with minimal preparation, from earth to sandy beaches, resulting in a high degree of unpredictability, or on durable concrete, sometimes covered by coir mats. From the eighteenth century, cricket matches in England were typically played on the village green, and this remained the romantic model well into the twentieth. At first the boundaries and surface of the field were the same as the green,

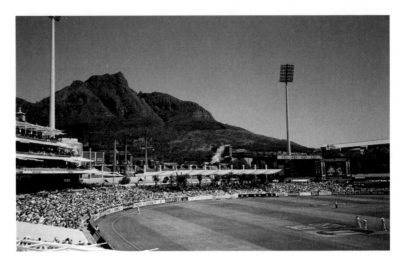

Newlands Cricket Ground, Cape Town, South Africa.

typically marked by trees, and the pitch could be located almost anywhere on the ground by agreement between opposing teams. Tales were told of fielders lacking clear sight of the pitch and the play. Similarly, in Barbados around 1900, it was said that many contests were 'fought out on a few square yards of pasture, with a quite well-prepared pitch on the only piece of level land . . . square leg out of sight in a gully, silly point standing on an outcrop of rock, and natural boundaries in the form of grazing goats and sheep'.[17]

The desire to create conditions of fair play in cricket had much to do with betting and gambling. Placing a bet depends on a level of predictability, but in the longer term encouraged match fixing and fraud. Initially low-scoring matches were the norm. Flattening the pitch shifted the advantage towards the batter. In England, the rolling or sweeping of a pitch before the commencement of an innings was first allowed in 1849, and this opened the way for over-arm bowling, legislated in 1864, leading to the rapid transformation of the pitch into a surface separate from nature. Gardeners became the first groundsmen, required to produce smooth surfaces without decorative elements. Lawnmowers – pushed by hand, pulled by horses and eventually motor-powered – smoothed the pitch and, less perfectly, the outfield. By the beginning of the twentieth century, the analogy could flow in the opposite direction, with flat Australian plains described as 'almost as level as a cricket pitch'.[18]

To enable drainage, the pitch is located near the centre of the field on a slightly raised surface, with a 360-degree camber to the boundary. Only at the end of the twentieth century did laser technology come to be used to create a perfectly uniform slope, removing minor humps and hollows. This was done for the first time at Sydney Cricket Ground in 2010.

Tennis played on a table – table tennis – involves hitting a ball with a bat, paddle or racquet, generally made of timber veneer and, increasingly, with a rubberized, dimpled surface. The table itself is made as flat as possible and the ball is completely smooth. Tennis played on grass or clay, or asphalt or concrete, has similar objectives, but uses racquets strung to create a resilient meshed surface to hit balls with a hairy fuzz. When the balls become too smooth, they are replaced. Although early varieties of tennis were often played in courtyards, without special preparation, by the sixteenth and seventeenth centuries the game was taken indoors by the European aristocracy and played in designated spaces. Today tennis is generally played outdoors, but the most sophisticated courts have the ability to close their roofs when it rains. Squash was also once played outside, but has largely retreated indoors and is played inside a cube with a flat floor and sides, using all of these surfaces.

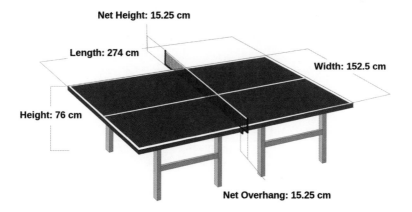

The standard dimensions of a table tennis table.

Badminton – using a shuttle rather than a ball – typically uses floors of rubber, vinyl or sprung hardwood to cushion impact.

In tennis, players seek to exploit the unpredictability of speed, bounce and direction of the ball when it connects with the surface of the court. Traditionally, the surface was either grass or clay. Grass, used at Wimbledon, the home of 'lawn tennis', allows fast speeds and low but variable bounce, the variability depending on the smoothness of the grass and its mowing, and increasing with wear and the appearance of bare patches. Clay, used in the French and Italian Open competitions, creates a slower speed and more uniform, higher bounce with top spin. For the u.s. and Australian Open matches, acrylic surfaces are the flattest of all, giving more predictable medium speed, medium height and uniform bounce with top spin. In the best-known international tournament, the Davis Cup, countries sometimes choose to play on a surface disliked by their competitors, particularly to confront lovers of clay with the unpredictability of grass.

Golf course, Reading Country Club, UK, 2005.

By the 1990s, drop-in grass courts were being created from portable squares, though this entailed new hazards caused by erosion along the joins between the units. Acrylic hard court tennis surfaces are said to possess micro-roughness in their topography, with increased traction (which can cause injury) and unpredictability due to differential wear (worn areas becoming smoother and easier to slide across), this local variation reducing the 'fairness' of a contest and making it more hazardous for players.

The ball game most often played in a 'natural' landscape is golf. Modern designed courses seek to replicate elements of this natural world, mixed with more precisely engineered sites. The fairway is smooth and has low-cut grass, but is undulating and bordered by a strip of 'rough', with trees or water hazards. The green is expected to have a smooth surface but not necessarily a flat one, so that a ball landing on the green may run off or roll back, and it is the player's task to 'read' the green's subtle slopes. Scottish golf courses preserved much from their varied landscapes, making play less predictable, in ways outsiders sometimes thought 'unfair'.

In 2004, the world's longest golf course was proposed: eighteen holes sited at intervals across the Australian desert, to be known as the 'Nullarbor Links'. The purpose was to break up the 1,400-kilometre journey across 'one of the world's driest, hottest, flattest and most monotonous deserts', often perceived as 'featureless and boring'. The fairways were necessarily composed of earth, and the greens were oiled sand. The course opened in 2009 and has flourished sufficiently to win tourism awards.[19]

Gaming

The contemporary passion for computer gaming has deep roots, stretching back to ancient warfare and sport. Wrestling and boxing were at first uninhibited in their violence and were performed on surfaces which were not necessarily levelled to create equal conditions for the contestants. Early war games similarly involved physical violence and injury, even death, as preparation for actual warfare. This style of dress rehearsal went out of fashion only in recent times, when the efficiency of the available firepower made such mock fighting too hazardous. However, alongside these theatrical performances, there developed in ancient times war games played on flat boards, using sculpted pieces that mimicked individual warriors or weapons, with the surface divided into territorial units of uniform size. The archetype is chess, with its origins in ancient India.

Chess is played on a square, flat board, with an eight-by-eight grid of alternately black and white squares. Early versions differed in dimensions and in some cases the boards were circular, divided into sectors. Modern transformations include hexagonal and rhombic patterns. With the exception of 'spherical chess', which sits on the margins of practice, the boards seem always to have been flat. In contrast, the pieces varied dramatically; they were often elaborately

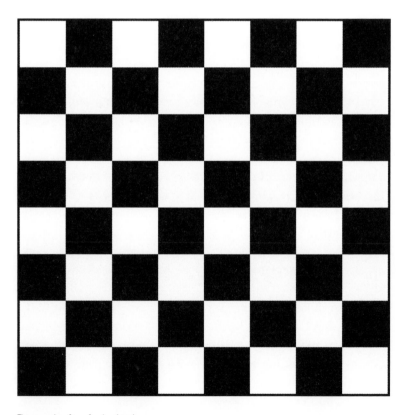

The squared surface of a chessboard.

carved and sometimes needed pegs, placed in holes in the board, in order to stand up. Myriad other board games exist – not all of them imitations of battle – spread widely across time and space, but most are played on a flat, gridded surface. Outdoor 'boards' might be painted or incised on stone or concrete, sometimes sited on the flat roofs of houses. Portable versions woven into mats were rolled out flat. Playing cards and dominoes, for example, share some of the same values, uniform (on one side) and flat, and typically played on top of a table to ensure fairness. The same applies to dice, with six flat sides, rolled on a flat surface, whether at home or in a casino.[20]

Chess has come to be regarded as the ideal war game, because it has nothing to do with the players' physical prowess and is not a matter of chance, but is a purely intellectual exercise. Perhaps for the same reasons, chess has never been the most popular of board games. The most popular war games are the most violent, with a capacity to kill and shed blood, though played today in electronic virtual reality (VR, born in the 1980s), on flat-panel display screens. These games happily give weight to chance, uneven terrain and the unexpected appearance of the enemy. Thus urban warfare, which is particularly deadly in real life, offers opportunities in video games which cannot be found on level, open battlefields, and connects with the diverse terrain of real-life warfare throughout history.[21]

The topographic variety of gaming in virtual reality sets it apart from modern sport. Most contact sports are now played on level fields that are relatively small in size and specially prepared with clear boundaries and limiting lines and zones. Gaming in virtual reality allows enhanced dimensionality and topographic variety, introducing unpredictable hazards such as chasms suddenly appearing in what seemed to be continuous flat surfaces. In full immersion, the experience comes to feel at least as real as the real world; the fact that it depends on a two-dimensional flat image is beside the point, part of the way flatness has been naturalized.

SEVEN

FLAT MATERIALS

'The world is complex, dynamic,
multidimensional; the paper is static, flat.'
Edward R. Tufte, 1990[1]

The increasingly rapid flattening of the world scene, in every aspect, from the construction of roads and railways to the levelling of lawns and football pitches, has gone hand in hand with the development of materials not found in nature, characterized by an artificial flatness. In many cases, these flat materials have been used in the flattening of the landscape and the built environment – concrete, glass, steel and aluminium, above all. Other 'unnatural' flat materials have entered our world less obtrusively but with intense ubiquity – paper and plastic stand out. Some of these materials have ancient antecedents, but others are completely modern, and for all of them, it has been in the modern world that their contributions have proved overwhelming. This contribution is both immediate and mediated through the application of regular geometries to the world at large.

Flat materials have had a central role in what Le Corbusier called the human ambition to apply geometric ordering in the midst of 'chaotic nature'. Although everyday experience requires negotiation and navigation through three-dimensional space, we are continuously 'caught up in the two-dimensionality of the endless flatlands of paper and video and screen'. Escaping this flat world, said Edward R. Tufte in 1990, is 'the essential task of envisioning information – for all the interesting worlds (physical, biological, imaginary, human) that we seek to understand are inevitably and

happily multivariate in nature. Not flatlands.'² Thus it is necessary
to attempt not only to explain the ways human beings have sought
to flatten the Earth and to mould the Earth's resources into artificial
flat things, but to expand the question to the broader problem of
why flat surfaces dominate our representations of information and
our pictures. The reasons for this dominance derive from the purely
practical aspect of flatness, which means both its functionality in
everyday life and its substantial contribution to economic efficiency
and financial gain.

Flatness means profits for manufacturers, distributors and
retailers. In distribution, flat materials have contributed notably to
the standardization of products, typically by regular surfaces and
geometries that enable close packing. From the bottom to the top –
from flat files, to the smallest frozen food box, to the offices in the
tallest skyscraper – space is divided into straight-sided units that can
be fitted together, in a refrigerator or on a container ship, in a filing
cabinet or state archive. Containers no longer necessarily reflect the
shape of their contents but present a flat uniformity. It is a rational,
machine-age image of space, a prerequisite of mass production and
transportation; the victory of abstract aestheticism over nature,
expressed in art and music as much as in architecture and the
making of commodities. The digital revolution has, very recently,
transformed the storage of information, but these technologies
persist in presenting the viewer with a flat image on a flat screen. At
the heart of all this is the essential flatness of the materials.

Wood, stone, earth

Most of the materials used in ancient technologies were natural
products. Only some societies adopted or invented artificial or
transformed forms of natural materials, such as in pottery and
metallurgy. Wood, stone, reeds, thatch, hides and ice – shaped with
tools to relative flatness or simply fitted or lashed together – were the
basis of architecture. The tools most used in roughly shaping timbers
were versions of the axe, the adze and the saw, while more precise
surfaces needed the plane. In every case, the materials retained

evidence of their former natural life – in knots in timbers and strata in stone – and in combination, they rarely formed a continuous, uniform surface. Mud, used widely in Africa and Asia, has plastic qualities when wet, so can be poured or patted to smoothness. Recently sheets of plaster or asbestos have been created from crushed materials in fluid form, often with toxic results. Organic materials have also been processed to create flat products – timber veneers, plywoods, fibreboard and pulpboard sheets, for example – but these generally betray their origins.

Pine wood floorboards, sawn flat and squared but revealing their knotty organic, arboreal origins.

None of these flat materials supported the construction of large, tall structures. The cost and instability of building helped to ensure the long-term relative flatness of urban settlements. Only rulers and institutions with access to large supplies of labour and resources were able to attempt such ambitious projects. In the ancient world, the biggest structures were pyramidal, made from stone or earth. Massive stone blocks, carefully squared, made the Great Pyramid, but earth and mud are much harder to shape and to stabilize and are therefore used to raise structures which are lower though not necessarily flatter. Bricks were made uniform with flat sides, and could be packed together with mortar to form consistent surfaces – especially when rendered – but proved unstable in earthquake zones and everywhere had limited vertical potential.

Textiles

Manufactured from natural materials, textiles possess a flexible flatness that has given them a variety of functions since ancient times, stretching back to 8,000 years ago. Their antiquity is brought out clearly in the way the creation of (flat) worlds is sometimes likened to the rolling out of a rug or carpet, and the magical flying carpet. Their flatness is a product of weaving technologies that typically depend on a loom to stretch the material taut and, through its warp and weft, make a gridded rectangle that potentially has great length but limited width. In these ways, woven textiles have much in common with papyrus and paper, and when used for clothing and writing they similarly replace less-modified materials such as the skins of animals. Likewise, the printing of designs on textiles can be done using either a flat screen or a rotary press, paralleling the evolution of letterpress printing from flatbed to offset.

Rugs and carpets come in many varieties, but a basic distinction is made between flat-woven and piled types. Whereas piled rugs feature designs created by tufted knots of varied colours, most flat-weaves carry patterns formed by drawing coloured wefts between the warps, so they are generally thinner and easier to roll up. Both are made on a loom – sometimes vertical, sometimes horizontal

– and both possess an essential flatness, whether created from spun wool, hair, silk or cotton. Traditionally, flat-weave was associated with poverty and penance, and the woolly softness of the pile with luxury and wealth. However, flat-weave types have a wider range of functions because of their flexibility: they are used not only as floor coverings (stretched over flat surfaces) but as prayer rugs, saddle pads and wall hangings, all of which can be easily rolled up, and even as clothing. This portability sees rectangular flat-weave rugs sometimes used to make tents, particularly among nomads living in desert regions such as the Middle East, where these textiles flourished, whereas the more rigid quality of piled rugs made them better suited to the tiled floors of city dwellers.[3]

New materials have entered the landscape through modelling based on the mathematical theory of minimal surfaces. Most often, the starting point is the plane, transformed by folding and bending, reminiscent of geological strata and the Platonic polyhedra. Similarly, the soap film principle has been applied to the use of flexible composite materials derived from textiles, most visibly in tent-like stretched canopies. Here the material is initially flat, stored as a roll, and then formed into polymorphic artefacts, just as clothing is made from flat, cut pieces. It is necessary first to define cutting lines on the projected three-dimensional architectural form, which generate non-planar 'strips' that must be 'flattened' before the correct material can be cut from fabric rolls. The fundamental problem is essentially the same as mapping the Earth onto a flat sheet of paper – just as it is impossible to form a sphere from a flat sheet – and the solutions applied in textile architecture are much the same as those attempted in cartography. Thus the greater the total curvature in the construction, the greater the number of flat strips required. As in cartography, none of the solutions are perfect, but textiles have the advantage of inherent flexibility.[4]

Concrete, glass, steel, aluminium, plastic

Lacking the organic flexibility of textiles, concrete and glass are similarly ancient products but did not become common until the late nineteenth century. Steel and aluminium were virtually unknown before this recent period. Plate glass was invented in England in the seventeenth century but remained expensive until produced by industrial methods, making its debut as a major building material in London, in the Crystal Palace of 1851. Aluminium waited until the late nineteenth century to be produced on an industrial scale, but its lightness quickly made it a gleaming symbol of 'aerodynamic modernism and supermobility'. Concrete was also an ancient medium, well known in some world regions by 100 BCE, but it took on new life when reinforced with steel and made into solid flat plates or slabs which could be suspended horizontally or vertically from concrete columns, to high standards of strength and stiffness. These materials only began to become relatively cheap in the nineteenth century and took on a new life in combination, making them agents of modernity and symbols of the invariance fundamental to flatness. Plastic is a more recent material, its production growing from just 1 million tonnes in 1950 to 265 million by 2010, when its volume was greater than that of steel.[5]

None of these modern materials possess a standard form but in a liquid, molten or heated state can be poured to flatness or shaped dramatically. Poured concrete shares characteristics with mud in its wet state but dries stronger and, when combined with steel, can stretch out horizontally and rise much higher. In Modernist architecture, the characteristic rectangular tower of plate glass and ferro-concrete defied gravity, yet in its fundamentals consisted of flattened surfaces made possible by materials that could flow when molten (glass) or be hot-milled (steel and aluminium), or be ground and polished to achieve the same smooth effect. Rather than heavily ornamented buildings of wood, mud, brick and natural stone, architecture in the Modernist style used concrete, steel, glass and aluminium to create flat or smooth planes with minimal decoration. The height and vertical flatness of these buildings impressed from the street but internally they supported horizontality. Thus Le Corbusier favoured open-plan buildings, with large glass windows stretched out in strips, and flat roofs, all made possible by reinforced concrete.

Glass and steel, the Comcast Tower, Philadelphia, USA, 2011.

Surfaces which are not truly flat can be smoothed by the application of cement rendering, plaster or paint. These materials may not actually flatten the surface but by making it uniform in texture and colour contribute to the impression of flatness. However, the success of this technique depends very much on lighting. Surfaces that appear flat in diffuse light can reveal stark imperfections when the sunlight hits them from a particular angle – though often only for a short period each day – or when a sidelight shines across them, especially when gloss paint is used. Further, houses originally built of brick rendered with concrete to create a smooth surface exacerbate the problem when trowel-work reveals itself in swipes and swirls. The cost of precision grinding is too great to be used in most housing projects, and the best that can be hoped for is an illusion of flatness through the appropriate use of decoration and glancing lighting. Residents are admonished, and told not to be precious about a little roughness.[6]

The flatness achieved with plastic materials in purist modernism was challenged in the 1970s, through 'postmodern' complexity, which preferred 'messy vitality over obvious unity'. Smoothness survived but might be transformed, as in the crumpled and destabilized digital manipulations of Frank Gehry (1929–). These buildings

Le Corbusier project, Maison Dom-ino, 1914, reconstructed for the Venice Architecture Biennale, 2014.

typically used the standard flat materials of modernist architecture – a kind of origami – but in his more recent projects a fresh challenge was attempted in applying traditional materials, particularly bricks, creating unexpected echoes of the crumpled surfaces.[7] A contrasting approach may be found in the distinctive buildings of Antoni Gaudí (1852–1926), who mixed modernism with traditional elements and organic forms a century earlier. However smoothed or crumpled the exteriors, all of these constructions respected the practicality and efficiency of flat floors.

Papyrus, parchment, paper

Pictorial representation in all its many forms has typically been inscribed on flat surfaces. Images that flow around a tree trunk or a stone pillar are relatively difficult to create and control, and hard to read. Like the walls of a cave and the sands of the desert, they lack portability. The invention of writing – and reading – dramatically increased the demand for flat surfaces. These needed to be capable of preserving marks made on them but lightweight and low in volume, in order to be able to exchange messages efficiently. From ancient times, writers have sought to fashion appropriate materials from what they could find around them. As we have seen, nature offers little help. Bark stripped from trees can be used but generally only after being heated and smoothed. The leaves of some plants, such as the palm and aloe, have been used, but appropriate large, flat leaves are not available everywhere, and even the most suitable require preparatory smoothing. The skins of animals too provided surfaces for writing and drawing but similarly needed smoothing and flattening. Bricks, wood, metals (such as copper and brass) and ceramics all offered smooth and often flat surfaces, but none of these bulky materials was practical in terms of packing, storage and incorporation.

From this great diversity of surfaces there emerged in ancient Egypt around 3000 BCE a new material, papyrus, which came to be

Plastered wall, painted.

Brick wall, painted silver.

the writing material of choice for literary texts for those who could obtain it. Made from thin sections of the stalk of the papyrus plant, laid across one another perpendicularly to create a grid, and then beaten or pressed, dried in the sun and polished with a stone to make the surface perfectly smooth, a number of sheets (generally twenty) could be joined and rolled up. Papyrus rolls came in standard widths and qualities, creating flat but flexible surfaces, generally coloured white or yellow, which were ideal for literary texts, written on with a reed brush or pen. At first the writing was in vertical lines, beginning at the right-hand end of the roll, but later in blocks of horizontal lines that followed the horizontal fibres of the papyrus on its inside (recto) surface. Generally only the inside was written on, but cost and scarcity led to palimpsests and reversals. Rolls proved durable when shipped in trade around the Mediterranean world, but had disadvantages for readers: they had to be rolled back in order to refer to an earlier passage, and the edges frayed.[8] They were insufficiently flat.

The roll came to be rivalled by the codex: a number of papyrus sheets stacked in a pile, folded down the middle, with writing on both sides of the sheet, continuing from front to back. The codex followed a principle applied to flat wax tablets or parchment as well as papyrus, the elements strung together along one edge. At first codices consisted of a single stack or 'quire', but gradually several quires came to be sewn together. There was a strong association between the rise of the codex and the spread of Christianity – partly because it coincided with a scarcity of papyrus – and by about 400 CE the codex had replaced the roll as the most common form for literary texts in the Mediterranean sphere. Both the codex and the papyrus roll were relatively expensive, and because papyrus was cultivated in only a small region, most of the world had no access to it. Equivalents were developed by some cultures, such as the Aztec and the Maya, but many remained committed to orality as their principal form of communication.

The vital breakthrough came with the invention of paper, 'one of the signature materials of the modern world'.[9] The essence of paper is that it is made from fibres reduced to individual filaments, then intertwined in thin, flat layers. The process involves the creation of a watery pulp, the fluidity of which enables it to create its own natural level, retained when dried out and reincorporated. In this characteristic, paper shares much with concrete, and the broader fluidity of molten sheet metals, glass and plastic. Thus paper can be thin yet strong, and, when sufficiently flat (though flexible), easily stacked or bound into books, capable of storing large quantities of data in small volumes. The cultural and intellectual implications were great. Writing technologies had long served to embed the word in space, but the paper book provided a 'container' for information and increasingly gave it a precise subject-matter.

Printing carried this process further, placing visual value on the spatial arrangement of words and pictures in typographic space, and enabling the production of multiple copies of page and book, each exactly identical. Texts became fixed. Maps were standardized and made into atlases. These innovations set the stage for universal scientific systems. Thus the repetition and homogeneity of the book, created from flat paper pages, contributed to the making of flat knowledge landscapes. In these ways, it paralleled the fundamental principle of invariance characteristic of flatness.[10]

Invented first in China sometime before 200 BCE, paper was in common use there by 600 CE, made from bark, bamboo, rattan, hemp and cloth. All of these papers were, however, made by hand, one sheet at a time, spread out and baked to dry. Their flatness came in different qualities. From China, these techniques spread first to Korea and Japan, cultures which preferred vertical rather than horizontal text. Only around 800 CE did papermaking technologies begin to spread west, to Eurasia, where they gradually replaced parchment and papyrus. On the western edge, paper was hardly known in England before the fourteenth century, and there parchment reigned supreme in formal record-keeping.[11]

Until the late nineteenth century, paper continued to be made in hand-held moulds, producing single sheets. The mould was simply a rectangular wooden frame with a wire mesh. A pulp made from beaten linen rags and water was poured in, and then turned onto a felt to dry. The side of the sheet in contact with the wire mesh was 'rough', whereas the side against the felt was 'smooth'. If not immediately obvious to the eye, the roughness of the mesh side of the paper can be easily seen by shining a light across the surface. The flatness of paper sheets was enhanced by pressing. The degree of refinement varied with use, which was by no means confined to writing and drawing. In Japan and Korea, very large sheets of thin paper were used in houses, instead of window glass, and thick, oiled ones for flooring. Wallpaper was introduced from China to Europe in 1550 CE.[12]

Mass production of paper to high standards of uniformity and at low prices began only in the late nineteenth century. This depended on continuous production techniques that made sheets of great length, rolled onto cylinders. The papyrus roll offered a model, of course, but the scale and system of production was vastly different. Demand caused a shift from rags to wood pulp, reducing the quality of the surface, but quantity increased dramatically, flooding the whole world with paper and paperboard to be used in a vast variety of contexts. Newspapers and 'pulp fiction' suddenly became cheap; the walls of houses were covered with wallpaper; containers were fashioned from cardboard (sometimes corrugated); and toilet paper was produced in rolls. All of these made flat surfaces, of one sort or another, part of the everyday life of almost everyone on Earth.

The availability of flat surfaces of record has played a significant role in global cultural development. Most immediately, the materials used to make these flat surfaces have had a direct impact on the development of writing forms. Thus stone, wood and clay are more easily inscribed with straight-line elements rather than soft curves, whereas papyrus, palm leaf or parchment permit the use of pen and brush to create calligraphic flourishes and cursive scripts. Secondly, the mechanical reproduction of images, whatever the technology of 'printing' – from block printing to Gutenberg and lithography – depended almost always on flat materials placed on flatbeds, and typically received the original pattern from another (inked) flat surface, notably moveable type and woodblocks. The original was sometimes an inked cylinder, rolled across a flat surface, and in modern rotary printing presses, from the late nineteenth century, paper could be spun off a roll to receive the inked image from a cylinder. Camera film was exposed and developed to create a negative, and then printed.

Whatever the process, flat materials were part of most stages of reproduction, and the final product was almost always a flat, folded newspaper or book or flat 'print' of some sort. Letterpress printing similarly demanded the standardization of typographic fonts, culminating in the sans serif simplicity of some ubiquitous twentieth-century letter forms, notably Helvetica, invented in 1957. Similarly, the relative economy of logographic Simplified Chinese, formally introduced in 1956, was innovative in being written horizontally from left to right, rather than the traditional vertical right-to-left pattern. Much the same occurred throughout East Asia, principally in response to Western influences and the rigid horizontality of letterpress technologies, rather than any biological advantage.[13]

During the twentieth century, new technologies emerged that seemed to challenge the dominance of flatness in communication, particularly in the electronic storage of data and its manipulation through computers. However, early computers depended on punched cards and tape, and microfilm and microfiche also retained an essential flatness. It may seem that digital technologies and laser printing have changed all this, but the predicted 'paperless' office has not come to be, and world production of paper continues to increase, almost doubling in the past twenty years. Equally, the electronic screens that now dominate daily communication are almost all flat surfaces, and horizontal texts written from left to right tend to dominate even when, as in the case of Japan, print media retain their verticality. Digital technologies have 'flattened' the concept of real space and created horizontal codes and sign-systems.[14]

The 'electronic page' maintains the flatness, rectangularity and architecture that began with the ancient tablet. The three-dimensional 'book' might be near death, but not the page, the essence of the plane surface, ideal for the inscription of everything from philosophy to financial accounts, the diagrams of science and the mind-bending equations of mathematics. Computer graphic devices create their images on flat, two-dimensional screens, with each point on the screen identified by two real numbers as coordinates, but with the potential for a third or even fourth data point and hence the possibility of generating easily visualized complex curved surfaces. The webpage has a virtual existence, and the *tablet* – with roots back to the surfaces on which the finger of God inscribed the Ten Commandments – remains current in the digital age.

In whatever manner data is stored, manipulated and delivered, the way in which we visualize it remains tied to an interpretation of a flat image of the world, spread out before us as a picture on a two-dimensional flat surface. The human visual system has evolved to use the depth cues in an image to construct the spatial arrangement of elements and the perception of three-dimensional properties, but distortions observed in computer-generated displays viewed on monitor screens can, in some cases, be explained by the presence of flatness cues. These cues to flatness occur because, in viewing a monitor, the focal distance is fixed and head movement constrained.[15] Distance is similarly underestimated in viewing large flat-screen immersive displays. In spite of these problems of perception and possible harm to eye and frame, whatever the message, the medium very often continues to be a flat surface.

In some cases, brute force is applied to the flattening of organic objects to enable their efficient storage. For example, the preservation of plant materials in herbaria has long depended on the drying of specimens placed on absorbent papers pressed between boards, and then, when fully dry, mounted on sheets of cartridge paper. Here the role of pressed flatness is both the practical one of reducing loss by breakage and an ultimate storage solution. Only specimens such as pine cones prove so recalcitrant that they escape flattening. Specimens from the animal kingdom do generally escape flattening, though it is often recommended that they be stored in flat-sided jars in order to avoid the visual distortion caused by cylindrical containers. Here it is useful to notice the unusual role of nature in preservation through flattening, in the particular example of palaeontology, where plant and animal impressions are found as sections in the geological record, the product of sedimentary stratigraphy and the laying down of flat sheets over very long periods of time. This mode of pressing reflects yet another facet of flatness, the fact that the form of the plant or animal is preserved as a fossilized absence or emptiness.

Flat packing

Almost equally ubiquitous in the modern world is the common flat-sided container, typically made of cardboard or strong paper. Just as flat-sided regular sheets of paper and whole books could be stacked and stored more efficiently than rolls and ceramic jars, so too modern packaging came to depend heavily on flat elements, in everything from envelopes to the (metal) containers carried on container ships. Flat-sided, standardized boxes provided secure protection not only for flat objects but for fragile and oddly shaped items. Further, the more these containers were limited to a small number of variants, the more tightly they could be packed. The application of automated cutting and folding technologies, particularly after about 1960, simplified processes, beginning with the initial materials, which increasingly were flat sheets of cardboard or strong paper. The entire container was stamped out from a single sheet.[16] An example is found in the familiar pizza box, cut from a flat sheet with minimum waste, folded into a flat box, to contain a flat disc; individual boxes stack efficiently one on top of another, concealing the microtopography of the pizza itself. Other seemingly simple boxes are cut from flat sheets using more complex templates and with greater waste.

The standardization and flattening of paper and cardboard packaging materials and modules also had a feedback effect, contributing to the flattening of the elements they contained. The best example here is 'flat pack' furniture, pioneered by the Swedish company IKEA in the late 1950s, in which bulky objects and pieces with inconvenient protrusions, such as legs, came to be disassembled so they could be made to fit into a simple flat-sided package, for more convenient transport and efficient storage. The puzzles of assembly were transferred to the customer, conceived as a person

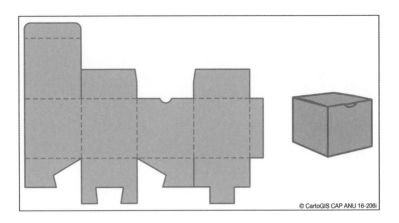

© CartoGIS CAP ANU 16-206i

Folded container cube and its pre-formed template: Top Tuck Auto-lock Bottom box style.

looking for something stylishly modern, perhaps a little funky yet unpretentious and cheap – a person capable of using an Allen key and following instructions.[17] The next stage was the redesign of the elements of the furniture itself, to make as many of the components as possible individually flat, so they could occupy the least space when packed. The cutting and shaping of flat elements – particularly in wood – was also least wasteful when cylinders and curves were reduced to the minimum. This connected with design trends – mostly Scandinavian – beginning with the minimalist art and artefacts of the early twentieth century. By the 1970s, raw wood, especially pine, had begun to displace upholstered surfaces.

The outcome, at its extreme, saw flat furniture filling flat-sided rooms, all delivered in flat packs, with curves at a minimum. Ultimately, entire houses could be purchased as flat packs, the elements prefabricated and transported on just one truck. Similar effects can be observed at smaller scales, in food for example. The purported marvellous invention of 'sliced bread' occurred in the 1920s, when a wide range of crust-cracked irregular shapes were replaced by standardized square slices, with perfect flatness on each machine-cut surface, ideal for packing in a lunch box. Flatbreads in many versions had, of course, been known from ancient times, in widespread places around the world, but all of these lacked the precise flatness achieved by machines. The same principles applied to the making of processed cheese slices, potato crisps packed in cylinders, the slicing of ham and bacon, the pounding of meat to make schnitzels, and the filleting of fresh fish and meat, the latter increasingly packed in flat polystyrene trays for efficient distribution to supermarket shelves. Further, the increased availability of fresh meat and cooking oil in modern times went together with a growing enthusiasm for frying on flat surfaces, where contact between meat and hot metal was maximized when both were flat.

Frank den Oudsten, *Red and Blue Chair*, from the Schröder House, Utrecht, by Gerrit Rietveld, 1918.

Although the flat pack is commonly associated with furniture, it also had an important place in the development of electronics from the 1960s, when ceramic flat-pack integrated circuits replaced round or cylindrical transistors.[18] The ubiquitous computer 'chip' is a tiny flat plate, typically square, with connections around its periphery. Problems arose in interactions between glass, metal and ceramic surfaces, but here the association with the flat world of paper is lost, and the resurgence of inorganic materials returns us to the multimedia lumpiness of ancient times.

Trans-shipment yards, full of shipping containers, can also resemble histograms, but loaded on a ship they tend to appear much more uniform. Because they generally have to be transferred to road or rail vehicles, containers are constrained in their dimensions; but this has, in turn, led to the widening and straightening of highways, and the local flattening of the landscape. Individually or locked together, shipping containers have also been used as the building blocks of functional modern architecture. The modules are standardized, on an international scale, imposing an essential uniformity.[19] All of these innovations travelled rapidly, spreading their particular varieties of flatness across the world.

EIGHT

PICTORIAL FLATTENING

'The irreducible essence of pictorial art consists in but
two constitutive conventions or norms: flatness and the
delimitation of flatness.'
Clement Greenberg, 1962[1]

Why do flat surfaces dominate our representations of information
and our pictures? The question is a central conceptual element in
explaining the dominance of flatness in the physical world of modernity. It was foreshadowed in the previous chapter, which traced
the growth to dominance of physical flatness in so many of the
material things that constitute the modern world and argued that
it stems largely from the functionality of flatness in everyday life
and its considerable contribution to economic efficiency and profit-
ability. The question also connects directly with the engineering
principles discussed in Chapter Five, the methods by which the
world's surface has been flattened. There, the creation of flat surfaces
derived from the rearrangement of physical materials; here, the task
is one of asking how the lumpiness of the real and imagined world
can be ironed out through pictorial representation.

Several subsidiary questions arise. First, how do we 'picture'
flatness? Images conjured in words and music, drawings and paintings all have a capacity for spatial representation but find different
solutions in their contrasting technologies. Second, how does the
dominance of flat surfaces play out across the wide range of pictorial
media, genre and subject matter? For example, how does flatness
work differently in photography, drawing, painting, printmaking
and animation; develop in modern painting traditions, from Realism

to Impressionism, to Abstract Expressionism; and inhabit portraiture, landscape art, map-making and diagrammatic illustration? All of these accommodate to representation on flat surfaces, whether sheets of bark or paper, stretched canvases or electronic screens. Third, does this requirement apply without regard to points of view? Do our pictures attempt to capture what we see with our eyes in the world around us, or represent things we see in our minds, or combine these seemingly distinct concepts in a single image?

At the core of the obsession with flat surfaces is one of the most fundamental problems of pictorial representation, namely the difficulty of translating three-dimensional figures (the pictures we see in our heads) to two-dimensional surfaces. Where the representation is itself three-dimensional – as in a globe or a hologram – the problem does not exist. Most often, however, in the modern world, we prefer pictures on flat surfaces. Atlases are preferred to globes, and photographic prints to mannequins. Full-body images derived from laser scans are confrontingly unnatural, and holograms remain an eerie rarity.[2] Why are we so obsessed with flat surfaces, and how is the problem of representation solved?

Answers to these questions, and the development of associated theory, have been preoccupations for millennia, from the problem of projection in cartography to the concept of linear perspective in art. The underlying assumption, however, is rarely questioned. Indeed, dictionaries define 'picture' as a representation on a surface, usually or typically flat. The urge to picture the three-dimensional world by means of two-dimensional pictorial representations dates back to the Palaeolithic and probably beyond. Typically the process assumes a flat platform, but in the case of mathematical cartography, the central problem becomes that of 'representing a portion of the curved surface of the earth on a flat piece of paper'.[3] Why is it assumed that cartographer and artist *must* choose a flat surface on which to depict what they see or imagine?

There are alternatives, some of them once very popular. The simplest is to represent the three-dimensional world at reduced scale. This is the solution offered to the cartographer by the globe and to the sculptor by the shaping of stone or wood. Modelling in clay is particularly appealing, and long-lasting when fired. Scale models of objects can be found in ancient archaeological sites – notably the tombs of the rich and powerful – and persist into modern dioramas and sculpture. Dramatic models similarly were once played out in arenas and theatres in the round. Navigational route maps can be constructed from sticks, threads, wires or the ribs of coconut palms, to show spatial relationships in two or three dimensions. Gradually or in some cases quite rapidly, these plastic representations of reality came to be largely replaced by art and cartography performed on flat surfaces, beginning with the walls of shelters and caves, and sandy ground.

Painting and drawing established the shift, and in the theatre the stage came to be viewed through an arch, much like looking at a framed painting. Photography and film, and electronic flat screens, merely confirmed the priority of the flat surface. Looking at the natural world, we see single frames, even if what is hidden is revealed by a mirror, but binocular vision and relative motion work together to enable the perception of depth and a three-dimensional picture of our reality. By contrast, pictures created on a flat surface have no access to these visual cues, and the artist must resort to a variety of devices to help the viewer achieve a sensation of spatiality. It is marvellous that a few lines or patches of colour on a flat surface can create mental representations of a three-dimensional scene, so that the viewer forgets to notice the flatness of the canvas.

The blank canvas or page is not only 'naturally' flat, it is also almost always rectangular. Why is this shape so obviously correct? Normal vision allows us to see a region of roughly 170° horizontally and 120° vertically but this space is curved (as seen from a point inside a sphere) rather than flat.[4] The 'blank' page or canvas seems to exist independently of art or communication, the work beginning only with the first stroke of brush or pen. Thus the shape of the pre-picture surface appears given, predetermined by its bounding horizontal and vertical lines. The rectangle can be rotated through 'portrait' and 'landscape' but remains a rectangle; with the square, rotation has no point. The picture plane or page might, however, be triangular or circular. In cartography, it has been common to represent the hemispheres of the Earth as circles, but almost always these are drawn on rectangular sheets. The reasons for the flatness of the sheets are essentially practical and economic; the reasons for rectangularity are very similar.

In modern times, the industrial production of paper and canvases has led to precise standard specifications, so that items can be packed efficiently, fed into printers and stored on shelves. These dimensional requirements match the fundamental practical advantages of flatness in ensuring cost-effectiveness and capitalist profit. Their flatness also mirrors the origins of much painting in fresco and mural on the surfaces of walls, and the efficient way framed works of art hang on the walls of galleries. The significance of this visual efficiency is made apparent when architects stray from the straight and narrow. Notoriously, Frank Lloyd Wright's Guggenheim Museum, opened in Manhattan in 1959, dispensed with flat surfaces, forming an essentially cylindrical structure. Artists and curators complained that paintings could not be hung in their true plane and had to contend with the tilt and curve of the walls as well as the inclined ramp that replaced the level floor.[5]

Unlike fragile scale models, images on flat surfaces can be packed and stacked, bound into volumes and easily transported long distances. They can be made from sturdy yet lightweight materials, with impressive longevity. Eventually they came also to be cheap and infinitely reproducible, as in modern printed paper. Although practicality may seem too simple a solution to the problem of pictorial representation, the flatness of blank surfaces contributed substantially to the ease of pictorial representation, its reduced cost and reproduction. At the same time, doing so required effort on the part of both artist and viewer, to depict the world with visual correctness and to understand what is displayed. This was no easy process. Whether or not regular flat surfaces have achieved their dominance by simple practical convenience rather than any logical necessity, the outcome had immense consequences.[6]

The use of flat surfaces also enabled new subjects. Whereas the creation of scale models – whether in sculpture, ceramics or glass – almost always focused on separate objects, pictorial representation on flat surfaces could attempt to capture whole scenes, ideally everything that came into view. This is particularly the case with 'landscape', which cannot easily be captured in scale models or the plastic arts, but can be painted on a flat canvas or photographed for viewing on a flat screen. In the West, art that is self-conscious about its relationship to the flatness of the surface of depiction is relatively modern, but in the East an awareness of the media – parallel to concepts of Abstract Expressionism – can, for example, be traced back through the heritage of Chinese brushwork, in calligraphy as well as misty mountain ink painting.

In moving images, three-dimensional film can successfully create the illusion of depth, and electronic devices – high-definition holograms and virtual reality headsets – enable us to inhabit other bodies. These, however, are of recent creation. They require special technologies to experience and place fresh demands on the observer.[7] For much of history, pictorial representations of the world have been actualized on flat surfaces, the artist only sometimes attempting to achieve a perspectival, three-dimensional illusion.

Cartography

If the Earth was flat, it would be easy enough to represent it pictorially, as a map. The task would be a simple one of reduction and scale, and a choice of what to include and what to omit. The map could be rolled up like a cylinder or carpet, and rolled out – as in some influential images of creation. Recognition that the Earth is, in fact, spherical created one of the great problems of early geometry. Attempting to depict the whole of the world on a single flat surface was, and remains, a challenge to visualization and technique. Although a simple solution might seem to be at hand in the globe, this immediately runs into practical difficulties of scale and representation, and always fails to provide an image of the world in a single view. The same applies to Earth itself, of course, seen from space, however wondrous the experience.

Pictorial representations of the Earth's surface created by indigenous peoples are often understood as aerial in their perspective and compared to the flat cartography of Western traditions. However, the Western cartographer achieves this knowledge by measurement and instrumentation, whereas Indigenous know-ledge comes from generations of living and moving within the space. As Aboriginal Australians declare: 'The land is a map.'[8] Often art, especially sand art, is created on the horizontal surface of the ground, never to be placed upright or separated from its envir-onment. It is part of country.

Most prehistoric maps represented relatively small worlds, in which the flatness or otherwise of the Earth's surface was not a problem. For practical purposes and for small areas, the assumption that the Earth's surface is flat introduces no serious error. However, these local maps sometimes coexisted with maps of the heavens, typically understood as a rounded cover, but flattened out to repre-sent two-dimensional graphs.[9] Cosmological maps also have been identified in prehistoric sites, but most of these images seem to relate to the idea of the world tree or celestial ladder, or to accept the notion that Earth is a flat disc or quadrilateral. Acceptance of a spherical model – emerging by the sixth century BCE – did not lead immediately to the use of celestial and terrestrial globes, and indeed the dating of their first use remains a subject of controversy. Rather, early understandings of sphericity were represented on plane surfaces by the circle, but easily misunderstood as images of a flat, inhabited world surrounded by an earth-ocean.[10]

Skipping over a great deal of the ancient history of cartography, we find a culmination in the work of the Greek astronomer Claudius Ptolemy (*c.* 100–168 CE), who synthesized the knowledge accumu-lated across his wider world and exerted a powerful influence on the study of astronomy and geography down to the Renaissance. His *Geography* is the only treatise on cartography to have survived from classical antiquity. Building on the achievements of ancient geometry and geodesy, Ptolemy was the first – as far as we know – to apply an understanding of latitude and longitude to the creation of sophis-ticated maps. He was also an innovator in using degrees (the 360 equal parts of the day and the zodiac, developed by the Babylonians) to measure arcs along parallels of latitude and meridians of longitude.

The fundamental problem of geometry faced by Euclid in his parallel postulate has practical effects in all attempts to project the Earth's curve onto a drawing surface. The parallels of latitude remain parallel to one another, forming circles, and each parallel lies in its own plane, at right angles to the axis of the Earth. In contrast, the meridians of longitude are semicircles, narrowing to meet at the poles, with their planes intersecting at the axis.

Ptolemy's map was built up from a vast accumulation of coordinates – points of intersecting latitude and longitude – from widespread localities. He never doubted that the world is spherical, and was well aware that using a globe offered the best means of preserving relative proportions. However, he also recognized the insoluble problem that such a spherical map could not be viewed at a single glance and understood the practical difficulty of scale. Particularly compelling, against the use of a globe, were the limits of Ptolemy's 'known world' (about one-quarter of the real world), which would have left the majority of the surface blank, wasted space.

The task was to find a method to satisfy the desire for relatively correct proportions and intervals, and to impart an impression of sphericity, all on a plane surface – probably a papyrus roll. The problem is essentially how best to plot the parallels and meridians on the map. This is performed by drawing a grid or graticule representing the parallels and meridians on a flat surface. Whatever the structure of the graticule, distortion is inevitable and compromise essential. Ptolemy chose to combine an impression of the Earth's curvature (using a modified conical projection, in which the parallels appear as concentric circles and the meridians are straight lines intersecting at a single point) with a limited distortion of relative distances. His objective was to create a chart to accompany his geographical itinerary, and he had no real interest in shape or area.[11]

In spite of these substantial advances, after Ptolemy, many cartographers in the Christian West regressed to a symbolic or religious model, notably the T-O world map, which sometimes included locations for the Garden of Eden. Occasional writers persisted in promoting the idea that Earth is a flat disc. In the Christian East, where the pagan inheritance was more completely rejected, the

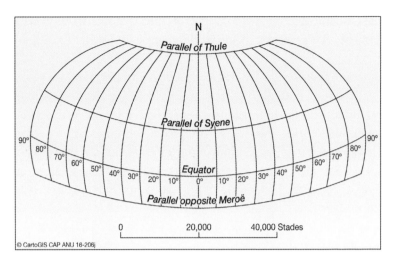

Ptolemy's second projection.

world was sometimes depicted as not only flat but rectangular – like a tabernacle – thus denying even the circle of the T-O model.[12]

The flourishing of the Islamic world, beginning in the eighth century CE, shifted the locus of cartographic production. In this tradition, maps of the habitable hemisphere were constructed by 'projection' onto a flat surface and thus depicted as a circle. The method of stereographic projection from a celestial globe onto a plane touching the earth at the equator was demonstrated in the planispheric mapping of the heavens, and in the 'flat' or 'flattened' astrolabe, which provided a two-dimensional model of the heavens. In the eleventh century, al-Bīrūnī mentioned seven different methods for projecting a sphere onto a flat surface – three of them his own invention – and he composed a small book on 'the projection of the constellations and the flattening of the sphere'. By the fourteenth century, Islamic cartographers were developing graticules, though sometimes using zonal 'climates' (based on the length of the day) rather than meridians and parallels, and they were too rigid to model the curvature of the earth's surface.[13]

Scientific cartography also experienced a period of creativity in China, in a form that was to continue uninterrupted until the seventeenth century. However, its fundamental assumptions were that China was at the centre of the world and that a practical map could be based on a rectangular grid of parallel lines in two dimensions, drawn on (multiple) flat sheets. Important for the conceptual history of flatness, early attempts at contour mapping begin to occur on Chinese maps from the seventeenth century, perhaps inspired by the large-scale landscape terracing of steep slopes for irrigated agriculture which dominated the visual field in many parts of China. Relief models, carved in wood, followed, but were apparently never made on a curved surface. Contact with the West from the seventeenth century brought the two traditions together, but Chinese cartographers only reluctantly surrendered their rectangular grid system, sometimes placing grid-lines and latitude–longitude lines on a single map.[14]

A similar reluctance to adopt Western models and knowledge occurred in Korea, where the scientifically naive and imaginative *chŏnhado* (map of all under heaven) remained popular into the nineteenth century. It depicted a flat world, an idea that Koreans either accepted or wanted to be true. Attempts to impose curved graticules over the *chŏnhado* marked the end of the style and, from the time of Japan's defeat of China in 1895, Korea's reluctance to accept Western ways dwindled rapidly, in cartography as in many other areas of culture.[15]

Skipping again over a great deal more of the history of cartography, in the West the fifteenth-century rediscovery of the Ptolemaic principles of projection and the use of grids of coordinates went hand in hand with European imperialism. For centuries, the drawing of boundary lines – whether counties, colonies or countries – was often made on the basis of quite empty flat maps. Viewed in metropolitan imperial offices or at peace conferences, the straight line – particularly along a meridian or parallel – was the easy solution in the absence of detailed topographic and cultural knowledge. The impact of these attitudes and practices was perhaps greatest in Africa. On the ground, the surveyor imposed geometric order, as well as collecting precise data on elevations which were the basis of scientific contour mapping. At a more symbolic level, the development of the world map proved one way of inflating imperial hubris.

Thus the great popularity of Mercator's projection in Great Britain, into the twentieth century, was said to result from the way it made the British Empire larger than it really was.[16]

Mercator's projection, produced in 1569, was cylindrical. It belongs to the class of world maps which use geometric perspective to project onto a plane, cone or cylinder – reminiscent of the papyrus roll and of a popular creation myth – but always 'opened out flat' by cutting along a preferred line. Most often, as in the case of Mercator, the axis of the cylinder is matched to the axis of the globe, and the lines of latitude and longitude are projected to create a rectangular grid, in which scale is correct along the meridians and along the equator, but increasingly exaggerated along the lines of latitude towards the poles. The poles themselves cannot be depicted because this would require infinite projection. Mercator's map was good for navigators, and remains so, since a straight line on the map is a line of constant bearing – a rhumb line – but the stretching of the earth's skin to create a flat and rectangular surface made Greenland appear larger than South America, whereas, in fact, South America is ten times as big. In spite of its distortions, Mercator's projection continues to dominate our image of the world, for its simple rectangularity and flatness. Alternatives often resemble the flattening of the skin of an orange on which a picture has been drawn, in which the skin breaks into segments. Most map users find such spatial incoherence disconcerting.[17]

Modifications of Mercator's projection have proved valuable in large-scale mapping. The most important of these is the 'transverse' Mercator projection, in which the cylinder is made to touch the globe along the great circle formed by a pair of opposite meridians, rather than touching at the equator. For small areas, with only a small range of longitude, this provides the base for a reliable ortho-morphic map, in which the shape of the land is preserved. The mathematician Gauss applied his concept of conformality to the problem, using 'double projection'. Following a method developed by Lagrange at the end of the eighteenth century, Gauss began by projecting an ellipsoid onto a sphere, and then, using Mercator's formulae, the sphere was projected onto a plane. In this version, the transverse Mercator is completely conformal, but the central meridian varies in scale.[18] However many projections, of however many varieties – and whether or not the map attempts to depict landforms are drawn, the final product is almost exclusively flat. Even relief models are typically moulded on a flat base, for the practical reason that they need to be mounted on a table or similar flat surface.

Generally, then, cartographers see flattening as the essence of their task, in full knowledge that the process creates distortion.[19] Failure to tell the truth with maps is not confined to the process of flattening, of course, but this is where the trouble starts. It is not a question of omission, generalization or scale, but a direct product of the lengths to which the cartographer is willing to go in order to transfer the real world to a flat surface. There seems little reason for the cartographer to reflect on the matter; flattening is simply the thing that has to be done. As in much of the history of flatness, the reasons are overwhelmingly practical. Viewing a sphere, cone or cylinder is challenging, and spheres, cones and cylinders do not pack together neatly, unlike map sheets or atlases. These benefits are sufficient to justify the sacrifice of reality for the practicality of a flat map sheet spread out before us. In any case, except in myth and imagination, the three-dimensional world cannot be observed in its entirety, with a single view, even from space.

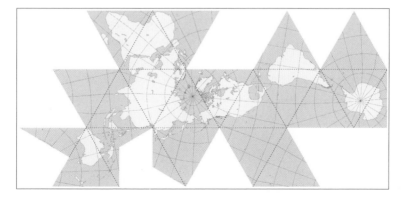

Icosahedral map projection of the Earth's continents, unfolded.

Aerial perspectives

Flight is a quintessentially modern experience, bringing together machine, functionalism and an original aesthetic. The sky was no longer the limit. Flight also created a sense of isolation or separateness from Earth, even a variety of surrealism or religious experience.[20] The curvature of the Earth was unmistakable but so too was the apparent flatness of the land when looking straight down at the ground, as in a vertical aerial photograph. The monotony of slow travel across flat landscapes was conquered and replaced by a new, modern image, one that could be captured in a photograph but also developed as a spatial and intellectual concept.

The aeroplane, or airplane, itself derived its very name from its ability to fly through the air, normally in a horizontal plane. Indeed, the *Oxford English Dictionary* finds the word 'aeroplane' used first in the 1860s, to describe the wings of insects, and later applied to the wing of an aircraft: 'a flattened structure, originally plane but later aerodynamically curved, that forms the principal lifting surface of an aircraft'. Slowly 'aeroplane' came to name the whole aircraft, and it then also revealed a new way of looking at the world, the aerial view that saw the land as plane, flat.

Air travel induced a 'cultural euphoria' in the early twentieth century that influenced artists and writers, photographers and film-makers, as well as city planners and architects. The French architect Le Corbusier, for example, was liberated by his aerial vision of Rio de Janeiro. He first travelled to Brazil in 1929, just two years after Lindbergh's miraculous crossing of the Atlantic, and immediately found in flight a new way to discover theoretically a 'hitherto unexplored plain', because it appeared as a flattened surface, a new 'geography'. Indeed, he claimed to have sketched his design for the city while looking down at it from a plane.[21] This was a perspective quite different from the traditional gaze from high points on land, however high, because from a plane the image could be vertical as well as oblique, thus providing an abstract, unnatural geometrical surface. It looked like a map yet was real, a cartographic 'facsimile'.[22]

The American writer Gertrude Stein, who first viewed the Midwest from a plane in 1934, was similarly inspired by the experience. By 'seeing everything as flat', she surmounted the 'arbitrary' grids and dividing lines, and the naming practices of cartographic representation. She used the flatness of the landscape and its blank physicality to reinterpret American identity, to see an unsegmented continuous surface, freed of narrative development.[23] Thus, for Stein, the flatness of the landscape viewed from above was liberating, and enabled the idea that the self was not fixed in time and space but rather free to develop, evolve. It was a way of denying the realities of division and difference that marked America so deeply.

When air travel became commonplace, beginning in the 1970s, the mystery of the experience faded. Travellers came to prefer looking at (flat) screens rather than the landscape, pulling down the shutters – if they were lucky enough not to be seated in the middle of the aircraft – even when offered wonderful, rare views of the real world, and complained of their discomfort. Most ceased to marvel.

Linear perspective

Before aerial perspectives and satellite imagery naturalized the cartographic model, pictorial representation depended on more grounded techniques. Perhaps the most important of these was linear perspective, a concept 'rediscovered' by the West and widely practised by imperial colonizers after Columbus. The basic principles of linear perspective are that lines parallel in reality appear to converge with distance and that objects that are further away appear smaller than when viewed close up. Fundamental to these rules is the assumption that the scene is viewed by a single observer, from a fixed point.[24] The principles were well known to the ancient Greeks, through geometry and geodesy. Pre-Euclidean styles, by contrast, composed pictures from multiple points of view and happily combined these with remembered images.

The rediscovery of linear perspective has commonly been located in Renaissance Florence, in the 1420s – just seventy years before the voyages of Columbus – but it can also be traced to developments in optics, derived from Arab science and to the preservation of Euclid in Arab texts. It is unsurprising that the technique shared many of its essential concepts and methods with land surveying and projective technical drawing. The broader importance of the concept of linear perspective – as a tool of imperialism and as the foundation of the modern world – is hotly debated, but there is no doubt of its significance within the more limited field of art history and landscape perception.[25]

There is an irony underlying the question of perspective in art. In the sighted person, a two-dimensional image is first laid down on the retina – a flat sheet of neural tissue – and then sent to the brain with cues that enable the construction of pictures in three dimensions. The artist does not have access to the flat retinal image but must recreate it on a flat canvas using only the perceived three-dimensional images. This can be achieved by applying the rules of perspective (as understood by the brain), together with shading, occlusion and haze. A further irony exists in the suggestion that artists with poor depth perception may excel at portraying it, because 'Seeing the world as flat just might be easier for them.'[26]

Linear perspective is important to the history of concepts of flatness in several ways. First, flat landscapes provide ideal settings for demonstration of the 'vanishing point' effect, in which, for example, parallel railway tracks appear to narrow to a point on the far horizon matching the observer's eye level. Second, early adopters of the rediscovered concept regularly included flat surfaces in the foregrounds of their pictures – typically piazzas of pavement blocks or chequerboard floors in which the grid they created could be used to demonstrate the new perspective in a simple (horizontal) geometric pattern. Indeed, it has been suggested that streetscape itself contributed to the invention of linear perspective. Third, descriptions of the system of perspective drawing generally showed the artist transferring what is seen in the real world to a flat sheet of paper, through the filter of a flat screen (the picture plane) divided into a grid of squares made up of string attached to a frame. The artist kept one eye closed, fooling the visual system into seeing the scene as flat.

The flatness of the picture plane was essential to the process, representing the way in which a drawing or painting was created from the plane's intersection of the 'visual pyramid' formed by rays or straight lines projecting out from the viewer's eye. Although unsupported by science, this was the model that best fitted the theory of vision that dominated before modern understanding of the way light enters the eye. These were principles that travelled along with Western colonialism, forced onto colonized peoples from early times, but sometimes resisted – as in the case of Japan – until the eighteenth century.[27] Ironically, the supposed flatness of Japanese art became attractive to European painters in the later nineteenth century, forming the foundation for flatness in several genres.

To North Americans and Western Europeans, argues Yi-Fu Tuan, the long tradition of Chinese landscape art often appears unreal – 'the pictorial symbol of Taoist nature mysticism' – but, in fact, represents precisely a common characteristic of Chinese topography. Indeed, said Tuan in 1970, most of China's people 'spend their lives on flat alluvial plains' from which steep-sided hills jut dramatically as shards and spires, shrouded in mist, with contorted conifers clinging to the tops and sides of the peaks. The art catches accurately the vertical and horizontal contrasts inherent to the landscape, and details of geological structure.[28] It also embodies ideas about the positive spiritual value of emptiness, in which Chinese theorists argued that the painter should always leave space for 'emptiness and hollowness' – allowing the viewer imaginative potential, with mists and clouds veiling the horizon and pointing to these opportunities, rather than a hard, flat line of closure. Chinese philosophy was not fearful of a world view that embraced the void, and saw emptiness and fullness as reciprocal.[29]

In the history of European art, the first independent landscapes – empty of people and lacking narrative – are generally attributed to painters working in the notoriously flat regions of the Netherlands and southern Germany, in the sixteenth and seventeenth centuries. Many of the innovations introduced in this work drew on Dutch marine painting: the low horizon, broad vista and play of light and weather working together through perspective to create atmospheric effects.[30] These motifs relate to Chinese landscape art, with its emphasis on the atmospheric sense of drifting mists, alternately revealing and blurring the relationship between emptiness and fullness, in a fluid space without borders, though typically in mountainous rather than flat landscapes.

In eighteenth-century Russia, untrained artists produced portraits in a 'plain painting' style, most obviously characterized by their 'flattened, almost two-dimensional' linear appearance. This full-frontal style contrasted strongly with that of the academy but matched the painting of Orthodox icons and many early Italian paintings, as well as the flatness that dominated in mixed drawing systems, as practised, for example, by Persian and Chinese artists from the tenth to the fifteenth century.[31]

In the U.S., artists in the Western tradition looked to the new nation's mountains, canyons, river valleys and waterfalls for subjects much more often than they envisioned the plains and prairies. The earliest known image of Niagara appeared in 1697 and was followed by many more, ranging from the fanciful to the wondrous. From the 1820s, however, painters began to attempt to put the falls into a wider context, but were challenged by its origin in 'endless flatness', resulting from the fact that Niagara is one of those waterfalls formed by differential erosion, so that its water flows gently over a broad plateau until suddenly thundering over the edge.[32] Even before the use of aerial perspective and aerial photography changed the way the land was viewed by artists, architects and planners, from the 1860s landscape photography in the U.S. began to offer images made mysteriously beautiful through their 'opulent flattening' of space.[33]

Modernist art

The Futurist painter Kazimir Malevich, working in Moscow before the First World War, employed Cubist non-Euclidean geometric techniques but became entranced by the notion of flight, which he saw as an escape from the constraints of time and space. In his painting *Aviator* (1914), Malevich saw the pilot as a man liberated from the limitations of gravity, the flatness of the painting's surface indicating 'a breakthrough toward infinity'. Quickly adopting a Suprematist style, Malevich turned to the painting of planes of colour on a white background, saying, 'I am transported into endless emptiness, where you sense around you the creative points of the universe'. His *Black Square* (1915) was 'entirely black and unabashedly flat', closing the door on perspective.[34]

The concept of 'flatness' dominated much discussion of the theory of art from the 1940s to the 1960s, particularly in the u.s., though its roots can be traced to late nineteenth-century France. It shifted attention away from the structure of pictorial representation – the scene – to the materials of the act of creation, and served as a metaphor for modernity. Partly in response to the threat posed by photography, painters in this style shifted the balance away from the creation of illusion towards a conscious awareness of the picture surface, towards 'flatness'. This flattening could be achieved through a variety of techniques, from suggesting uniformity of texture to the use of principles of projection lacking depth clues, thus disconnecting the system of pictorial symbols from the optic array.[35] Although the separation between the illusion and the picture surface came to seem artificial, flatness played an important role in the philosophy of art.

What has been called 'the closed box of modernist painting', associated with the vision of a 'unified field of flatness', can also be questioned by looking at works at different scales. Thus, whereas key works of Malevich, for example, may possess a 'painterly flatness' viewed from a distance, they take on local roughness when seen close-up, independent of the illusion of depth. Artists, observes Hannah B. Higgins, 'often speak of music or sculptural effects in relation to their seemingly flat works – a concern that clearly speaks of physical engagement through multidimensional touch or listening'.[36] Viewers tend to adopt an accepted distance – even within the controlled limits of behaviour allowed in galleries, where alarms go off if the viewer gets too close – seeing the painting as a whole and

Kazimir Malevich, *Black Square*, 1923–9, oil on linen canvas, 79.5 x 79.5 cm.

not very interested in the fact that it may shift between flat and
not-flat with changes in distance and scale.

In the u.s., the concept of flatness entered the core of criticism
in the writings of Clement Greenberg, whose reputation peaked in
the 1960s. He saw flatness as the defining characteristic of painting,
particularly in the minimalist practice of American artists, such as
Mark Rothko (1903–1970), whose work decried everything pictorial. Numerous works affected an explicit emptiness, as in *Alpha-Phi*,
created in 1961 by Morris Louis (1912–1962), an exponent of Colour
Field painting who 'simply' poured lines of paint down the sides of
a 'blank' canvas. The objective was to emphasize the flatness of the
painting and its definitively non-representational reality. Only the
'coloristic illusion' – called 'opticality' by Greenberg – saved such
art from going over the edge, thus avoiding the 'total flatness' that

Mark Rothko, *1957 #20*, 1957, oil on canvas, 233 cm x 193 cm.

followed the exposure of the empty canvas, yet somehow respecting 'the flatness of the picture plane'.[37]

Some of these artists – notably Jackson Pollock – sought to deny even the concept of composition by painting on a horizontal canvas, standing it upright only when the work was complete. The formal ambition of such work was 'flatness', something not easily subjected to illusionistic interpretation but ideally understood two-dimensionally in order to show respect for the physical act of painting on a two-dimensional surface. Here the act of painting becomes the vital value, rather than seeing the work as a picture or evocation of landscape.[38]

T. J. Clark, in 1999, emphasized the paradox underlying the flatness/depth dichotomy, arguing that admitting the fundamental truth that the picture is a plane surface could only be achieved by 'discovering what it was in flatness that could be put utterly at the service of the depiction of depth'.[39] Further, the very notion of depth could be questioned, along with changing understandings of the geometry of space and the mathematics of curvature. In the manner of projective cartography, Cubism hammered reality so flat that it broke up into fragments. In his efforts to convey the manifold planes and mass of space, by transforming the dimensions so that the back and front of an object could be seen at the same time, the Cubist painter Georges Braque (1882–1963) drew directly on Poincaré's non-Euclidian geometry. Modernists sought to leave behind the idea that it was necessary to apologize for the materiality of the work of art – 'two dimensions pretending to be three' – and to go forward with an assurance that 'brought flatness back to the picture plane in a way not seen since medieval icons'. The Cubists and the Futurists imagined a new way of representing the three-dimensionality of their subjects, attempting to see all of an object's surfaces at once, thus making the problem of flatness the very subject of their work.[40]

As exemplified in the work of Piet Mondrian (1872–1944), flatness might also be used in a way suggestive of the spatial contin-uity found in nature, with truncated lines pointing to a landscape that extends beyond the bounds of the picture's frame. Mondrian was, after all, a Dutch painter, and he began with the landscape of 'the flat Zeeland coast'. By 1911 Mondrian was showing Zeeland images in 'broad planes' of pure colour, with 'linear exaggeration'. But soon after his exposure to the early Cubist art of Picasso, Mondrian moved to Paris, where he painted subjects marked by their rectangularity and planarity – courtyards, roofscapes and abandoned buildings. By early 1914 he could declare with confidence, 'I construct complexes of lines and colors on a flat plane so as to plastically express universal beauty – as consciously as possible.' Mondrian moved to New York in 1940, and in the final months of his life focused on the design of his apartment, making his own (flat) furniture and locating planes of coloured card on the walls. Mondrian's contribution to 'complex modernist design' in the Netherlands was celebrated because 'he summed up the whole place in what appears to be a flat and empty canvas but which is both spiritually and monetarily worth a fortune'.[41]

Similarly, the use of plate glass, sheet steel, aluminium and Perspex in sculpture enabled both transparency and the illusion of emptiness. The boundaries between painting and sculpture dissolved, encouraged by the plastic, emotionless emptiness of photography and Pop art. Further, when painting became 'totally flat', it necessarily began to relate more to its environment – the wall on which it was hung – than to the elements within the framed picture. The hazard was that 'the plane of the picture might be assimilated to the wall'. But here the art remained separate, portable, formed from the same flat materials as the architectural mass. In many societies, portable art might be painted on bark or a skin lying flat on the ground, and rotated during the process so that there is no fixed viewing orientation. Modernist art sometimes returned to these techniques, but typically it found its way onto a wall.[42]

On the other hand, the human shaping of the landscape includes both ancient and modern forms of 'earth art', works inscribed on the surface of the land in situ. Recent self-conscious works of this sort – emerging in the 1960s – had purely aesthetic intentions, and in some cases, rather than creating raised shapes on flat surfaces, were dug into a dry lake or plain (in places like Arizona) to make linear depressions in which the art's 'dimensionality' appeared 'entirely horizontal'. Other artists made terraces, and some 'mapped' the land with grids that mimicked latitude and longitude, implicitly flattening the ground to parallel maps drawn on paper or canvas.[43] Public art does not always meet public approval.

Photographic flatness

The optical path in a camera is similar to the process of vision in the human eye, in which an illuminated object creates a wave with all the information about it. This object wave can be made visible in a plane of the optical path, by using a screen, for example, but the light field would be incomprehensible to an observer. If photographic film is placed in the position of the screen, the object wave darkens during processing, but only the intensity of the light is recorded – its amplitude or brightness – resulting in a two-dimensional image. All of the phase information – regarding the shape of the object – is lost. The same applies if the object is imaged on film through a lens.

Photography has passed through a series of technical innovations since its practical beginnings in 1839. Initially, latent images were captured in photographic emulsion coating a flat glass plate or flat celluloid film. When 'developed' and printed, the images were generally transferred to other flat materials for viewing or projecting. Digital photography, which rapidly came to dominate the technology in the twenty-first century, changed the way light was captured, but the final product – on paper or screen – remained a flat one.

Whether still photography or moving pictures – or viewing a scene with the eye from a fixed point – the outcome is always a flat image. The exception is holography, in which the object wave is reconstructed completely, thus permitting the projection of what an observer sees as a three-dimensional image of the object. Holography uses laser light, and records on film, but the perceived image is not flat, not limited to a flat screen. However, although the principles were known by the early nineteenth century – when photography was emerging – the first practical application was not until 1963, and viewing holograms remains an uncommon experience.[44]

Digital technologies returned the grid to photography, with rows of pixels – picture elements – composing an image from myriad units of colour and brightness, rather like the flatness and two-dimensionality of collage. This electronic technique is thoroughly flat in its format, but the quality of the image, and its capacity to signify depth, increases with the fineness of the grid or dpi (dots per inch) and the resulting denial of its flatness. Colourless images of distant planets and galaxies, recorded by space telescopes, are brought to life by the application of hue and brightness values, following choices in much the same way as a modernist painter or animator who uses colour to vivify a flat geometry.[45]

The problem of movement

Painting, drawing, earth art and still photography enable flatness, because they are all 'snapshots', essentially devoid of movement. Moving images make flatness more difficult to achieve. Stereoscopic photography bridged the gap to some extent by providing images with apparent (though unnaturally exaggerated) three-dimensional depth, derived from sequential overlapping pairs. Longer sequences of photographs enabled movement, first through card-spinning, peephole devices, and then with film and its more recent digital derivatives. In almost every case, however, the illusion of movement – sometimes called the fourth dimension – depended on the projection of flat images onto a flat screen. Photography, even more than painting, depended on flat, smooth surfaces for developing and printing images, hence the frighteningly realistic apparent three-dimensionality of early moving pictures. The later use of 3D, beginning in the 1950s, had much less dramatic impact.

Before the moving picture show, drama was long performed 'in the round', on a level surface surrounded by raked, terraced seating, or on a raised stage in the midst of a standing or sitting audience. In seventeenth-century China, theatrical performance spaces were typically mobile and temporary, enabled by the simple rolling out of a red carpet, either indoors or outdoors, with open boundaries and spectators wandering about to gain varied perspectives. Performances were also sometimes staged on water, in canals and lakes. By the eighteenth century, however, in the West, theatres had generally adopted the concept of the proscenium arch, opening a window onto a flat stage, not unlike the illusion created by *trompe l'oeil* painting on a flat canvas. It was three-dimensional yet dependent on a deep, horizontal plane, and the floor plane constituted the most important element in stage design.[46] The same principles applied in ballet.

There is an interesting relationship between the emergence of minimalist art and the rapid development of photography in the late nineteenth century. Western art commenced a battle with its role as representational and hence 'theatrical', as opposed to its aesthetic purity. Artists sought to demonstrate awareness that pictures are indeed flat objects, rather than windows on a pictorial world of depth and volume. Whereas Picasso and Matisse, for example, offered 'decorative flatness', significant strands of modernist art turned away from lush qualities of depth to embrace an emptied-out, ineluctable flatness far away from the romantic realism of the picture theatre.[47]

Not all moving film presented images drawn from nature or acted-out drama, and there was, from the earliest days, a vital genre of animation that depended on abstract two-dimensional figures rather than attempting to imitate real life. Animated images drew inspiration from traditional art practice in the East, as well as from fine art in the West (some of it drawing in turn on flat Japanese styles), and combined these elements with ingredients drawn from popular culture. In this way, commercial and avant-garde styles overlapped and interacted, blurring the boundaries between fine and popular art, the surreal and the subconscious. From these roots developed a prolonged conflict, played out in the work of Walt Disney, between acceptance of the flatness of the medium and its playful potential – the world of *Felix the Cat* – and a desire to restore perspective and the laws of gravity to a real three-dimensional world, as shown by *Snow White and the Seven Dwarfs*. After the

Second World War, high art critics sought to deny the role of elements derived from 'cartoon trash' that had filtered into 'fine art' minimalism; even though, as Esther Leslie argues, 'Cartooning was the place where research into flatness and illusion and abstraction was most conscientiously carried out.'[48]

The composition of images in (Japanese) anime entails a flattening and 'dehierarchization' of layers. Because these images lack an obvious centre, the eyes are encouraged to scan and scuttle across the surface, through 'lateral movement'. The consequence, argues Thomas Lamarre, is 'a proliferation of flattened planes on a single plane', lacking priority and lacking depth. However, anime involves animation, and once movement is portrayed, the moving element naturally gains priority and gets pushed to the foreground of the viewer's perception, creating depth by moving across or penetrating the surrounding flatness.[49]

In the West, directors of 'art' films sometimes gained a reputation for making movies boring and thus 'flat'. Because boredom is alien to the modernity of 'busy-time', there was a new demand for constantly changing – flickering – images. A frame of film held too long becomes boring and 'begins to look flat', in much the same way that the monotony and repetition at the centre of Samuel Beckett's plays can be viewed as tedious and boring, and empty.[50] Beckett (1906–1989), throughout his career, grappled with the concept of depth, constantly drawing attention to 'the media of art, the surface of paintings, the frame of the stage, the flatness of film, the television box, and language itself', yet always maintaining a self-conscious awareness of his characters, in the presence of an audience.

In Beckett's *Endgame* (1957), the robotic servant Clov views the outside world – the world outside Hamm's brain – through a spyglass, but sees 'zero, zero, zero'. In *Lessness* (1970), Beckett sees only 'flatness endless'. As Alan Ackerman puts it, 'Beckett sees nothing at all, yet all that is he sees.'[51] Meaning is not easy to find. The reality is that much of life is indeed made up of repetitive elements, and survival depends directly on their flatness and predictability. If reality were the virtual world of computer games – a world in which we must leap across chasms as the earth opens up beneath our feet – our lives would be short. The everyday practicality of flatness, noticed at several points in this study, is underpinned by the security it supplies.

Before Beckett, in 1927 E. M. Forster devoted a good deal of thought to an analysis of 'flat characters' in fiction writing, the people included in order to portray a single idea or quality – rather like Clov – and never allowed a rounded or complex existence. Later commentators have often read Forster negatively but, in fact, he believed that flat characters played a useful role, providing readers with the comfort of permanence. Such one-dimensional characters had the advantage of being dependable and easily remembered. The people created by Charles Dickens were 'nearly all flat', said Forster, and this was no bad advertisement. Round characters, on the other hand, need to be capable of surprising, but in a convincing manner. This is no easy task for the writer. It requires a contrasting consistency in the behaviour of the flat characters. As in all flatness metaphors, flat characters cannot diverge from their established models – they must be consistently wicked or consistently woeful.[52]

Whereas Beckett's flat characters and empty landscape reflected Cold War fears of atomic annihilation, the twenty-first century rediscovered his melancholic mental model in the growing dominance of electronic/digital technologies that took monotonous repetition to a new level. Images captured on digital cameras, iPhones and the like rapidly accumulated to immense numbers, instantly shared across the world but often limited in subject matter and seemingly trivial, as well as self-referential (the 'selfie'). Similarly, the sameness of pornography means it can quickly cease to stimulate, but contemporary communications technologies encourage the repeated viewing of scenes, series and sitcoms. Thus the 2013 Oberhausen Short Film Festival took as a theme 'Flatness: Cinema after the Internet', exploring flatness as 'a contemporary ontological category, an emotional state and a digital morphology'. The films or 'moving image works' – more than fifty of them – charted 'what it feels like to be always plugged in and always on the hedonic treadmill of our consumerist entertainment network'. The emotional flatness of the films was characterized by 'a lack of subjective expression', reflecting a world in which people become replicable 'units' and the man-machine threatens humanity rather than Beckett's bomb.[53] These psychopathologies can be interpreted as the end result of the mass production of goods, including images, which began in the eighteenth century.

Musical flatness

Musicians have often understood their works as reflective of particular landscapes – as much as emotions or events – yet they struggle to explain exactly how these places are conveyed in sound without the aid of programme notes. Like its painters, composers in the u.s. looked for inspiration to the Hudson River, Niagara and the Grand Canyon more often than to the prairies or the Great Plains. Music provided the possibility of building from the gentle flatness of the plateau to the roar of the waterfall that was missing from the visual art. Landscapes that lacked the opportunity to orchestrate such drama were less attractive, taken as subjects only within wider themes such as the frontier. The busyness of the city also trumped flat lands. Even Steve Reich, who sought to bring together the 'flattened-out' contours of American speech and melody, focused on New York City. Although *The Desert Music* (1984) was based on his rapid transits across the Mojave, the work was explicitly rooted in the poetry of William Carlos Williams rather than visual imagery. Reich claimed it contained no 'picturesque evocation' of the desert but admitted that at least one part of it made him think: 'Out on the plain, running like hell.' It was unlike the minimalist music for which he is known but spoke more of emptiness than metaphorical flatness.[54]

Where flatness was a more dominant feature of the natural landscape, so it had a better chance of entering musical life. Strongly influenced by his nation's landscape, the Australian composer Peter Sculthorpe (1929–2014) connected national characteristics of music and speech. Both indigenous and white varieties of music, he thought, possessed 'a particularly broad time-span', meaning music with few events and 'a very slow rate of harmonic change, regardless of whether the music is quick or slow', and he identified 'a certain flatness and elongation of melodic shape'. Sculthorpe also commented that a musical score often 'sounds just as it looks', and thought that much of his own music looked 'horizontal: its elongated, overlapping shapes almost give the appearance of a geological map of this continent'. In 1998 Vincent Plush described Sculthorpe's *Sun Music* series, composed in the 1960s, as evoking the 'vastness' of Australia and the 'overweening flatness of the continent'.[55] Sculthorpe came to introduce the sound of the didgeridoo, with its characteristic low frequencies, into all of his compositions by the early twenty-first century, arguing that Aboriginal music had been formed by the landscape over many millennia.

Traditional – indigenous – music is sometimes attributed a 'flatness' when it emphasises sonority or repetitive sound, or the persistent monotony of a drone. On the other hand, music possesses a richness in the way it is heard, as an immediate feeling, that visual art struggles to achieve. Music, and all sound, engulfs, whereas visual art always requires a surface – generally a flat surface with a tactile materiality. Sound is transitory, even when it is annoyingly repetitive. Visual art may also be short-lived, as in sand painting, but in the right conditions can survive for millennia.

Modernist music shared many elements with modernist art and architecture, and emerged around the same time in response to similar influences, in the early twentieth century. These elements included unity and simplicity in composition, with clean lines and an almost machine-like regularity, in which electronic instruments could come to play a part. Didier Maleuvre sees a neutrality and 'flatness of tone' entering 'the collage compositions' of Igor Stravinsky (1882–1971) with his score for *The Firebird* (1910), which expected the listener to hear the instruments separately. The music historian Robert Fink, on the other hand, sees in Stravinsky a series of prolongations and progressions, understood in landscape terms: 'each plateau is impressed on the ear by its internal repetition, and the plateaux line up, one after another, in an almost unbroken stepwise succession.' Other composers adopted atonality as a rejection of the concept of a single centre of perception, in the manner of Cubism, while serial music depended on a strict mathematical approach, along the lines of Malevich and Mondrian.[56]

After the Second World War, the style was further distilled, particularly in serialism and minimalism, exemplified by the early compositions of John Cage and Reich. Cage's famous 4′33″, first performed in 1952, embodied relative notions of space-time that mirrored minimalist art. The score was, in this version, measured out on grand staff pages, though lacking notes, but in 1953 Cage produced a graphic version with straight lines drawn on a blank sheet, explicitly referencing the white paintings. Further, the environmental aurality of Cage's composition – different on every listening – denied the absence of sound and the possibility of silence. According to Cage, speaking in 1957, 'There is no such thing as an empty space or an empty time. There is always something to see, something to hear.' Further, 'This openness exists in the fields of modern sculpture and architecture. The glass houses of Mies van der Rohe reflect their environment, presenting to the eye images of clouds, trees, or grass.'[57]

Focus on the surface constituted an emptying of content, reduced ultimately to an immobile two-dimensional flatness, but pure, free-floating and therefore radical and disorientating. One leading critic, Fredric Jameson, distinguishes between 'the high-modernist and postmodernist moment', and identifies the most obvious formal feature as 'the emergence of a new kind of flatness or depthlessness, a new kind of superficiality in the most literal sense'. For Jameson, this flatness occurs alongside a waning of affect – sometimes called a 'flattening of affect' – that can be seen in art and architecture as well as music, and in the theatre of Samuel Beckett. Its form is expressed in concrete and glass, and intolerable silences, not merely in spatial metaphors. Jameson, says Fink, 'hammers postmodernism absolutely flat'.[58]

Minimalism was not confined to 'classical' music but had a place in electronic, experimental, ambient, noise and popular genres. Most of these styles depended ultimately on obsessive repetition, pushing the listener's patience to the edge. As Western musical creations, these elements can be traced back to monophonic monastic plainsong and the German composers Richard Wagner and Gustav Mahler, and carried forward by the American minimalists Philip Glass and Reich – among many others – but in a global context, hypnotic drones and repetitive clapping and drumming have a vastly deeper history. The music of Asia and Africa was highly influential, most obviously the Western adoption of traditional Indian instrumental music, often identified with Ravi Shankar. All of these threads were synthesized in Brian Eno's invention of ambient music in 1975.[59] Eno's brother Roger later drew on classical sources – notably Debussy and Satie – in his own ambient compositions, particularly a CD titled *The Flatlands* (1998), which included tracks called 'Elevation' and 'Palimpsest', as well as 'Flatlands'. Objekt's debut album, *Flatland* (2014), combines 'rippling techno rhythms and electro-funk scuttling', the tracks having no obvious connection with the spatial concepts of flatness. Electro-acoustic music stretched the silences, opening spaces for imagination and (Zen) emptiness, creating a kind of flatness marked by occasional peaks of aural activity, like the cityscapes of Le Corbusier.

The German group Kraftwerk sought to develop 'a pure electronic aesthetic'. Their early iconic concepts replicated the rhythms of the motorway and the railway. *Autobahn* (1974) brought together wanderlust, modernity and the freedom of the road – together with the speed enabled by its smooth surface – and the hypnotic techno/mechanical rhythm of pure, robotic electronic sound, larded with sonorous lyrics. The album became famous for its cover artwork, the original German sleeve designed by Emil Schult taking the driver's perspective, dominated by the road surface itself reeling relentlessly into the distance where the sun rose over a wide valley.[60] Video versions emphasized the painted lines that demarcated the lanes, turning them into flat, white and rectangular planes floating above the asphalt. Later Kraftwerk performances made much use of visual images, marked by mechanical or robotic flatness but drawing consciously on the art of Dadaism and constructivism, and the architecture of the Bauhaus.

As in art and architecture, musical modernism was followed by postmodernism, the music becoming playful and eclectic. This

Kraftwerk performing onstage for their album *Autobahn* (1974).

did not necessarily mean the end of flatness, however. Indeed, postmodern painting has been described as simply a 'psychological flatness' or superficiality characterized by pastiche and simulation. Something similar can be seen in architecture. As David Joselit contends, 'the flatness or depthlessness we experience in our globalized world is more than an optical effect'; it serves as 'a powerful metaphor for the price we pay in transforming ourselves into images – a compulsory self-spectacularization which is the necessary condition of entering the public sphere in the world of late capitalism'.[61] So the whole world has been made flat.

NINE

FUTURE FLATNESS

'"Super flatness" is the stage to the future.'
Takashi Murakami, 2000[1]

Anthropic projects to engineer the flattening of the Earth's surface and to insinuate flat geometric surfaces into almost every aspect of modern life appear puny in the face of the remaking of the landscape implied in prophecy and on cosmological time-scales. Long-term geological transformation and the anger of gods seem set to alter fundamentally the surface of the Earth in a distant future, but predictions of future flatness are much closer at hand.

Apocalyptic flattening

Visions of the end of the world take many forms, a final flattening being simply one of the more prominent ideas. Typically, historic texts portray this apocalyptic event as achieved by the levelling of mountains. In the Revelation of John, for example, a great earthquake removes every mountain and island, and the sky is rolled up like a scroll. The social hierarchy and ruling classes are reduced to a common level, coincident with the geophysical flattening. In the Qur'an, the Day of Judgment sees the Earth made flat, and the people gathered together, naked, to face the wrath of the divine. In contrast, Buddhist eschatology sees the (Chinese) world made 'very flat and even' – in a utopian image – and the people 'equal in all respects'. Ancient Iranian (Zoroastrian) texts typically regard mountains as sacred places but, occasionally, their making is seen

THE STEAM ROLLER

American suffragettes aboard a steamroller, flattening opposition to their egalitarian political agenda of social levelling, 1917.

as an assault by the Evil Spirit on the original good creation, which had exhibited a level terrain.[2]

In these radical versions, the world is flattened at the end of time. At the centre is the notion of restoring the perfection of a flat Earth – without 'up' and without 'down' – when evil is finally overcome and all humanity become one, speaking a single language. The levelling is egalitarian, matching the topographic transformation with the end of vertical hierarchies in society and governance, and the revolutionary dismantling of imperial enterprises. These are themes that resonate with radical ideologies promoting the 'levelling' of society through 'the humbling of the mighty and the exaltation of the low'.[3]

Some of the most powerful Old Testament prophecies occur in Isaiah 40:1–5. These verses are seen by Christians as foretelling the coming of John the Baptist and of salvation through the Lord (Jesus), and they provide the opening scene of Handel's Messiah (1743). Here the suffering people of Zion are told to heed:

> The voice of him that crieth in the wilderness, Prepare ye the way of the Lord, make straight in the desert a highway for our God. Every valley shall be exalted, and every mountain and hill shall be made low: and the crooked shall be made straight, and the rough places plain.

This world, writes Christopher Connery, 'will look like a sheet of graph paper: featureless, two-dimensional, abstract'. However, the levelling and straightening were preliminary to making prominent the 'holy mountain' or 'mountain of the Lord' that has a central role in several of Isaiah's prophecies.[4]

In the early medieval world, Christian thinkers opposed to the spherical and heliocentric model of the universe warned their detractors of the horror they would experience, in the last days, when the stars fell from the heavens and the truth of the Earth's shape was revealed, when they would be punished for their wickedness in believing otherwise. However, the Hellscape is typically characterized by its vastness and emptiness – ultimate uniformity – rather than any physical flatness.[5] Alternative models more firmly rooted in fears for real physical futures are easy enough to find, on Earth itself.

Sea-level change

Apocalyptic visions sometimes conceive an Earth completely covered by water. It happened before, in the book of Genesis: first, in the original Creation, prior to God's separation of land and sea, and second, in the Flood or Deluge, an event remembered by many cultures. The Old Testament version of the Flood, however, saw the retreat of the waters revealing the once smooth earth as a ruin, now marked by high mountains and a wild sea threatening to invade the land. On the other hand, the Book of Revelation (21:1) foreshadows a final state in which 'there was no more sea', and the old had given way to 'a new heaven and a new earth'.[6] In the contemporary world, the implications of rising sea levels induced by climate change are similarly threatening, though less absolute. Whatever the cause, rising sea levels always increase the 'flatness' of the Earth's surface overall but tend to reduce the flatness of the terrestrial component – because the flattest land is likely to be the first covered.

The possibility of inundation is more strongly correlated with altitude than flatness, but the strong association between lowness and flatness means that the first to go under will be small, low, flat islands. Very low places are always flat. Thus the Tibetan Plateau is immune in spite of its flatness, whereas islands such as Tuvalu in the Pacific are highly vulnerable. In the Indian Ocean, the Maldives, a group of more than one thousand islands lying less than three metres above sea level, are similarly threatened. Quite small changes can mean the end of island life, and at current rates of change, most of the islands will be destroyed by about 2030. Sea level rise also threatens existing coastal wetlands, whether natural, such as the Everglades of Florida, or engineered, such as the polders of the Netherlands. The effects are not confined to human cultures, of course; plants and animals typically colonize the shore in horizontal bands, in adaptation to variations in temperature and exposure.

Globally, the long-term drift of population to coastal regions, in association with urbanization, has increased the significance of sea-level change for human societies. This demographic drift reflects the many advantages of living near the sea, particularly for trade and travel, and the fact that natural geological processes have often created flat and fertile land at about the present sea level, acting as a magnet to human settlement. Some flat coastal strips experience large daily and seasonal changes in sea level as a result of tidal variation, and sometimes these effects extend far up estuaries and streams. Where the land is not naturally flat, engineering works have sometimes opened corridors through elevated coastal barriers, creating the potential for saltwater to spread inland when sea levels

Malé, the Maldives, Indian Ocean, 2004.

rise. These cuttings, tunnels and graded slopes – designed to suit roads and railways – are in themselves only small-scale elements of local landscape flattening, but constitute conduits or weak links for a more dramatic increase in the extent of the ocean's watery flatness and in its share of the Earth's surface.

Storms sweeping across low-lying coasts are often devastating. People have adapted to these patterns fairly easily, and indeed take advantage of annual floods. Tsunamis have more catastrophic impacts, 'flattening' everything in their path, but, fortunately, are rare.[7] The great deltas of the Nile and the Ganges support some of the most densely populated regions of the world, but their lowness and flatness make them highly vulnerable, and the cost of building effective defences may prove too costly, as well as requiring complex engineering. Where more money is available for investment, heroic short-term strategies may be attempted. In the Maldives, a new capital – Hulhumale – was commenced in 1997, on a rectangular island, built on top of a submerged reef using ground coral.

If sea-level rise is sufficiently large, the impact will spread beyond coastal societies and ecosystems to affect inland continental regions. In Australia, the 'flattest continent', a rise of 70 metres – the level predicted following the melting of the world's ice caps and glaciers – would be enough to create large inland lakes. Such an ice-free world would see the loss of Bangladesh, the Netherlands and Denmark, and large populated regions of China. Long before this extreme is reached, however, rises of 1 or 2 metres would be enough to disrupt many large cities seriously, from New York to Melbourne.

Global warming and nuclear futures

Final flatness might also be a direct product of global warming. An example of this vision is found in the science fiction novel *October the First is Too Late,* written by the British cosmologist Fred Hoyle. He explores concepts of time and space from the perspective of an anachronistic Earth made up of copies of regions, some as they had been in earlier times, some as they would be in the future. Thus, in Hoyle's novel, North America is somewhere in the eighteenth century, while France is mired in 1917. Only England finds itself in 1966, the year of the book's publication. Flying east to investigate the geomorphology of this 'strange new world', investigators find a vast, empty, iridescent flat plain. Somewhere over 'what should have been the Ural Mountains', they decide to land: 'There was no problem finding a flat place, it was all flat.'[8] On the ground, the absence of any idea of scale proves 'bewildering and distinctly frightening', but after much consideration, the scientists conclude that this 'huge Plain of Glass' represents the 'ultimate fate of the Earth' – reminiscent of the 'sea of glass' in the Book of Revelation (4:6, 15:2). Whereas this apocalyptic sea of glass is 'mingled with fire', the surface of Hoyle's Plain of Glass is fused by extreme heat resulting from the warming of the Sun (rather than nuclear war). It is a world without people, empty. Here flatness serves as one possibility in a world of alternative universes, perhaps a beginning as much as a final state.[9]

North American movies with a nuclear theme often point to Armageddon and the Apocalypse, entailing the catastrophic flattening of urban landscapes. Cities are inundated by immense tsunamis or drifting sands slowly covering the pretentious tall buildings of man, creating a new surface level. Once again, the scouring of the Earth creates the possibility of return to the beginning, often with just a few individual survivors faced with the task of repopulation. In Japanese movies, Godzilla flattens by clumsy stomping and fiery breath. However, the spatiality of the flatness is not as important as the symbolic destruction of everything that civilization had built up and held dear.[10] Rather than an apocalyptic levelling of mountains, it is the modern city that is flattened, its own internal fascination with flat surfaces trampled by beasts and ferocious weather events.

Australian landscape flatness has contributed to a variety of film genres, typically drawing out the horror of isolation and the terror it can feed. *Ground Zero* (1987) found its site and story in the desert of South Australia, where, in the 1950s, the British carried out nuclear tests that caused long-term health problems and deaths in the indigenous population. The central character, struggling to expose the truth that governments seek to hide, undergoes a personal journey of self-discovery, his comprehension heightened by nuclear holocaust.[11] The site of the actual Ground Zero is marked by an obelisk. From the point of view of the British and Australian govern-ments, the bombs changed the landscape little; they saw it as already flat and 'empty', making it an ideal place to test weapons. On the other hand, the *Mad Max* trilogy, set in another Australian desert, takes the landscape for granted, bare and barren, with abundant space for bizarre characters.

Fears of population growth, resource depletion, climate change and meteor strikes have encouraged Earth's peoples to look for solutions beyond the limited landscape of the planet's surface. For example, a relatively hopeful vision of future flatness occurs in the science fiction movie *When Worlds Collide* (1951), in which a handful of survivors of the destruction of life on Earth make it to a new planet, where they see their future symbolized in 'a vast, flat lawn of idyllic, flat grass that stretches to the horizon.'[12] Grass offered something nearer to the savannah than the resourceless prospect of Hoyle's Plain of Glass.

Monument at the hypocentre (ground zero), Nagasaki, 2008. The cenotaph was erected in 1956 to honour those lost in the atomic bomb blast.

Parallel to changes in the world landscape, at every scale, there has, since the nineteenth century, been a growing recognition of the positive values contained in flat lands. Indeed, a celebration of the value of flatness can be identified among the settler communities of Australia, North America and Russia, linked to emerging concepts of national identity. Typically, this appreciation begins within artistic communities, including among photographers, and flourishes next in literature, before coming to be understood in geophysical terms. The aeroplane and aerial photography have a vital role in seeing the world in a different way, revealing the topographical complexity of flat landscapes, which could not previously be appreciated because there were no mountains to look down from (as well as no hills to which to lift up one's eyes). The consequence is a complex interaction between visual perception, spiritual notions and geological and geomorphological truths.

Dispossessed indigenous people lament not only the loss of their ancestral land but the way in which Western settler societies have sealed ancient sacred landscapes under pavements of concrete and asphalt, the flatness of the new surfaces concealing the significance of what lies beneath. It is the end of a landscape of subtle and spiritual meaning – replaced by nothing more than an appalling flattened encrustation.

Flatscape

Elemental fears are often associated with loss and nostalgia, over-shadowed by our inability to know the future. In the modern world, the rich tapestry of the past is supplanted by the flatness of plastic. Thus, in his classic work *Place and Placelessness*, first published in 1976, Edward Relph regrets the diminished opportunity for authentic experience of diverse places in most contemporary cultures. Instead the world is becoming increasingly uniform and standardized: 'The trend is towards an environment of few significant places – towards a placeless geography, a flatscape, a meaningless pattern of buildings.'[13] He borrowed the term 'flatscape' from Christian Norberg-Schulz, who used it first in 1969 in his critique of the emptiness of contemporary urbanism. For Relph, it means a landscape 'lacking intentional depth and providing possibilities only for commonplace and mediocre experiences'.[14]

Looking beyond the flatness of future landscapes, a strong case can be mounted for the role of planarity in the making of hierarchical societies based on literacy, planning and spatial order. The standardization of the material world is found at every spatial level – and not confined to flatness – but represented most coherently in the rise of linearity and the application of grid lines across the spectrum, from the pixels of a screen to rectangular survey.[15] Grids are seen to 'flatten out the world', diminishing the natural variety found in human culture and society, yet at the same time possessing creative possibilities and the emergence of new symbols and systems of knowledge.[16] Certainly grids have proved productive in everything from science to art, enabling precise measurement, spatial location, projection and scaling. However, attributing creativity to geometric grids depends on seeing flatness as two-dimensional, whereas the points and lines of the grid can be extended into other dimensions. Further, it may be argued that flatness as a landscape metaphor is being replaced by the spatial continuity created by global connectivity and its non-places, together with the abstract plane of cyberspace enveloping the Earth.

Recent trends in technology point towards a world that is less flattened than in the modern model investigated in this book. The future appears likely to be modelled around natural, biological shapes and – in biomimicry and biotechnology – applied to many different objects, from organic bodies to machines and surfaces. Aerial technologies have many advantages, because they do not need to interface so directly with the surface of the Earth, thus giving a large potential role for small-scale drones in agriculture, sweeping in swarms like insects across uneven land, seeding, fertilizing and harvesting.

The development of 3D printing also heralds a more plastic world, in which products may take advantage of the properties of minimal surfaces without requiring the rigidity of older planar technologies and materials. Similarly, the application of rapid throughput electron microscopy imaging systems to the mapping of the human body offers opportunities to explore the anatomy, taking advantage of technologies developed by Google Maps. These developments emphasize once more the way in which 'landscapes' can be viewed at an immensely wide range of scales, from the whole of Earth to the human body and its smallest regions. What remains constant is the way in which – at least for the present and with the exception of holograms – almost all of these images are viewed on flat surfaces.

The predominance of flat surfaces in the contemporary built environment has significant implications for modelling the 'outdoor' urban scene. Although the capacity to collect massive amounts of digital data enables the finely detailed visualization and analysis of the urban landscape, in all its geometrical complexity, in practice the use of 'point clouds' and 'dense meshes' serves rather to shroud the underlying 'semantic structure' of the architectural mass. Particularly for planning purposes, effective models can be constructed by viewing the world as a series of textured planar surfaces. This works well in the contemporary city, because the simplifying assumption does not greatly contradict the real world, and small numbers of data points prove adequate for most purposes. The 'flattening' of such urban surfaces does not distort the visual image, falling well within the tolerances appropriate to the task.

Automation is said to proceed most rapidly where two flat surfaces can interface. This applies in manufacturing, where strong bonds are required between materials by pasting or welding, and it applies to the automation of tasks such as the mobile cleaning robot sweeping cleanly across a flat carpet. The principle can also be seen at work in transactional technologies, such as the interfacing of plastic identity or credit cards, and barcodes, held against flat sensors. Scanners may be less obviously flat, but they work best when reading from flat surfaces: this is why the cashier at your supermarket has to manually key in the digits from a barcode sticker when it has been wrapped around a block of cheese reduced for quick sale.

The original curved surface of the television and indeed almost all electro-optical display devices has been rapidly flattened since the 1970s. The principal reasons for this shift are that flat panels can be made thin and light, thus enabling easy portability. The quality of the image is not necessarily improved and in some cases panels can only be viewed straight-on. Flat-panel displays have become ubiquitous in everything from mobile phones to laptops, digital watches, notebooks, digital cameras and tablets, and they have remained flat as the light source shifted from cathode ray tube to liquid crystal, plasma and organic materials. Globally by the year 2000 there were two billion flat-panel display devices. More and more, people spent large parts of each day staring at the two-dimensional images delivered by these devices, living less and less in the world of three-dimensional pictorial representation, and ignoring the morphological diversity of the natural world, including natural flatness. For those who become addicted to this flattened two-dimensional virtual world, the psychological and physiological effects can be catastrophic. In Japan, the addiction has a name, *hikikomori*, typically associated with young men unwilling to leave home – or even their bedrooms – preferring the virtual over the real world, sometimes suffering death by starvation, neglect or suicide. Whether this will become an international problem remains to be seen.[17]

Although these tendencies appear universal, progress towards a flat-world or level-playing-field vision of the future – driven by technology and globalization – is not shared equally by all peoples and all cultures. Indeed, the ubiquity of flat surfaces in the constructed material world appears to be rarely noticed, as an everyday reality, whereas the metaphorical 'flat world' of economy and society which has caught our attention is, in fact, much more illusory. Globalization has not contributed to the uniform spread of economic activity, the equalization of wages or the reduction of inequalities in wealth. Rather, the loci have shifted to new regions. Some indicators – such as global income distribution – have indeed become more unequal. Population growth is most rapid in the poorest states and regions. Rural populations are now outnumbered by urban ones, and the desperation of people to move to the centres of wealth and opportunity is both evidence of existing disparities and a contributor to the widening of the gaps. When migrants follow these paths in mass movements, barriers are thrown in their way to prevent the erosion of existing advantage. The world economy remains marked by peaks of prosperity and ravines of poverty.[18]

Thus there were strong reactions to the publication in 2005 of *The World Is Flat: A Brief History of the Globalized World in the Twenty-first Century*, written by Thomas L. Friedman, a columnist with the *New York Times*. For Friedman, 'the flattening of the world' signals the interconnectedness of the globe brought about by telecommunications, the internet, outsourcing and offshoring, the commoditization of labour, cargo containerization and dramatically reduced transport costs. For critics such as Edward E. Leamer, however,

> Flat featureless planes of competition are the preferred spaces for the mathematical modeling of geographical competition, not because flatness closely resembles nature but because modeling of competition in real geographies with rivers and oceans and hills and mountains is beyond the reach of algebra.

All of this makes Friedman's flatness a 'nonsense metaphor', striking in its boldness and capacity to reinforce fears but not rooted in the realities of global economic patterns. Friedman's argument was interpreted as a justification for the inevitability of neo-liberal globalization – really Americanization – and linked with a series of discredited social theories, back to Social Darwinism.[19]

Superflatness

In 2000 Takashi Murakami asserted, 'The world of the future might be like Japan today – super flat.' In Japan, he says, society, culture, customs and art had all become 'extremely two-dimensional', as displayed in anime, manga, poster art and computer games, in which distinct layers could be merged into one. For Murakami, 'super flatness' constitutes 'an original concept of Japanese who have been completely Westernized', particularly through international travel, thus creating a worldview linking past, present and future. In art, it appears in extreme planarity, with colour dripped into a finely delineated grid.[20] This is a relationship that, as we have seen, is equally significant in the opposite direction – as exemplified by the influence of Hokusai on Manet in the middle of the nineteenth century, at the birth of flatness in Western modernist painting. Links with the u.s. version of flatness in art theory in the 1960s also appear probable, and with the postmodern theory of the gaze, yet the notion of the super flat is claimed as an essentially pure Japanese creation. Murakami sketches an idea of 'Japan' as a 'super flat' image, constructed of disparate planes across which the gaze flits, following an eccentric route.

Hiroki Azuma argues that the 'super flat' concept emerged from an art exhibition mounted in 1999 titled 'Ground Zero Japan', which pointed to 'the leveling of high culture and subculture, the dissolving of borders between genres and the successive descent into irrelevance of existing learning and criticism – as a return to "zero"'. It referenced the threshold of a new millennium, a return to zero, in 2000.[21] However, the term 'superflat' was, in fact, first used in the early 1980s in reference to the levelling of concrete floors, by grinding. Here, everyday practical understandings of flatness intersect with metaphorical meanings, demonstrating once again how the challenging abstraction that planarity entails has become an essentially intuitive, natural concept.

'Super flat' is not so much a physical attribute or even an absence of materiality, but rather a worldview in which linearity has little meaning, and there is a postmodern disjunction between the eye and the visualization of topological space. This sets up an opposition between Western modernity and Japanese postmodernity, but depends on the assumption that the Renaissance conception of single-point perspective was fundamentally modernizing. It also points to a rethinking of two key elements of flatness: repetition/ continuity and absence/emptiness.

Continuity is often cast negatively as simply an absence of change or variation, the long silence between tectonic events,

Jeffrey Smart, *Labyrinth*, 2011, oil on canvas, 100 cm x 100 cm.

whether geological or historical. Alternatively, continuity can be understood as the connecting chain that holds together past and present, the rough with the smooth. Modern flatness has, however, often served the cause of capitalism and colonialism, spreading non-renewable 'artificial' materials across the landscape, sealing off what went before, denying its spiritual continuity and desecrating the virtues of the natural world, while replacing it with a uniform surface of desolation.[22] The stratigraphy of the Earth is rearranged in the cause of creating flat surfaces on which human beings can comfortably walk, drive, communicate and play; in the pursuit of profit and pleasure; and in the making of civilization. Thus flatness, in all its guises, seems set to continue its ambiguous role in determining the character of everyday life on Earth. It is something to crave, yet dread.

REFERENCES

ONE **Conceptualizing Flatness**

1 David Summers, *Real Spaces: World Art History and the Rise of Western Modernism* (London, 2003), p. 343.
2 Yi-Fu Tuan, *Topophilia: A Study of Environmental Perception, Attitudes, and Values* (Englewood Cliffs, NJ, 1974), p. 86.
3 Richard Trim, 'Conceptual Networking Theory in Metaphor Evolution: Diachronic Variations in Models of Love', in *Historical Cognitive Linguistics*, ed. Kathryn Allan, Heli Tissari and Margaret E. Winters (Berlin, 2010), p. 225 (pp. 223–60).
4 S. C. Woodhouse, *English–Greek Dictionary: A Vocabulary of the Attic Language* (London, 1954).
5 Terry Regier, *The Human Semantic Potential: Spatial Language and Constrained Connectionism* (Cambridge, MA, 1996), pp. 18–19; David P. Wilkins, 'Towards an Arrernte Grammar of Space', in *Grammars of Space: Explorations in Cognitive Diversity*, ed. Stephen C. Levinson and David P. Wilkins (Cambridge, 2006), p. 62 (pp. 24–62).
6 C. W. Huntington Jr, *The Emptiness of Emptiness: An Introduction to Early Indian Mādhyamika* (Honolulu, HI, 1989), p. 59; Steven W. Laycock, *Nothingness and Emptiness: A Buddhist Engagement with the Ontology of Jean-Paul Sartre* (Albany, NY, 2001), pp. 96–7.
7 Susanna Millar, *Space and Sense* (Hove, 2008), p. 18.
8 Vitruvius, *Ten Books on Architecture*, trans. Ingrid D. Rowland (Cambridge, 1999), p. 74.
9 Michael Seul, Lawrence O'Gorman and Michael J. Sammon, *Practical Algorithms for Image Analysis* (Cambridge, 2000), p. 76.
10 Rachel Kaplan and Stephen Kaplan, *The Experience of Nature: A Psychological Perspective* (Cambridge, 1989), pp. 37–8.

TWO The Dimensions of Flatness

1 Edwin Abbott Abbott, *Flatland: A Romance in Many Dimensions*
   (Princeton, NJ, 1991), pp. 3–4.

2 John O'Keefe, 'Kant and the Sea-horse: An Essay in the
   Neurophilosophy of Space', in *Spatial Representation: Problems
   in Philosophy and Psychology*, ed. Naomi Eilan, Rosaleen McCarthy
   and Bill Brewer (Oxford, 1993), p. 61 (pp. 43–64).

3 Jean Piaget and Bärbel Inhelder, *The Child's Conception of Space* [1948]
   (London, 1956), pp. 447–51; Stanislas Dehaene, Véronique Izard,
   Pierre Pica and Elizabeth Spelke, 'Core Knowledge of Geometry
   in an Amazonian Indigene Group', *Science*, CCCXI (20 January 2006),
   pp. 381–4.

4 George Lakoff and Rafael E. Núñez, *Where Mathematics Comes From:
   How the Embodied Mind Brings Mathematics into Being* (New York,
   2000), pp. xii–xiii.

5 Jeremy Gray, *Henri Poincaré: A Scientific Biography* (Princeton,
   NJ, 2013), pp. 97–9.

6 D'Arcy Wentworth Thompson, *On Growth and Form* (Cambridge,
   1917); Wallace Arthur, *The Origin of Animal Body Plans: A Study
   in Evolutionary Developmental Biology* (Cambridge, 1997).

7 Yi-Fu Tuan, *Space and Place: The Perspective of Experience*
   (Minneapolis, MN, 1977), pp. 36–40; Jay Appleton, *The Symbolism of
   Habitat: An Interpretation of Landscape in the Arts* (Seattle, WA, 1990),
   pp. 28–32.

8 David R. Olson and Ellen Bialystok, *Spatial Cognition: The Structure
   and Development of Spatial Relations* (Hillsdale, NJ, 1983), pp. 69–77;
   Jean M. Mandler, 'On the Birth and Growth of Concepts', *Philosophical
   Psychology*, XXI/2 (2008), pp. 207–30.

9 Olson and Bialystok, *Spatial Cognition*, p. 69.

10 Jan L. Souman, Ilja Frissen, Manish N. Sreenivasa and Marc E. Ernst,
   'Walking Straight into Circles', *Current Biology*, XIX/18 (29 September
   2009), pp. 1–5.

11 J. M. Kinsella-Shaw, Brian Shaw and M. T. Turvey, 'Perceiving
   "Walk-on-able" Slopes', *Ecological Psychology*, IV/4 (1992), pp. 223–39.

12 I. P. Howard and W. B. Templeton, *Human Spatial Orientation*
   (London, 1966), pp. 71–138.

13 George Mather, *Foundations of Sensation and Perception* (Hove, 2009),
   p. 170; Howard and Templeton, *Human Spatial Orientation*, pp. 43–6;
   John Wylie, 'Depths and Folds: On Landscape and the Gazing Subject',

Environment and Planning D: Society and Space, XXIV/4 (2006), pp. 519–35.

14   Margaret Livingstone, *Vision and Art: The Biology of Seeing* (New York, 2002), p. 100; Jenny C. A. Read and Bruce G. Cumming, 'Does Depth Perception Require Vertical-Disparity Detectors?', *Journal of Vision*, VI/12 (2006), pp. 1323–55.

15   Mather, *Foundations of Sensation and Perception*, pp. 299–300; Mark Wagner, *The Geometries of Visual Space* (Mahwah, NJ, 2006), pp. 30–49.

16   James E. Cutting and Robert T. Millard, 'Three Gradients and the Perception of Flat and Curved Surfaces', *Journal of Experimental Psychology*, CXIII/2 (1984), pp. 198–216; Sibylle D. Steck, Horst F. Mochnatzki and Hanspeter A. Mallot, 'The Role of Geographical Slant in Virtual Environment Navigation', in *Spatial Cognition III: Routes and Navigation, Human Memory and Learning, Spatial Representation and Spatial Learning*, ed. Christian Freksa, Wilfried Brauer, Christopher Habel and Karl F. Wender (Berlin, 2003), pp. 62–76.

17   Lynn S. Liben, 'Perceiving and Representing Horizontals: From Laboratories to Natural Environments and Back Again', *Ecological Psychology*, XXVI/1–2 (2014), pp. 158–66.

18   Edmund Leach, *Culture and Communication: The Logic by which Symbols are Connected: An Introduction to the Use of Structural Analysis in Social Anthropology* (Cambridge, 1976), pp. 51–2; Tim Ingold, *Lines: A Brief History* (London, 2007), p. 155.

19   Peter Janich, *Euclid's Heritage: Is Space Three-dimensional?* (Dordrecht, 1992), p. 4.

20   Ludwig Boltzmann, *Theoretical Physics and Philosophical Problems* (Dordrecht, 1974), p. 259.

21   James Franklin, *An Aristotelian Realist Philosophy of Mathematics: Mathematics as the Science of Quantity and Structure* (London, 2014), p. 157.

22   Susanna Millar, *Space and Sense* (Hove, 2008); Edward Relph, 'Geographical Experiences and Being-in-the-world: The Phenomenological Origins of Geography', in *Dwelling, Place and Environment: Towards a Phenomenology of Person and World*, ed. David Seamon and Robert Mugerauer (Dordrecht, 1985), pp. 15–31.

23   Vesselin Petkov, ed., *Relativity and the Dimensionality of the World* (Dordrecht, 2007).

24   Tony Robbin, *Shadows of Reality: The Fourth Dimension in Relativity, Cubism, and Modern Thought* (New Haven, CT, 2006), pp. 45–7.

25   Immanuel Kant, *Critique of Pure Reason* [1781, 1787], trans. Norman
     Kemp Smith (London, 2007), pp. 67–70; O'Keefe, 'Kant and the
     Sea-horse', p. 45.

26   Dean Rickles and Maria Kon, 'Interdisciplinary Perspectives on
     the Flow of Time', *Annals of the New York Academy of Sciences*,
     MCCCXXVI/1–8 (2014), pp. 1–8; Claudia Zaslavsky, *Africa Counts:
     Number and Pattern in African Culture* (Boston, MA, 1973); Iain
     Morley and Colin Renfrew, eds, *The Archaeology of Measurement:
     Comprehending Heaven, Earth and Time in Ancient Societies*
     (Cambridge, 2010).

27   Olson and Bialystok, *Spatial Cognition*, p. 250.

28   Franklin, *Aristotelian Realist Philosophy of Mathematics*, p. 150; Janich,
     Euclid's Heritage, pp. 15–16; Carl B. Boyer, *A History of Mathematics*
     (New York, 1968), pp. 111–18.

29   Boyer, *History of Mathematics*, p. 94; Germaine Aujac, 'The
     Foundations of Theoretical Cartography in Archaic and Classical
     Greece', in *The History of Cartography*, vol. I, ed. J. B. Harley and David
     Woodward (Chicago, IL, 1987), p. 137 (pp. 130–47).

30   Raymond P. Mercier, 'Geodesy', in *The History of Cartography*, vol. II,
     Book One, ed. J. B. Harley and David Woodward (Chicago, IL, 1992),
     p. 175 (pp. 175–88).

31   Joseph Needham, *Science and Civilisation in China*, vol. III:
     Mathematics and the Sciences of the Heavens and the Earth
     (Cambridge, 1959), pp. 91–5; Michael P. Closs, ed., *Native American
     Mathematics* (Austin, TX, 1986); Zaslavsky, *Africa Counts*.

32   David A. Singer, *Geometry: Plane and Fancy* (New York, 1998),
     pp. 1–6.

33   G. Waldo Dunnington, *Carl Friedrich Gauss: Titan of Science* (New
     York, 1955), pp. 28, 122–5, 137–8; Tord Hall, *Carl Friedrich Gauss*
     (Cambridge, MA, 1970), pp. 21–4; W. K. Bühler, *Gauss: A Biographical
     Study* (Berlin, 1981), p. 96.

34   Dunnington, *Carl Friedrich Gauss*, p. 164; Bühler, *Gauss*, pp. 100–103.

35   Thomas F. Banchoff, 'Flatland: A New Introduction', in Edwin Abbott
     Abbott, *Flatland: A Romance in Many Dimensions* (Princeton, NJ,
     1991), p. 34.

36   Hermann von Helmoltz, *Popular Lectures on Scientific Subjects*
     (New York, 1881), p. 34.

37   Marvin Jay Greenberg, *Euclidean and Non-Euclidean Geometries:
     Development and History* (San Francisco, CA, 1980), pp. 140–48.

38   Jeffrey R. Weeks, *The Shape of Space* (New York, 2002), p. 37.

39   Karl Friedrich Gauss, *General Investigations of Curved Surfaces*
     (New York, 1965), p. 47.

40   Abbott, *Flatland*; K. G. Valente, 'Transgression and Transcendence:
     Flatland as a Response to "A New Philosophy"', *Nineteenth-century
     Contexts*, xxvi/1 (2004), p. 61 (pp. 61–77).

41   Burkard Polster and Günter Steinke, *Geometries on Surfaces*
     (Cambridge, 2001), p. 11.

42   Abbott, *Flatland*, p. 72.

43   Ibid., p. 93.

44   Ibid., pp. 8–17; Rosemary Jann, 'Abbott's *Flatland*: Scientific
     Imagination and "Natural Christianity"', *Victorian Studies*, xxviii/3
     (1985), pp. 475–6 (pp. 473–90); Christopher White, 'Seeing Things:
     Science, the Fourth Dimension, and Modern Enchantment', *American
     Historical Review*, cxix/5 (2014), p. 1482 (pp. 1466–91).

45   Jann, 'Abbott's *Flatland*', p. 473; Thomas F. Banchoff, 'From *Flatland* to
     Hypergraphics: Interacting with Higher Dimensions', *Interdisciplinary
     Science Reviews*, xv/4 (1990), pp. 364–72; Dionys Burger, *Sphereland:
     A Fantasy about Curved Spaces and an Expanding Universe* (New
     York, 1965); A. K. Dewdney, *The Planiverse: Computer Contact with a
     Two-dimensional World* (London, 1983); Ian Stewart, *Flatterland: Like
     Flatland Only More So* (London, 2001).

46   Marcel Berger, *Geometry Revealed: A Jacob's Ladder to Modern Higher
     Geometry* (Heidelberg, 2010), pp. 250, 381–4; Ulrich Dierkes, Stefan
     Hildebrandt and Friedrich Sauvigny, *Minimal Surfaces* (Berlin, 2010).

47   William H. Meeks iii, Antonio Ross and Harold Rosenberg, *The
     Global Theory of Minimal Surfaces in Flat Spaces* (Berlin, 2002).

48   Martin H. Trauth, matlab® *Recipes for Earth Sciences* (Berlin, 2006),
     p. 35; Peter H. Westfall, 'Kurtosis as Peakedness, rip', *American
     Statistician*, lxviii/3 (2014), pp. 191–5.

49   K. Drouiche, 'A Test for Spectrum Flatness', *Journal of Time Series
     Analysis*, xxviii/6 (2007), pp. 793–806; N. Madhu, 'Note on Measures
     for Spectral Flatness', *Electronics Letters*, xlv/23 (5 November 2009),
     pp. 1195–6.

50   BlueScope Steel Ltd, *Product Dimensional Tolerance Handbook*
     (Sydney, 2003).

51   Berger, *Geometry Revealed*, p. 399.

52   U. Prisco and W. Polini, 'Flatness, Cylindricality and Sphericity
     Assessment Based on the Seven Classes of Symmetry of the Surfaces',
     Advances in Mechanical Engineering, ii (2010), article 154287.

53   Philip Stein, 'How Flat Is Flat?', *Quality Progress*, xxxv (2002), pp. 77–81.

54 Joseph Whitworth, 'On Plane Metallic Surfaces, or True Planes'
    [1840], in Joseph Whitworth, *Miscellaneous Papers on Mechanical
    Subjects* (London, 1858); Frédéric Bosché and Emeline Guenet,
    'Automating Surface Flatness Control Using Terrestrial Laser Scanning
    and Building Information Models', *Automation in Construction*, XLIV
    (2014), p. 213 (pp. 212–26).

55 Joan D. Hayhurst and J. W. Bell, *Calculation of the Flatness of Surfaces
    by Electronic Computer* (Melbourne, 1968), pp. 3–4.

56 Bosché and Guenet, 'Automating Surface Flatness', pp. 212–26.

57 Lionel R. Baker, *Metrics for High-quality Specular Surfaces*
    (Bellingham, WA, 2004), pp. 29–35; Gerhard K. Ackermann and
    Jürgen Eichler, *Holography: A Practical Approach* (Weinheim, 2007),
    p. 203; G. Ehret, M. Schulz, M. Stavridis and C. Elster, 'Deflectometric
    Systems for Absolute Flatness Measurements at PTB', *Measurement
    Science and Technology*, 23 (2012), pp. 1–8.

58 Mercier, 'Geodesy', pp. 182–4.

59 M.A.R. Cooper, *Modern Theodolites and Levels* (London, 1982),
    pp. 1–5.

60 C. Fleming, S. H. Marsh and J.R.A. Giles, eds, *Elevation Models for
    Geoscience* (London, 2010); John P. Wilson and John C. Gallant, eds,
    Terrain Analysis: Principles and Applications (New York, 2000), p. 3.

61 N. Gonga-Saholiariliva, Y. Gunnell, C. Petit and C. Mering,
    'Techniques for Quantifying the Accuracy of Gridded Elevation
    Models and for Mapping Uncertainty in Digital Terrain Analysis',
    Progress in Physical Geography, XXXV/6 (2011), pp. 739–64.

62 Erwin Raisz, *General Cartography* (New York, 1948), p. 279;
    K. M. Clayton, *Slopes* (Edinburgh, 1972), pp. 183–4; Ian S. Evans,
    'An Integrated System of Terrain Analysis and Slope Mapping',
    Zeitschrift für Geomorphologie, Supp. 36 (1980), p. 279 (pp. 274–95).

63 Vernor C. Finch and Glenn T. Trewartha, *Elements of Geography:
    Physical and Cultural* (New York, 1942), p. 305; Arthur N. Strahler,
    Physical Geography (New York, 1951), p. 110.

64 Edwin H. Hammond, 'Small-scale Continental Landform Maps',
    Annals of the Association of American Geographers, XLIV/1 (1954),
    pp. 33–42.

65 Glenn T. Trewartha, Arthur H. Robinson and Edwin H. Hammond,
    Fundamentals of Physical Geography [1961] (New York, 1968),
    pp. 227–30.

66 Clayton, *Slopes*, pp. 172–4.

67 Brian T. Bunting, *The Geography of Soil* (London, 1967), p. 67.

68 R.A.G. Savigear, 'A Technique of Morphological Mapping', *Annals of the Association of American Geographers*, LV/3 (1965), pp. 514–38; Bunting, *Geography of Soil*, p. 72.

69 Jerome E. Dobson and Joshua S. Campbell, 'The Flatness of U.S. States', *Geographical Review*, CIV/1 (2014), pp. 2–3 (pp. 1–9).

70 Paul Henderson and Gideon M. Henderson, *The Cambridge Handbook of Earth Science Data* (Cambridge, 2009), p. 35; Frank Close, *Nothing: A Very Short Introduction* (Oxford, 2009), p. 36.

71 Barry Smith and David M. Mark, 'Do Mountains Exist? Towards an Ontology of Landforms', *Environment and Planning B: Planning and Design*, XXX/3 (2003), pp. 411–27.

THREE Flatness in Earth History

1 Jill Ker Conway, *The Road From Coorain* (New York, 1989), p. 5.

2 Yi-Fu Tuan, *Topophilia: A Study of Environmental Perception, Attitudes, and Values* (Englewood Cliffs, NJ, 1974), pp. 35–6; Kim Plofker, 'Humans, Demons, Gods, and Their Worlds: The Sacred and Scientific Cosmologies of India', in *Geography and Ethnography: Perceptions of the World in Pre-modern Societies*, ed. Kurt A. Raaflaub and Richard J. A. Talbert (Chichester, 2010), pp. 32–42.

3 Mineke Schipper, 'Stories of the Beginning: Origin Myths in Africa South of the Sahara', in *Imagining Creation*, ed. Markham J. Geller and Mineke Schipper (Leiden, 2008), p. 110 (pp. 103–38); Abdullah Yusuf Ali, *The Holy Qur'an: Text, Translation and Commentary* (Lahore, 1938), vol. II, pp. 640 (15:19), 800 (20:53); Tarif Khalidi, *The Qur'an: A New Translation* (New York, 2008), pp. 250 (20:53), 430 (51:48), 481 (71:19), 494 (78:6).

4 Nicolas Wyatt, 'A Royal Garden: The Ideology of Eden', *Scandinavian Journal of the Old Testament*, XXVIII/1 (2014), pp. 8–10 (pp. 1–35); Jean Delumeau, *History of Paradise: The Garden of Eden in Myth and Tradition* (New York, 1995), pp. 5–17, 50–55, 98; Monique Mosser, 'The Saga of Grass: From the Heavenly Carpet to Fallow Fields', in *The American Lawn*, ed. Georges Teyssot (New York, 1999), pp. 41–2 (pp. 41–63).

5 Nicholas Campion, *Astrology and Cosmology in the World's Religions* (New York, 2012), p. 29; David A. Leeming, *Creation Myths of the World: An Encyclopedia* (Santa Barbara, CA, 2010), pp. 1–24; George Fowler, *The Biblical Heavens and Earth, And a Controversy on, Is The Earth Flat?* (Sydney, c. 1925).

6   W. G. Lambert, *Babylonian Creation Myths* (Winona Lake, IN, 2013),
    p. 198; Leeming, *Creation Myths of the World*, pp. 1–24.

7   Arthur Demarest, *Ancient Maya: The Rise and Fall of a Rainforest
    Civilization* (Cambridge, 2004), p. 179; Miguel León-Portilla, *Time and
    Reality in the Thought of the Maya* (Norman, OK, 1988), p. 57.

8   Tuan, *Topophilia*, pp. 31–44.

9   M. R. Wright, *Cosmology in Antiquity* (London, 1995); Malcolm
    Schofield, 'The Ionians', in *Routledge History of Philosophy*, vol. I: *From
    the Beginning to Plato*, ed. C.C.W. Taylor (London, 1997), pp. 48–50
    (pp. 47–87).

10 Daniela Dueck, *Geography in Classical Antiquity* (Cambridge, 2012),
    pp. 69–70; David Sedley, *Creationism and Its Critics in Antiquity*
    (Berkeley, CA, 2007), pp. 97, 118; E. J. Dijksterhuis, *The Mechanization of
    the World Picture: Pythagoras to Newton* (Princeton, NJ, 1986), pp. 32–5.

11 Joseph Needham, *Science and Civilisation in China*, vol. III:
    Mathematics and the Sciences of the Heavens and the Earth
    (Cambridge, 1959), pp. 210–21.

12 Barbara Ryden, *Introduction to Cosmology* (San Francisco, CA, 2003),
    pp. 192–5; Andrew Liddle, *An Introduction to Modern Cosmology*
    (Hoboken, NJ, 2013), pp. 47–52; P. M. Okouma, Y. Fantaye and
    B. A. Bassett, 'How Flat is Our Universe Really?', *Physics Letters B*, 719
    (2013), pp. 1–4.

13 Carl B. Boyer, *A History of Mathematics* (New York, 1968), pp. 650–53;
    George F. Ellis, 'The Shape of the Universe', *Nature*, CDXXV (9 October
    2003), pp. 566–7.

14 Richard Lieu, 'Has Inflation Really Solved the Problems of Flatness
    and Absence of Relics?', *Monthly Notices of the Royal Astronomical
    Society*, CDXXXV (2013), pp. 575–83.

15 León-Portilla, *Time and Reality in the Thought of the Maya*, pp. 85–6;
    Mary W. Helms, *Ulysses' Sail: An Ethnographic Odyssey of Power,
    Knowledge, and Geographical Distance* (Princeton, NJ, 1988), pp. 33–49.

16 Hans C. Ohanian, 'The Real World and Space-Time', in *Relativity
    and the Dimensionality of the World*, ed. Vesselin Petkov (Dordrecht,
    2007), p. 99 (pp. 81–100).

17 Liddle, *Introduction to Modern Cosmology*, p. 16.

18 J.-Ch. Hamilton, 'What Have We Learned from Observational
    Cosmology', *Studies in the History and Philosophy of Modern Physics*,
    XLVI (2014), pp. 70–85.

19 Jeffrey Burton Russell, *Inventing the Flat Earth: Columbus and
    Modern Historians* (New York, 1991), pp. 74–5; Valerie I. J. Flint,

The Imaginative Landscape of Christopher Columbus (Princeton, NJ, 1992), pp. 23–6; C. Raymond Beazley, *The Dawn of Modern Geography* [1897] (New York, 1949), vol. I, pp. 273–81.

20 Natalia Lozovsky, '*The Earth is Our Book*': Geographical Knowledge in the Latin West, ca. 400–1000 (Ann Arbor, MI, 2000), pp. 120–22; Naomi Reed Kline, *Maps of Medieval Thought: The Hereford Paradigm* (Woodbridge, 2001), pp. 30–34.

21 Christine Garwood, *Flat Earth: The History of an Infamous Idea* (New York, 2007), pp. 36–45.

22 Fowler, *The Biblical Heavens and Earth*.

23 Garwood, *Flat Earth*, pp. 201–6.

24 Ibid., p. 256; David Adam, 'Flat Earth Society', *The Guardian* (24 February 2010).

25 Kendrick Oliver, *To Touch the Face of God: The Sacred, the Profane, and the American Space Program, 1957–1975* (Baltimore, MD, 2013), pp. 46–51.

26 Edward R. Tufte, *Visual Explanations: Images and Quantities, Evidence and Narratives* (Cheshire, CT, 1997), p. 24.

27 Ala Samarapungavan, Stella Vosniadou and William F. Brewer, 'Mental Models of the Earth, Sun, and Moon: Indian Children's Cosmologies', *Cognitive Development*, XI/4 (1996), pp. 491–521; Georgia Panagiotaki, Gavin Nobes and Robin Banerjee, 'Is the World Round or Flat? Children's Understanding of the Earth', *European Journal of Developmental Psychology*, III/2 (2006), pp. 124–41.

28 Schipper, 'Stories of the Beginning', p. 110; Peter Sutton, ed., *Dreamings: The Art of Aboriginal Australia* (New York, 1989), p. 91; T.G.H. Strehlow, *Central Australian Religion* (Adelaide, 1978), pp. 14–16.

29 Andrea Seri, 'The Role of Creation in Enūma eliš', *Journal of Ancient Near Eastern Religions*, XII (2012), pp. 8–16 (pp. 4–49).

30 Campion, *Astrology and Cosmology in the World's Religions*, pp. 24, 29.

31 Marjorie Hope Nicolson, *Mountain Gloom and Mountain Glory: The Development of the Infinite* [1959] (New York, 1963), pp. 81–90.

32 Alessandro Scafi, *Mapping Paradise: A History of Heaven on Earth* (Chicago, IL, 2006), pp. 160–62; Dijksterhuis, *Mechanization of the World Picture*, pp. 92–3.

33 Nicolson, *Mountain Gloom and Mountain Glory*, p. 161.

34 Clarence J. Glacken, *Traces on the Rhodian Shore: Nature and Culture in Western Thought from Ancient Times to the End of the Eighteenth Century* (Berkeley, CA, 1967), pp. 406–9; Nicolson, *Mountain Gloom and Mountain Glory*, chapters 5 and 6.

35 Dijksterhuis, *Mechanization of the World Picture*, pp. 464–80.

36 John Ray, *Three Physico-theological Discourses*, 3rd edn [1713] (New York, 1978), pp. 34–5, 356–7.

37 Robert Macfarlane, *Mountains of the Mind* (New York, 2003), p. 149.

38 John Ruskin, *Modern Painters*, vol. IV: *Of Mountain Beauty* [1856] (London, 1897), p. 98; Nicolson, *Mountain Gloom and Mountain Glory*, pp. 4–5; Alicia Lubowski-Jahn, 'A Comparative Analysis of the Landscape Aesthetics of Alexander von Humboldt and John Ruskin', *British Journal of Aesthetics*, LI/3 (2011), pp. 321–33.

39 Ruskin, *Modern Painters*, vol. IV: *Of Mountain Beauty*, pp. 86, 94–6, 399.

40 Needham, *Science and Civilisation in China*, vol. III, p. 598; Jacques Gernet, *China and the Christian Impact: A Conflict of Cultures* (Cambridge, 1985), pp. 201–13.

41 Gina L. Barnes, 'Buddhist Landscapes of East Asia', in *Archaeologies of Landscape: Contemporary Perspectives*, ed. Wendy Ashmore and A. Bernard Knapp (Oxford, 1999), p. 113 (pp. 101–23).

42 George F. Adams, ed., *Planation Surfaces: Peneplains, Pediplains, and Etchplains* (Stroudsburg, PA, 1975), p. 1; Nicolson, *Mountain Gloom and Mountain Glory*, pp. 111–12.

43 Walther Penck, *Morphological Analysis of Land Forms: A Contribution to Physical Geology* (London, 1953), pp. 120–21, 138; Richard J. Chorley, Antony J. Dunn and Robert P. Beckinsale, *The History of the Study of Landforms or The Development of Geomorphology* (London, 1964–2008); K. M. Clayton, *Slopes* (Edinburgh, 1972), pp. 25–40.

44 Adams, *Planation Surfaces*, p. 1.

45 William Morris Davis, *Elementary Physical Geography* (Boston, MA, 1902), p. 133.

46 Yoav Rappaport, D. F. Naar, C. C. Barton, Z. J. Lui and R. N. Hey, 'Morphology and Distribution of Seamounts Surrounding Easter Island', *Journal of Geophysical Research*, CII (1997), pp. 713–29.

47 Jonathan I. Lunine, *Earth: Evolution of a Habitable World* (Cambridge, 1999), pp. 208–9; Geoffrey F. Davies, *Dynamic Earth: Plates, Plumes and Mantle Convection* (Cambridge, 1999), p. 77.

48 Peter John Cattermole, *Mars: The Mystery Unfolds* (Oxford, 2001), p. 19; Paul D. Lowman Jr and James B. Garvin, 'Planetary Landforms', in *Geomorphology from Space: A Global Overview of Regional Landforms*, ed. Nicholas M. Short and Robert W. Blair, Jr (Washington, DC, 1986), p. 610.

FOUR Very Flat Places

1   Maxim Gorky, *On the Russian Peasantry* (Berlin, 1922), in *Journal of Peasant Studies*, IV (1976), p. 13 (pp. 11–27).

2   John Ruskin, *Modern Painters*, vol. IV: *Of Mountain Beauty* (London, 1897), p. 356.

3   Gordon H. Orians, 'Habitat Selection: General Theory and Applications to Human Behavior', in *The Evolution of Human Social Behavior*, ed. Joan S. Lockard (New York, 1980), p. 60 (pp. 49–66); Susan R. Schrepfer, *Nature's Altars: Mountains, Gender, and American Environmentalism* (Lawrence, KS, 2005), pp. 1–2.

4   Don Hinrichsen, *Coastal Waters of the World: Trends, Threats, and Strategies* (Washington, DC, 1998), p. 1.

5   Don Mitchell, 'The Lure of the Local: Landscape Studies at the End of a Troubled Century', *Progress in Human Geography*, XXV/2 (2001), p. 270 (pp. 269–81); Kenneth Robert Olwig, *Landscape, Nature, and the Body Politic: From Britain's Renaissance to America's New World* (Madison, WI, 2002), pp. 214–16; Jay Appleton, *The Symbolism of Habitat: An Interpretation of Landscape in the Arts* (Seattle, WA, 1990), p. 21.

6   Anna A. Adevi and Patrik Grahn, 'Preferences for Landscapes: A Matter of Cultural Determinants or Innate Reflexes that Point to Our Evolutionary Background?', *Landscape Research*, XXXVII/1 (2012), pp. 27–49; Steven C. Bourassa, Martin Hoesli and Jian Sun, 'What's in a View?', *Environment and Planning A*, XXXVI (2004), p. 1446 (pp. 1427–50).

7   Samuel Johnson, *Dictionary of the English Language*, HeinOnline World Constitutions Illustrated (1785 edition). Languages other than English do not always have direct equivalences to these meanings of landscape: Katrin Gehring and Ryo Kohsaka, '"Landscape" in the Japanese Language: Conceptual Differences and Implications for Landscape Research', *Landscape Research*, XXXII/2 (2007), pp. 273–83.

8   Rob J. F. Burton, 'Understanding Farmers' Aesthetic Preference for Tidy Agricultural Landscapes: A Bourdieusian Perspective', *Landscape Research*, XXXVII/1 (2012), pp. 51–71, ref on pp. 65–6.

9   Orians, 'Habitat Selection', pp. 51–4; Steven C. Bourassa, *The Aesthetics of Landscape* (London, 1991), p. 67.

10 Orians, 'Habitat Selection', p. 64; Anthony Vidler, *Warped Space: Art, Architecture, and Anxiety in Modern Culture* (Cambridge, MA, 2000), pp. 25–50.

11 Jay Appleton, *The Experience of Landscape* (Chichester, 1975),
    pp. 68–74; Adevi and Grahn, 'Preferences for Landscapes', p. 28;
    Bourassa, *Aesthetics of Landscape*, pp. 83–8; Rachel Kaplan and
    Stephen Kaplan, *The Experience of Nature: A Psychological Perspective*
    (Cambridge, 1989).

12 Kenneth R. Olwig, 'Liminality, Seasonality and Landscape', *Landscape
    Research*, xxx/2 (2005), pp. 259–71.

13 Ellen Churchill Semple, *Influences of Geographic Environment:
    On the Basis of Ratzel's System of Anthropo-geography* (New York, 1911),
    pp. 477–82, 521; Arthur N. Strahler, *Physical Geography* (New York,
    1951), p. 109; Ellsworth Huntington, *Principles of Human Geography*
    (New York, 1951, first edition 1920), pp. 218, 227; Albert L. Seeman,
    Physical Geography (New York, 1942), pp. 96–100, 156–60.

14 John Pethick, *An Introduction to Coastal Geomorphology* (London,
    1984), pp. 58–60, 214.

15 A. G. Bolam, *The Trans-Australian Wonderland* (Melbourne, 1924),
    p. 47; Peter Bishop, 'Gathering the Land: The Alice Springs to Darwin
    Rail Corridor', *Environment and Planning D: Society and Space*, xx/3
    (2002), p. 307.

16 Adrian A. Borsa, Bruce G. Bills and Jean-Bertrand Minster, 'Modeling
    the Topography of the Salar de Uyuni, Bolivia, as an Equipotential
    Surface of Earth's Gravity', *Journal of Geophysical Research – Solid
    Earth*, cxiii (2008), article 10408; Thomas T. Veblen, Kenneth R.
    Young and Antony R. Orme, eds, *The Physical Geography of South
    America* (Oxford, 2007), p. 70.

17 Eric Fielding, Bryan Isacks, Muawia Barazangi and Christopher
    Duncan, 'How Flat is Tibet?', *Geology*, xxii/2 (1994), pp. 163–7; R.
    Gloaguen and L. Ratschbacher, eds, *Growth and Collapse of the
    Tibetan Plateau* (London, 2011).

18 Mark Fonstad, William Pugatch and Brandon Vogt, 'Kansas Is Flatter
    Than a Pancake', *Annals of Improbable Research*, ix (2003), pp. 16–17.

19 Jerome E. Dobson and Joshua S. Campbell, 'The Flatness of u.s.
    States', *Geographical Review*, civ (2014), pp. 1–8; Edwin H. Hammond,
    'Small-scale Continental Landform Maps', *Annals of the Association
    of American Geographers*, xliv/1 (1954), pp. 33–42.

20 Charles Dickens, *American Notes for General Circulation* [1842]
    (Harmondsworth, 2004), pp. 201–2; Dorothy Anne Dondore,
    *The Prairie and the Making of Middle America: Four Centuries of
    Description* [1926] (New York, 1961), pp. 267, 292–3, 340; Walter
    Prescott Webb, *The Great Plains* (Boston, MA, 1931), pp. 488–9.

21   Orians, 'Habitat Selection', p. 60.

22   William Morris Davis, *Elementary Physical Geography* (Boston, MA,
     1902), pp. 158–60; Webb, *Great Plains*, pp. 3–5, 495–6.

23   David J. Wishart, ed., *Encyclopedia of the Great Plains* (Lincoln, 2004),
     pp. 373, 385–6; Robert L. Dorman, 'From the Middle of Nowhere
     to the Heartland: The Great Plains and American Regionalism', in
     Literature and Place, 1800–2000, ed. Peter Brown and Michael Irwin
     (Oxford, 2006), pp. 179–98; Jay Appleton, *How I Made the World:
     Shaping a View of Landscape* (Hull, 1994), p. 163; Marilynne Robinson,
     Gilead (London, 2005), p. 281.

24   Gerald Friesen, *The Canadian Prairies: A History* (Toronto, 1984),
     pp. 5–6.

25   Yi-Fu Tuan, *Space and Place: The Perspective of Experience*
     (Minneapolis, MN, 1977), pp. 52, 56; Gorky, *On the Russian Peasantry*,
     p. 12.

26   Valerie A. Kivelson, 'Mapping Serfdom: Peasant Dwellings on
     Seventeenth-century Litigation Maps', in *Picturing Russia: Explorations
     in Visual Culture*, ed. Valerie A. Kivelson and Joan Neuberger (New
     Haven, CT, 2008), pp. 47–50; Valerie A. Kivelson, *Cartographies of
     Tsardom: The Land and Its Meanings in Seventeenth-century Russia*
     (Ithaca, NY, 2006), pp. 61, 71–2.

27   Kivelson, *Cartographies of Tsardom*, pp. 67–70.

28   David Jackson and Patty Wageman, eds, *Russian Landscape* (Schoten,
     Belgium, 2003).

29   Anton Chekhov, 'Across Siberia', in *The Unknown Chekhov: Stories and
     Other Writings*, trans. A. Yarmolinsky (New York, 1969), pp. 267 and
     295, quoted in Valerii Tiupa, 'The Mythologeme of Siberia: On the
     Concept of a Siberian Motif in Russian Literature', *Orbis Litterarum*,
     LXI (2006), pp. 443–60.

30   Glenn T. Trewartha, Arthur H. Robinson and Edwin H. Hammond,
     Fundamentals of Physical Geography [1961] (New York, 1968), p. 231.

31   N. R. Wills, ed., *Australia's Power Resources* (Melbourne, 1955),
     pp. 63, 74.

32   J. N. Jennings and J. A. Mabbutt, 'Physiographic Outlines and
     Regions', in *Australia: A Geography*, ed. D. N. Jeans (Sydney, 1977),
     p. 38. Emphasis in original.

33   *Year Book of Australia*, No. 70 (Canberra, 1986), p. 28.

34   John F. McCoy, *Geo-data: The World Geographical Encyclopedia*
     (Detroit, MI, 2003), p. 31; David Johnson, *The Geology of Australia*
     (Cambridge, 2004), pp. 11–12.

35 Geoscience Australia, *Shaping a Nation: A Geology of Australia* (Canberra, 2012), pp. 25–6, 234–48.

36 Henk van Os, *The Discovery of the Netherlands: Four Centuries of Landscape Painting by Dutch Masters* (Rotterdam, 2008), p. 14; Steve Meacham, 'Better Red than Dead', *Sydney Morning Herald* (15 December 2004), p. 16.

37 Jill Ker Conway, *The Road from Coorain* (New York, 1989), pp. 5, 24–5, 98–9, 184–5, 201.

38 Graham Swift, *Waterland* (London, 1984), pp. 2, 34; Peter Toohey, *Boredom: A Lively History* (New Haven, CT, 2011), p. 27.

39 Appleton, *How I Made the World*, pp. 30, 90, 162.

FIVE Flattening the World

1 Pierre von Meiss, *Elements of Architecture: From Form to Place* (London, 1990), p. 143.

2 Stuart Piggott, *The Earliest Wheeled Transport: From the Atlantic Coast to the Caspian Sea* (Ithaca, NY, 1983), p. 63; Salvatore Ciriacono, *Building on Water: Venice, Holland and the Construction of the European Landscape in Early Modern Times* (New York, 2006); David Bourdon, *Designing the Earth: The Human Impulse to Shape Nature* (New York, 1995), p. 57.

3 Roger LeB. Hooke, 'On the History of Humans as Geomorphic Agents', *Geology*, XXVIII/9 (2000), pp. 843–6.

4 Andrew Goudie, *The Human Impact on the Natural Environment* (Oxford, 1990), p. 206; Hooke, 'On the History of Humans as Geomorphic Agents', p. 844.

5 Arthur N. Strahler, 'The Nature of Induced Erosion and Aggradation', in *Man's Role in Changing the Face of the Earth*, ed. William L. Thomas, Jr (Chicago, IL, 1956), pp. 621–38.

6 Jijun Zhao and Jan Woudstra, '"In Agriculture, Learn from Dazhai": Mao Zedong's Revolutionary Model Village and the Battle against Nature', *Landscape Research*, XXXII/2 (2007), p. 194 (pp. 171–205).

7 John Clancy, *Site Surveying and Levelling* (London, 2011), p. 301.

8 Adam Rome, *The Bulldozer in the Countryside: Suburban Sprawl and the Rise of American Environmentalism* (Cambridge, 2001), p. 151.

9 H. C. Darby, *The Draining of the Fens* (Cambridge, 1956), pp. 28, 38–45, 94–119.

10 Michael Williams, *Deforesting the Earth: From Prehistory to Global Crisis* (Chicago, IL, 2003), pp. 420–21.

11 Ibid., pp. 37–8; John F. Richards, 'Land Transformation', in *The Earth as Transformed by Human Action: Global and Regional Changes in the Biosphere over the Past 300 Years*, ed. B. L. Turner II (Cambridge, 1990), p. 164 (pp. 163–78).

12 R. Douglas Hurt, *American Farm Tools from Hand-power to Steam-power* (Manhattan, KS, 1985), p. 111.

13 Thorstein Veblen, *The Theory of the Leisure Class: An Economic Study of Institutions* (New York, 1953), pp. 98–9.

14 Virginia Scott Jenkins, *The Lawn: A History of an American Obsession* (Washington, DC, 1994), p. 3; Maggie Keswick, *The Chinese Garden: History, Art and Architecture* (London, 1986), p. 18.

15 Jean Delumeau, *History of Paradise: The Garden of Eden in Myth and Tradition* (New York, 1995), pp. 121–8.

16 Karen R. Jones and John Wills, *The Invention of the Park: Recreational Landscapes from the Garden of Eden to Disney's Magic Kingdom* (Cambridge, 2005), pp. 21–4.

17 Ibid., pp. 47–52; Kenneth T. Jackson, *Crabgrass Frontier: The Suburbanization of the United States* (New York, 1985), pp. 54–61.

18 Jenkins, *The Lawn*, p. 63.

19 P. J. Hurley, *An Encyclopaedia for Australian Gardeners* (Sydney, 1949), p. 139; J. L. Rees, *Lawns, Greens, and Playing Fields: Their Making and Maintenance* (Sydney, 1962), pp. 91–2; Geoff Stebbings, *Lawns and Ground Cover* (London, 1999), p. 16.

20 Rees, *Lawns, Greens, and Playing Fields*, pp. 208–9.

21 Paul Robbins, *Lawn People: How Grasses, Weeds, and Chemicals Made Us Who We Are* (Philadelphia, PA, 2007); Jenkins, *The Lawn*, p. 63; Georges Teyssot, 'The American Lawn: Surface of Everyday Life', in *The American Lawn*, ed. Georges Teyssot (New York, 1999), pp. 10, 30–31 (pp. 1–39).

22 Ken Worpole, *Last Landscapes: The Architecture of the Cemetery in the West* (London, 2003), p. 144.

23 David Charles Sloane, *The Last Great Necessity: Cemeteries in American History* (Baltimore, MD, 1991), pp. 159–71.

24 Robin T. Underwood, *Road Engineering Practice* (Melbourne, 1995), p. 91.

25 Joseph A. Amato, *On Foot: A History of Walking* (New York, 2004), pp. 230–31.

26 K. D. White, *Greek and Roman Technology* (Ithaca, NY, 1984), pp. 93–7; Hooke, 'On the History of Humans as Geomorphic Agents', pp. 843–4.

27 James J. Flink, *The Automobile Age* (Cambridge, MA, 1988), pp. 169–70.

28   William F. Laurance et al., 'A Global Strategy for Road Building',
      Nature, DXIII (11 September 2014), pp. 229–32.

29   Christof Mauch and Thomas Zeller, eds, *The World Beyond the
      Windshield: Roads and Landscapes in the United States and Europe*
      (Athens, OH, 2008); Michael Martone, *The Flatness and Other
      Landscapes* (Athens, GA, 2000), p. 2.

30   John A. Jakle and Keith A. Sculle, *Lots of Parking: Land Use in Car
      Culture* (Charlottesville, VA, 2004), pp. 1–10.

31   Ibid., p. 108.

32   Wolfgang Schivelbusch, *The Railway Journey: The Industrialization
      of Time and Space in the 19th Century* (Berkeley, CA, 1986), p. 22.

33   Vaclav Smil, *Making the Modern World: Materials and
      Dematerialization* (Chichester, 2014), p. 28.

34   Schivelbusch, *Railway Journey*, pp. 57–60.

35   William L. Graf, 'Dam Nation: A Geographic Census of American
      Dams and their Large-scale Hydrologic Impacts', in *Physical
      Geography*, vol. IV, ed. K. J. Gregory (London, 2005), pp. 153–66.

36   Bourdon, *Designing the Earth*, pp. 70–72; Charles R. Ortloff, *Water
      Engineering in the Ancient World: Archaeological and Climate
      Perspectives on Societies of Ancient South America, the Middle East,
      and South-east Asia* (Oxford, 2009), pp. 64–6.

37   R. D. Martienssen, *The Idea of Space in Greek Architecture*
      (Johannesburg, 1956), p. 3; Amos Rapoport, *House Form and Culture*
      (Englewood Cliffs, NJ, 1969), pp. 28–31; David Leatherbarrow,
      Uncommon Ground: Architecture, Technology, and Topography
      (Cambridge, MA, 2000), pp. 10–11.

38   Rapoport, *House Form and Culture*, p. 36; Francis D. K. Ching,
      Architecture: Form, Space, and Order (New York, 1996), pp. 3, 18–19;
      Leatherbarrow, *Uncommon Ground*, p. 10.

39   Robert Venturi, *Complexity and Contradiction in Architecture*
      (New York, 1977), p. 52.

40   Richard Weston and John Pardey, 'Platform: Explorations
      of an Architectural Idea', *Architectural Research Quarterly*, VI/2
      (2002), pp. 145–57; Richard Weston, 'From Place to Planet: Jørn
      Utzon's Earthbound Platforms and Floating Roofs', in *Constructing
      Place: Mind and Matter*, ed. Sarah Menin (London, 2003),
      pp. 241–52.

41   Jørn Utzon, 'Platforms and Plateaus', *Zodiac*, X (1962), pp. 113–41;
      Grant Hildebrand, *Origins of Architectural Pleasure* (Berkeley, CA,
      1999), pp. 21–2, 68–70.

42   Edward Popko, *Geodesics* (Detroit, MI, 1968), p. 7; Hugh Kenner,
     Geodesic Math and How to Use It (Berkeley, CA, 2003), pp. 48–53.

43   Leatherbarrow, *Uncommon Ground*, pp. 27–8; von Meiss, *Elements
     of Architecture*, p. 143.

44   John Huxley, 'The Very Height of Ambition', *Sydney Morning Herald*
     (13 January 2006), p. 9.

45   Wang Jun, *Beijing Record: A Physical and Political History of Planning
     Modern Beijing* (Singapore, 2011), pp. 27–33, 146, 370–78.

46   Bernd Hüppauf, 'Spaces of the Vernacular: Ernst Bloch's Philosophy
     of Hope and the German Hometown', in *Vernacular Modernism:
     Heimat, Globalization, and the Built Environment*, ed. Maiken Umbach
     and Bernd Hüppauf (Stanford, CA, 2005), p. 97 (pp. 84–113).

47   Bill Hubbard Jr, *American Boundaries: The Nation, the States, the
     Rectangular Survey* (Chicago, IL, 2009), p. 183; David M. Scobey,
     Empire City: The Making and Meaning of the New York City Landscape
     (Philadelphia, PA, 2002), pp. 120–31.

48   Le Corbusier, *The City of Tomorrow and Its Planning* (London, 1971),
     pp. 16–22, 280, 297, italics in original; Richard Weston, 'From Place
     to Planet: Jørn Utzon's Earthbound Platforms and Floating Roofs',
     in *Constructing Place: Mind and Matter*, ed. Sarah Menin (London,
     2003), pp. 241–52; A. J. Brown and H. M. Sherrard, *Town and Country
     Planning* (Melbourne, 1951), p. 43.

49   Peter Hall, ed., *Von Thünen's Isolated State* (Oxford, 1966), p. 7; Peter
     Haggett, *Locational Analysis in Human Geography* (London, 1965),
     pp. 21–2, 162; Alfred Weber, *Theory of the Location of Industries*
     (Chicago, IL, 1929), pp. 42–7.

50   Walter Christaller, *Central Places in Southern Germany* (Englewood
     Cliffs, NJ, 1966), pp. 28, 43–5; August Lösch, *The Economics of Location*
     (New Haven, CT, 1954), pp. 109–10.

51   George Kingsley Zipf, *Human Behavior and the Principle of Least
     Effort: An Introduction to Human Ecology* (New York, 1949), pp. 348–9.

52   Trevor J. Barnes and Claudio Minca, 'Nazi Spatial Theory: The Dark
     Geographies of Carl Schmitt and Walter Christaller', *Annals of the
     Association of American Geographers*, CIII/3 (2013), pp. 669–87;
     Constantinos A. Doxiadis, *Ekistics: An Introduction to the Science
     of Human Settlements* (London, 1968), pp. 133–40.

53   Isla Forsyth, 'Designs on the Desert: Camouflage, Deception and the
     Militarization of Space', *Cultural Geographies*, XXI/2 (2014), pp. 247–
     65; Rachel Woodward, 'Military Landscapes: Agendas and Approaches
     for Future Research', *Progress in Human Geography*, XXXVIII (2014),

pp. 40–61; Gareth L. Pawlowski, *Flat-tops and Fledglings: A History of American Aircraft Carriers* (New York, 1971), pp. 17–23.

54   Edward T. Linenthal, Jonathan Hyman and Christine Gruber, eds, *The Landscapes of 9/11: A Photographer's Journey* (Austin, TX, 2013), pp. 133, 167.

55   I. L. Finkel and M. J. Seymour, eds, *Babylon: Myth and Reality* (London, 2008), p. 219.

56   L. J. Hogan, *Man-made Mountain: Your Life, Your Land Australia* (Sydney, 1979), pp. 69–74; *Sydney Morning Herald* (22 August 2011), p. 20.

57   Wang Jun, *Beijing Record: A Physical and Political History*, pp. 200–201.

58   John Romer, *The Great Pyramid: Ancient Egypt Revisited* (Cambridge, 2007), pp. 269, 310–15, 451; Christopher Bartlett, 'The Design of the Great Pyramid of Khufu', *Nexus Network Journal*, XVI/2 (2014), pp. 299–311.

SIX   Level Playing Fields

1   Bernard Cache, *Earth Moves: The Furnishing of Territories* (Cambridge, MA, 1995), p. 25.

2   John Bale, *Landscapes of Modern Sport* (Leicester, 1994), pp. 67–8; David A. Singer, *Geometry: Plane and Fancy* (New York, 1998), p. 148.

3   J. A. Mangan and Fan Hong, *Sport in Asian Society: Past and Present* (London, 2003).

4   John Vrooman, 'Two to Tango: Optimum Competitive Balance in Professional Sports Leagues', in *The Econometrics of Sport*, ed. Plácido Rodríguez, Stefan Késenne and Jaume García (Cheltenham, 2013), pp. 3–5 (pp. 3–34).

5   'Soccer Corruption Indictments', www.c-span.org, 27 May 2015.

6   David Gilman Romano, *Athletics and Mathematics in Archaic Corinth: The Origins of the Greek Stadion* (Philadelphia, PA, 1993), pp. 16–17, 21, 33, 77.

7   Bale, *Landscapes of Modern Sport*, pp. 108–9.

8   John A. Hawley, ed., *Running: Olympic Handbook of Sports Medicine* (Chichester, 2008), p. 36.

9   Bale, *Landscapes of Modern Sport*, pp. 59–60.

10   Ibid., p. 68.

11   C. B. Daish, *The Physics of Ball Games* (London, 1972), pp. 16, 73, 92.

12   Matt Caple, Iain James and Mark Bartlett, 'Spatial Analysis of

the Mechanical Behaviour of Natural Turf Sports Pitches', *Sports Engineering*, XV/3 (2012), pp. 143–57.

13   Bale, *Landscapes of Modern Sport*, p. 23.

14   Jacques Gernet, *A History of Chinese Civilization* (Cambridge, 1982), pp. 283, 331.

15   Bale, *Landscapes of Modern Sport*, p. 72.

16   D. M. James, M. J. Carré and S. J. Haake, 'Predicting the Playing Character of Cricket Pitches', *Sports Engineering*, VIII/4 (2005), pp. 193–207.

17   Hilary McD. Beckles, 'The Origins and Development of West Indies Cricket Culture in the Nineteenth Century: Jamaica and Barbados', in *Liberation Cricket: West Indies Cricket Culture*, ed. Hilary McD. Beckles and Brian Stoddart (Kingston, Jamaica, 1995), p. 42 (pp. 33–43).

18   J. M. Taylor, *Geography of New South Wales* (Sydney, 1912), p. 33.

19   Robert Wainwright, 'Holes on the Road Won't Handicap Journey', *Sydney Morning Herald* (30–31 October 2004), p. 11.

20   H.J.R. Murray, *A History of Chess* (Oxford, 1913); R. C. Bell, *Board and Table Games from Many Civilizations* (London, 1960); Andrew Topsfield, ed., *The Art of Play: Board and Card Games of India* (Mumbai, 2006).

21   Martin van Creveld, *Wargames: From Gladiators to Gigabytes* (Cambridge, 2013), pp. 20–22, 140–42.

SEVEN **Flat Materials**

1   Edward R. Tufte, *Envisioning Information* (Cheshire, CT, 1990), p. 9.

2   Le Corbusier, *The City of Tomorrow and Its Planning* (London, 1971), pp. 28–9; Tufte, *Envisioning Information*, p. 12.

3   Parviz Tanavoli, *Persian Flatweaves: A Survey of Flatwoven Floor Covers and Hangings and Royal Masnads* (Woodbridge, Suffolk, 2002), p. 30; Arend Bandsma and Robin Brandt, *Flatweaves of Turkey* (Bathurst, Australia, 1995), p. 13.

4   Bernard Maurin and René Motro, 'Textile Architecture', in *Flexible Composite Materials: In Architecture, Construction and Interiors*, ed. René Motro (Basel, 2013), pp. 26–38; Michele Emmer, 'Minimal Surfaces and Architecture: New Forms', *Nexus Network Journal*, XV/2 (2013), pp. 227–39; Andrea Casale, Graziano Mario Valenti, Michele Calvano and Jessica Romor, 'Surfaces: Concept, Design, Parametric Modelling and Prototyping', *Nexus Network Journal*, XV/2 (2013), pp. 271–83.

5   Mimi Sheller, *Aluminum Dreams: The Making of Light Modernity*
    (Cambridge, MA, 2014), p. 147; Edward S. Hoffman, David P. Gustafson
    and Albert J. Gouwens, *Structural Design Guide to the ACI Building
    Code* (Boston, MA, 1998), p. 76; Vaclav Smil, *Making the Modern World:
    Materials and Dematerialization* (Chichester, 2014), pp. 41–2.

6   Bob Cameron, *Illumination and Decoration of Flat Surfaces*
    (Collingwood, Australia, 2009).

7   Robert Venturi, *Complexity and Contradiction in Architecture*
    (New York, 1977), p. 16; Anthony Vidler, *Warped Space: Art,
    Architecture, and Anxiety in Modern Culture* (Cambridge, MA, 2000),
    pp. 6–8.

8   Jaroslav Černý, *Paper and Books in Ancient Egypt* (Chicago, IL, 1985);
    Roger S. Bagnall, ed., *The Oxford Handbook of Papyrology* (Oxford,
    2009), pp. 3–29; Albertine Gaur, *A History of Writing* (London, 1992).

9   Smil, *Making the Modern World*, p. 50.

10 Walter J. Ong, *Orality and Literacy: The Technologizing of the Word*
    (London, 2015), first published 1982, pp. 121–6.

11 M. T. Clanchy, *From Memory to Written Record: England, 1066–1307*
    (Oxford, 1993), p. 120.

12 Dard Hunter, *Papermaking: The History and Technique of an Ancient
    Craft* (New York, 1947); Joseph A. Dane, *What Is a Book? The Study of
    Early Printed Books* (Notre Dame, IN, 2012), pp. 49–50.

13 Yasuko Obana, 'Vertical or Horizontal? Reading Directions in
    Japanese', *Bulletin of the School of Oriental and African Studies*, LX
    (1997), pp. 86–94.

14 Alicia Imperiale, *New Flatness: Surface Tension in Digital Architecture*
    (Basel, 2000), p. 15.

15 Peter Stoicheff and Andrew Taylor, eds, *The Future of the Page*
    (Toronto, 2004); Fulvio Domini, Rajesh Shah and Corrado Caudek,
    'Do We Perceive a Flattened World on the Monitor Screen?', *Acta
    Psychologica*, CXXXVIII (2011), pp. 359–66.

16 Joost Hölscher and Joost Baardman, *Structural Package Designs*
    (Amsterdam, 2003).

17 Staffan Bengtsson, *IKEA: The Book* (Stockholm, 2010).

18 R. L. Zielasko, 'Ceramic Flat Packs: Design and Construction',
    American Ceramic Society Bulletin, XLVI (1967), p. 385.

19 Han Slawik, Julia Bergmann, Matthias Buchmeier and Sonja Tinney,
    eds, *Container Atlas: A Practical Guide to Container Architecture*
    (Berlin, 2010).

EIGHT Pictorial Flattening

1   Clement Greenberg, 'After Abstract Expressionism', *Art International*,
    VI (25 October 1962), p. 30.

2   Alicia Imperiale, *New Flatness: Surface Tension in Digital Architecture*
    (Basel, 2000), p. 8.

3   Stephen Grossberg, 'The Art of Seeing and Painting', *Spatial Vision*,
    XXI/3–5 (2008), p. 463 (pp. 463–86); John Milnor, 'A Problem in
    Cartography', *American Mathematical Monthly*, LXXVI/10 (1969),
    p. 1101.

4   Bob Nickas, *Painting Abstraction: New Elements in Abstract Painting*
    (London, 2009), p. 5; Mark Wagner, *The Geometries of Visual Space*
    (Mahwah, NJ, 2006), p. 24.

5   Michel Henry, *Seeing the Invisible: On Kandinsky* (London, 2009),
    pp. 57–9.

6   Tim Ingold, *The Perception of the Environment: Essays on Livelihood,
    Dwelling and Skill* (London, 2000), p. 241.

7   Alan M. MacEachren, *How Maps Work: Representation, Visualization,
    and Design* (New York, 2004), pp. 370–76.

8   Peter Sutton, ed., *Dreamings: The Art of Aboriginal Australia*
    (New York, 1989), p. 19; David Turnbull, *Masons, Tricksters and
    Cartographers: Comparative Studies in the Sociology of Scientific and
    Indigenous Knowledge* (Amsterdam, 2000), pp. 97–8; Howard Morphy,
    'Seeing Indigenous Australian Art', in *Anthropologies of Art*, ed. Mariët
    Westermann (Williamstown, MA, 2005), pp. 126–7 (pp. 124–42).

9   Catherine Delano Smith, 'Cartography in the Prehistoric Period in the
    Old World: Europe, the Middle East, and North Africa', in *The History
    of Cartography*, ed. J. B. Harley and David Woodward (Chicago, IL,
    1987), vol. I, pp. 54–101. The several volumes of *The History
    of Cartography* provide a comprehensive account of the subject.

10 Germaine Aujac, 'The Foundations of Theoretical Cartography
    in Archaic and Classical Greece', in *The History of Cartography*,
    ed. Harley and Woodward, vol. I, pp. 130–47.

11 J. Lennart Berggren and Alexander Jones, *Ptolemy's 'Geography':
    An Annotated Translation of the Theoretical Chapters* (Princeton, NJ,
    2000); O.A.W. Dilke, 'The Culmination of Greek Cartography in
    Ptolemy', in *The History of Cartography*, ed. Harley and Woodward,
    vol. I, pp. 177–200.

12 David Woodward, 'Medieval *Mappaemundi*', in *The History
    of Cartography*, ed. Harley and Woodward, vol. I, pp. 318–21

(pp. 286–370); Alessandro Scafi, *Mapping Paradise: A History
   of Heaven on Earth* (Chicago, IL, 2006), pp. 160–63.

13   Emilie Savage-Smith, 'Celestial Mapping', in *The History
   of Cartography*, ed. Harley and Woodward, vol. II, Book 1, pp. 18, 34–6
   (pp. 12–70); Gerald R. Tibbetts, 'Later Cartographic Developments', in
   The History of Cartography, ed. Harley and Woodward, vol. II, Book 1,
   pp. 148–50 (pp. 137–55).

14   Joseph Needham, *Science and Civilisation in China*, vol. III:
   Mathematics and the Sciences of the Heavens and the Earth
   (Cambridge, 1959), pp. 539, 586.

15   Gari Ledyard, 'Cartography in Korea', in *The History of Cartography*,
   ed. Harley and Woodward, vol. II, Book 1, p. 256 (pp. 235–345).

16   George P. Kellaway, *Map Projections* (London, 1946), p. 37.

17   John P. Snyder, *Flattening the Earth: Two Thousand Years of Map
   Projections* (Chicago, IL, 1993).

18   Ibid., pp. 98–9.

19   Mark Monmonier, *How to Lie with Maps* (Chicago, IL, 1991), p. 1.

20   Kendrick Oliver, *To Touch the Face of God: The Sacred, the Profane, and
   the American Space Program, 1957–1975* (Baltimore, MD, 2013), pp. 82–6.

21   Adnan Morshed, 'The Cultural Politics of Aerial Vision: Le Corbusier
   in Brazil (1929)', *Journal of Architectural Education*, LV/4 (2005),
   pp. 201–10; Anthony Vidler, *Warped Space: Art, Architecture, and
   Anxiety in Modern Culture* (Cambridge, MA, 2000), p. 10; Robert
   Wohl, *A Passion for Wings: Aviation and the Western Imagination,
   1908–1918* (New Haven, CT, 1994), pp. 253–5.

22   David Leatherbarrow, *Uncommon Ground: Architecture, Technology,
   and Topography* (Cambridge, MA, 2000), pp. 13–15.

23   Elliott L. Vanskike, '"Seeing Everything as Flat": Landscape in
   Gertrude Stein's *Useful Knowledge* and *The Geographical History
   of America*', *Texas Studies in Literature and Language*, XXXV/2 (1993),
   p. 152 (pp. 151–67).

24   Fred Dubery and John Willats, *Perspective and Other Drawing Systems*
   (London, 1972); Robert W. Gill, *Basic Perspective* (London, 1974).

25   Samuel Y. Edgerton, *The Mirror, the Window, and the Telescope: How
   Renaissance Linear Perspective Changed Our Vision of the Universe*
   (Ithaca, NY, 2009), pp. xiii–xv; Hans Belting, *Florence and Baghdad:
   Renaissance Art and Arab Science* (Cambridge, MA, 2011), pp. 1–3;
   Veronica della Dora, '*Topia*: Landscape before Linear Perspective',
   Annals of the Association of American Geographers, CIII/3 (2013),
   pp. 688–709.

26   Margaret Livingstone, *Vision and Art: The Biology of Seeing*
      (New York, 2002), pp. 100–104.

27   Daryn Lehoux, *What Did the Romans Know? An Inquiry into Science
      and Worldmaking* (Chicago, IL, 2012), pp. 111–16; Belting, *Florence
      and Baghdad*, pp. 42–5.

28   Yi-Fu Tuan, *China* (London, 1970), pp. 1–6; Needham, *Science and
      Civilisation in China*, vol. III, p. 593.

29   François Jullien, *The Great Image Has No Form, or On the Nonobject
      through Painting* (Chicago, IL, 2009), pp. 76–7, 85–6, 121–2.

30   Christopher S. Wood, *Albrecht Altdorfer and the Origins of Landscape*
      (London, 1993), p. 9; Alan Chong, 'Landscape', in *Dutch Art: An
      Encyclopedia*, ed. Sheila D. Muller (New York, 1997), pp. 213–16.

31   David L. Ransel, 'Neither Nobles nor Peasants: Plain Painting
      and the Emergence of the Merchant Estate', in *Picturing Russia:
      Explorations in Visual Culture*, ed. Valerie A. Kivelson and Joan
      Neuberger (New Haven, CT, 2008), pp. 76–80; John Willats, *Art
      and Representation: New Principles in the Analysis of Pictures*
      (Princeton, NJ, 1997), pp. 228–35.

32   Denise Von Glahn, *The Sounds of Place: Music and the American
      Cultural Landscape* (Boston, MA, 2003), pp. 17–27.

33   Rosalind E. Krauss, *The Originality of the Avant-garde and Other
      Modernist Myths* (Cambridge, MA, 1985), pp. 131–3.

34   Wohl, *A Passion for Wings*, pp. 158–78; Didier Maleuvre, *The Horizon:
      A History of Our Infinite Longing* (Berkeley, CA, 2011), p. 270.

35   Wassily Kandinsky, *Point and Line to Plane* (New York, 1979), p. 115;
      Henry, *Seeing the Invisible*, pp. 57–9; Willats, *Art and Representation*,
      pp. 221, 247.

36   Hannah B. Higgins, *The Grid Book* (Cambridge, MA, 2009), pp. 266–9.

37   Jonathan Harris, *Writing Back to Modern Art: After Greenberg, Fried
      and Clark* (London, 2005), p. 64; James Meyer, *Minimalism: Art and
      Polemics in the Sixties* (New Haven, CT, 2001), pp. 111, 213; Johanna
      Drucker, *Theorizing Modernism: Visual Art and the Critical Tradition*
      (New York, 1994), p. 65; Clement Greenberg, *Homemade Esthetics:
      Observations on Art and Taste* (New York, 1999), pp. 125–6. Cf. Joseph
      Masheck, 'The Carpet Paradigm: Critical Prolegomena to a Theory
      of Flatness', *Arts Magazine*, LI (1976), pp. 82–109.

38   Lucian Krukowski, *Art and Concept: A Philosophical Study*
      (Amherst, MA, 1987), p. 40.

39   T. J. Clark, *Farewell to an Idea: Episodes from a History of Modernism*
      (New Haven, CT, 1999), pp. 204–5.

40 Maleuvre, *The Horizon*, pp. 269–71, 283; Linda Dalrymple Henderson, *The Fourth Dimension and Non-Euclidean Geometry in Modern Art* (Princeton, NJ, 1983), p. 275; Tony Robbin, *Shadows of Reality: The Fourth Dimension in Relativity, Cubism, and Modern Thought* (New Haven, CT, 2006), pp. 28–40.

41 Harry Holtzman and Martin S. James, eds, *The New Art – The New Life: The Collected Writings of Piet Mondrian* (Boston, MA, 1986), pp. 9–14; Wolfgang Stechow, *Dutch Landscape Painting of the Seventeenth Century* (Oxford, 1966); Aaron Betsky and Adam Eeuwens, *False Flat: Why Dutch Design is so Good* (London, 2004), p. 358; Nancy J. Troy, *The Afterlife of Piet Mondrian* (Chicago, IL, 2013), pp. 13–14; Nickas, *Painting Abstraction*, pp. 96–103.

42 Philip Leider, 'Literalism and Abstraction: Frank Stella's Retrospective at the Modern', in *Abstract Art in the Late Twentieth Century*, ed. Frances Colpitt (Cambridge, 2002), p. 19 (pp. 11–24); Frank Stella, *Working Space* (Cambridge, MA, 1986), p. 28; Wally Caruana, *Aboriginal Art* (London, 1993), pp. 22–5.

43 Edward S. Casey, *Earth-Mapping: Artists Reshaping Landscape* (Minneapolis, MN, 2005), pp. 47–75; David Bourdon, *Designing the Earth: The Human Impulse to Shape Nature* (New York, 1995), p. 8.

44 Gerhard K. Ackermann and Jürgen Eichler, *Holography: A Practical Approach* (Weinheim, 2007), pp. 4–7.

45 Edgerton, *The Mirror, the Window, and the Telescope*, p. 172.

46 Sophie Volpp, *Worldly Stage: Theatricality in Seventeenth-century China* (Cambridge, MA, 2011), pp. 71–7; Nicholas Wood, 'Flatness and Depth: Reflections', in *The Potentials of Spaces: The Theory and Practice of Scenography and Performance*, ed. Alison Oddey and Christine White (Bristol, 2006), pp. 61–5.

47 Harris, *Writing Back to Modern Art*, p. 172.

48 Esther Leslie, *Hollywood Flatlands: Animation, Critical Theory and the Avant-garde* (London, 2002), pp. 148–9, 299.

49 Thomas Lamarre, *The Anime Machine: A Media Theory of Animation* (Minneapolis, MN, 2009), pp. 111, 126–7.

50 Rachel June Torbett, 'The Quick and the Flat: Walter Benjamin, Werner Herzog', in *Essays on Boredom and Modernity*, ed. Barbara Dalle Pezze and Carlo Salzani (New York, 2009), pp. 155–76.

51 Alan Ackerman, 'Samuel Beckett's *Spectres du Noir*: The Being of Painting and the Flatness of Film', *Contemporary Literature*, XLIV/3 (2003), p. 438 (pp. 399–441).

52   E. M. Forster, *Aspects of the Novel* (London, 1949), pp. 65–75; George
     R. Clay, 'In Defense of Flat Characters', *Midwest Quarterly*, XLII/1–2
     (2001), pp. 271–80.

53   John Beagles, 'Fear of a Flat Planet', *Sight and Sound*, XXIII/7 (2013),
     pp. 52–3.

54   Denise Von Glahn, *The Sounds of Place: Music and the American
     Cultural Landscape* (Boston, MA, 2003), pp. 27, 252–60.

55   Peter Sculthorpe, *Sun Music: Journeys and Reflections from a
     Composer's Life* (Sydney, 1999), pp. 199–200, 263; Vincent Plush,
     'Notes from the Great South Land: The Origins of Contemporary
     Music in Australia, 1788 to the 1950s', in *Australia: Exploring the
     Musical Landscape*, ed. Caitlin Rowley (Sydney, 1998), p. 48.

56   Maleuvre, *The Horizon*, pp. 272–3; Robert Fink, 'Going Flat: Post-
     hierarchical Music Theory and the Musical Surface', in *Rethinking
     Music*, ed. Nicholas Cook and Mark Everist (Oxford, 1999), p. 117
     (pp. 102–37).

57   Julia Robinson, 'John Cage and Investiture: Unmanning the System',
     in *John Cage*, ed. Julia Robinson (Cambridge, MA, 2011), pp. 193–5
     (pp. 171–216); Liz Kotz, *Words to Be Looked At: Language in 1960s Art*
     (Cambridge, MA, 2007), pp. 18–22; John Cage, 'Experimental Music',
     in *Silence: Lectures and Writings by John Cage* (Middletown, CT, 2011),
     p. 8.

58   Fredric Jameson, *Postmodernism, or, The Cultural Logic of Late
     Capitalism* (Durham, NC, 1991), p. 9; Fink, 'Going Flat', p. 102.

59   Keith Potter, *Four Musical Minimalists: La Monte Young, Terry
     Riley, Steve Reich, Philip Glass* (Cambridge, 2000), pp. 10–17; Mark
     Prendergast, *The Ambient Century: From Mahler to Trance – The
     Evolution of Sound in the Electronic Age* (New York, 2000), pp. 91–5.

60   Prendergast, *Ambient Century*, p. 297; David Buckley, *Kraftwerk
     Publikation: A Biography* (London, 2012), p. 56; Thomas Zeller,
     'Building and Rebuilding the Landscape of the Autobahn, 1930–70',
     in *The World Beyond the Windshield: Roads and Landscapes in the
     United States and Europe*, ed. Christof Mauch and Thomas Zeller
     (Athens, OH, 2008), p. 125 (pp. 125–42).

61   David Joselit, 'Notes on Surface: Toward a Genealogy of Flatness',
     Art History, XXIII/1 (2000), pp. 19–34; Jane Piper Clendinning,
     'Postmodern Architecture/Postmodern Music', in *Postmodern Music/
     Postmodern Thought*, ed. Judy Lochhead and Joseph Auner
     (New York, 2002), pp. 119–40.

NINE Future Flatness

1 Takashi Murakami, *Super Flat* (Tokyo, 2000), p. 1.

2 Bruce Lincoln, '"The Earth Becomes Flat" – A Study of Apocalyptic Imagery', *Comparative Studies in Society and History*, XXV/1 (1983), pp. 136–53.

3 Ibid., pp. 136–53.

4 Christopher Connery, '*There was No More Sea*: The Supersession of the Ocean from the Bible to Cyberspace', *Journal of Historical Geography*, XXXII/3 (2006), p. 498 (pp. 494–511); John F. A. Sawyer, 'Isaiah', in *The Oxford Handbook of the Reception History of the Bible*, ed. Michael Lieb, Emma Mason and Jonathan Roberts (Oxford, 2011), pp. 54–5.

5 C. Raymond Beazley, *The Dawn of Modern Geography* (New York, 1949), vol. I, p. 293 (first published 1897); Darren Oldridge, *The Devil: A Very Short Introduction* (Oxford, 2012), p. 84.

6 Connery, '*There was No More Sea*', pp. 494–511.

7 David Pugh, *Changing Sea Levels: Effects of Tides, Weather and Climate* (Cambridge, 2004), p. 1.

8 Fred Hoyle, *October the First is Too Late* (Harmondsworth, 1968), p. 84.

9 Ibid., pp. 76–95, 140–43, 164–6.

10 Jerome F. Shapiro, *Atomic Bomb Cinema: The Apocalyptic Imagination on Film* (New York, 2002).

11 Ibid., p. 12.

12 Mark Wigley, 'The Electric Lawn', in *The American Lawn*, ed. Georges Teyssot (New York, 1999), p. 189 (pp. 155–95).

13 E. Relph, *Place and Placelessness* (London, 1976), p. 117.

14 Christian Norberg-Schulz, 'Meaning in Architecture', in *Meaning in Architecture*, ed. Charles Jencks and George Baird (New York, 1970), p. 228 (pp. 214–29); Relph, *Place and Placelessness*, p. 79.

15 John Demos, *Circles and Lines: The Shape of Life in Early America* (Cambridge, MA, 2004); David Summers, *Real Spaces: World Art History and the Rise of Western Modernism* (London, 2003), p. 344.

16 Hannah B. Higgins, *The Grid Book* (Cambridge, MA, 2009), pp. 275–7.

17 Joseph A. Castellano, *Liquid Gold: The Story of Liquid Crystal Displays and the Creation of an Industry* (Hackensack, NJ, 2005); S. M. Kelly and J. A. Connor, *Flat Panel Displays: Advanced Organic Materials* (Cambridge, 2000).

18 Harm de Blij, *The Power of Place: Geography, Destiny, and Globalization's Rough Landscape* (Oxford, 2009), pp. 3–5.

19 Thomas L. Friedman, *The World is Flat: A Brief History of the Globalized World in the Twenty-first Century* (London, 2005); Edward E. Leamer, 'A Flat World, a Level Playing Field, a Small World After All, or None of the Above? A Review of Thomas L. Friedman's *The World is Flat*', *Journal of Economic Literature*, XLV (2007), pp. 87, 122 (pp. 83–126).

20 Murakami, *Super Flat*, pp. 1–11.

21 Hiroki Azuma, 'Super Flat Speculation', in Murakami, *Super Flat*, p. 139.

22 Murakami, *Super Flat*, pp. 23–5; Michael Darling, 'Plumbing the Depths of Superflatness', *Art Journal*, LX/3 (2001), pp. 76–89; Thomas Lamarre, *The Anime Machine: A Media Theory of Animation* (Minneapolis, MN, 2009), pp. 113–22; Morgan Meyer, 'Placing and Tracing Absence: A Material Culture of the Immaterial', *Journal of Material Culture*, XVII (2012), pp. 103–10; Alicia Imperiale, *New Flatness: Surface Tension in Digital Architecture* (Basel, 2000), p. 9; Edwin Abbott Abbott, *Flatland: A Romance in Many Dimensions* (Princeton, NJ, 1991).

SELECT BIBLIOGRAPHY

Ackermann, Gerhard K., and Jürgen Eichler, *Holography: A Practical Approach* (Weinheim, 2007)

Appleton, Jay, *The Experience of Landscape* (Chichester, 1975)

—, *How I Made the World: Shaping a View of Landscape* (Hull, 1994)

—, *The Symbolism of Habitat: An Interpretation of Landscape in the Arts* (Seattle, WA, 1990)

Bale, John, *Landscapes of Modern Sport* (Leicester, 1994)

Beazley, C. Raymond, *The Dawn of Modern Geography* (New York, 1949)

Berger, Marcel, *Geometry Revealed: A Jacob's Ladder to Modern Higher Geometry* (Heidelberg, 2010)

Betsky, Aaron, and Adam Eeuwens, *False Flat: Why Dutch Design is so Good* (London, 2004)

Bourassa, Steven C., *The Aesthetics of Landscape* (London, 1991)

Bourdon, David, *Designing the Earth: The Human Impulse to Shape Nature* (New York, 1995)

Boyer, Carl B., *A History of Mathematics* (New York, 1968)

Campion, Nicholas, *Astrology and Cosmology in the World's Religions* (New York, 2012)

Colpitt, Frances, *Minimal Art: The Critical Perspective* (Seattle, 1990)

Dierkes, Ulrich, Stefan Hildebrandt and Friedrich Sauvigny, *Minimal Surfaces* (Berlin, 2010)

Franklin, James, *An Aristotelian Realist Philosophy of Mathematics: Mathematics as the Science of Quantity and Structure* (London, 2014)

Friedman, Thomas L., *The World is Flat: A Brief History of the Globalized World in the Twenty-first Century* (London, 2005)

Garwood, Christine, *Flat Earth: The History of an Infamous Idea* (New York, 2007)

Greenberg, Clement, *Homemade Esthetics: Observations on Art and Taste* (New York, 1999)

Harley, J. B., and David Woodward, eds, *The History of Cartography*, vol. I (Chicago, IL, 1987)

Henderson, Linda Dalrymple, *The Fourth Dimension and Non-Euclidean Geometry in Modern Art* (Princeton, NJ, 1983)

Higgins, Hannah B., *The Grid Book* (Cambridge, MA, 2009)

Howard, I. P., and W. B. Templeton, *Human Spatial Orientation* (London, 1966)

Imperiale, Alicia, *New Flatness: Surface Tension in Digital Architecture* (Basel, 2000)

Janich, Peter, *Euclid's Heritage: Is Space Three-dimensional?* (Dordrecht, 1992)

Jenkins, Virginia Scott, *The Lawn: A History of an American Obsession* (Washington, DC, 1994)

Jones, Karen R., and John Wills, *The Invention of the Park: Recreational Landscapes from the Garden of Eden to Disney's Magic Kingdom* (Cambridge, 2005)

Jullien, François, *The Great Image Has No Form, or On the Nonobject through Painting* (Chicago, IL, 2009)

Kandinsky, Wassily, *Point and Line to Plane* (New York, 1979)

Kaplan, Rachel, and Stephen Kaplan, *The Experience of Nature: A Psychological Perspective* (Cambridge, 1989)

Krauss, Rosalind E., *The Originality of the Avant-garde and Other Modernist Myths* (Cambridge, MA, 1985)

Lamarre, Thomas, *The Anime Machine: A Media Theory of Animation* (Minneapolis, MN, 2009)

Le Corbusier, *The City of Tomorrow and Its Planning* (London, 1971)

Leatherbarrow, David, *Uncommon Ground: Architecture, Technology, and Topography* (Cambridge, MA, 2000)

Leslie, Esther, *Hollywood Flatlands: Animation, Critical Theory and the Avant-garde* (London, 2002)

Liddle, Andrew, *An Introduction to Modern Cosmology* (Hoboken, NJ, 2013)

Livingstone, Margaret, *Vision and Art: The Biology of Seeing* (New York, 2002)

Maleuvre, Didier, *The Horizon: A History of Our Infinite Longing* (Berkeley, CA, 2011)

Meiss, Pierre von, *Elements of Architecture: From Form to Place* (London, 1990)

Millar, Susanna, *Space and Sense* (Hove, 2008)

Monmonier, Mark, *How to Lie with Maps* (Chicago, IL, 1991)

Murakami, Takashi, *Super Flat* (Tokyo, 2000)

Needham, Joseph, *Science and Civilisation in China*, vol. III: *Mathematics and the Sciences of the Heavens and the Earth* (Cambridge, 1959)

Nicolson, Marjorie Hope, *Mountain Gloom and Mountain Glory:*
    The Development of the Infinite [1959] (New York, 1963)
Olson, David R., and Ellen Bialystok, *Spatial Cognition: The Structure*
    and Development of Spatial Relations (Hillsdale, NJ, 1983)
Prendergast, Mark, *The Ambient Century: From Mahler to Trance –*
    The Evolution of Sound in the Electronic Age (New York, 2000)
Raisz, Erwin, *General Cartography* (New York, 1948)
Rapoport, Amos, *House Form and Culture* (Englewood Cliffs,
    NJ, 1969)
Relph, E., *Place and Placelessness* (London, 1976)
Robbin, Tony, *Shadows of Reality: The Fourth Dimension in Relativity,*
    Cubism, and Modern Thought (New Haven, CT, 2006)
Ruskin, John, *Modern Painters*, vol. IV: *Of Mountain Beauty* [1856]
    (London, 1897)
Russell, Jeffrey Burton, *Inventing the Flat Earth: Columbus and Modern*
    Historians (New York, 1991)
Schivelbusch, Wolfgang, *The Railway Journey: The Industrialization*
    of Time and Space in the 19th Century (Berkeley, CA, 1986)
Shapiro, Jerome F., *Atomic Bomb Cinema: The Apocalyptic Imagination*
    on Film (New York, 2002)
Smil, Vaclav, *Making the Modern World: Materials and Dematerialization*
    (Chichester, 2014)
Snyder, John P., *Flattening the Earth: Two Thousand Years of Map*
    Projections (Chicago, IL, 1993)
Summers, David, *Real Spaces: World Art History and the Rise of Western*
    Modernism (London, 2003)
Sutton, Peter, ed., *Dreamings: The Art of Aboriginal Australia*
    (New York, 1989)
Thomas, William L., Jr, ed., *Man's Role in Changing the Face of the Earth*
    (Chicago, IL, 1956)
Tuan, Yi-Fu, *Space and Place: The Perspective of Experience*
    (Minneapolis, MN, 1977)
—, *Topophilia: A Study of Environmental Perception, Attitudes, and Values*
    (Englewood Cliffs, NJ, 1974)
Tufte, Edward R., *Envisioning Information* (Cheshire, CT, 1990)
—, *Visual Explanations: Images and Quantities, Evidence and Narratives*
    (Cheshire, CT, 1997)
Turner, B. L., II, ed., *The Earth as Transformed by Human Action: Global*
    and Regional Changes in the Biosphere over the Past 300 Years
    (Cambridge, 1990)

Vidler, Anthony, *Warped Space: Art, Architecture, and Anxiety in Modern Culture* (Cambridge, MA, 2000)

Von Glahn, Denise, *The Sounds of Place: Music and the American Cultural Landscape* (Boston, 2003)

Wagner, Mark, *The Geometries of Visual Space* (Mahwah, NJ, 2006)

Willats, John, *Art and Representation: New Principles in the Analysis of Pictures* (Princeton, NJ, 1997)

Williams, Michael, *Deforesting the Earth: From Prehistory to Global Crisis* (Chicago, IL, 2003)

Wright, M. R., *Cosmology in Antiquity* (London, 1995)

ACKNOWLEDGEMENTS

In writing this book, I have depended on the research findings of authors cited and uncited, and on guidance from friends and colleagues named and unnamed. Almost all of the work has been done at the Australian National University, where I first aired some of my ideas in 2002 in a seminar presented to the History Program of the Research School of Social Sciences, on 'Australia as a Flat Place'. For suggestions and references, I thank Laurence Brown, Milton Cameron, Lizzie Collingham, Tania Colwell, Diana Wood Conroy, Ian Dalziell, Ros Dalziell, Kirsty Douglas, Mark Fonstad, Tom Griffiths, Pat Jalland, Howard Johnson, Shino Konishi, Jeanine Leane, Jacquie Lo, Alan MacEachern, Martin Parry, James Robertson, Don Rowland, Carolyn Strange and Brandon J. Vogt. For help with images, I thank Kay Dancey, Ann Gibbs-Jordan, Harry Gilonis, Sophie Napier, Karina Pelling and Geraldine Woodhatch. Alexandra Lord, Trevor McClaughlin, Ann McGrath and Ruth Waller kindly read all or part of the manuscript and gave much-valued comment and criticism. I also thank the myriad of friends who have happily talked about flatness, in informal situations, when they might easily have preferred other topics. In particular, I thank Karen Fog Olwig and Kenneth Olwig for extended dialogue I enjoyed in their garden grove in 2013, which decided me to tackle the writing of this book ahead of alternative, seductive options.

PHOTO ACKNOWLEDGEMENTS

The author and publishers wish to express their thanks to the below sources of illustrative material and/or permission to reproduce it. (Some locations uncredited in the captions for reasons of brevity are also given below.)

Photos author: pp. 158, 164 top; photo Andrew Beeston: p. 164 foot (this file is licensed under the Creative Commons Attribution 2.0 Generic license: any reader is free to share – to copy, distribute and transmit the work, or to remix – to adapt the work, under the following conditions: you must attribute the work in the manner specified by the author or licensor, but not in any way that suggests that they endorse you or your use of the work: note that you may not apply legal terms or technological measures that legally restrict others from doing anything the license permits); illustration by Begoon: p. 151; photo Julien Carnot: p. 92 (this file is licensed under the Creative Commons Attribution-Share Alike 2.0 Generic license: any reader is free to share – to copy, distribute and transmit the work, or to remix – to adapt the work, under the following conditions: you must attribute the work in the manner specified by the author or licensor, but not in any way that suggests that they endorse you or your use of the work); from Maurice Courant, *Bibliographie Coréenne*, vol. II (Paris, 1895): p. 61 (photo Australian National University Library); photo Jean-Pierre Dalbéra: p. 163 (this file is licensed under the Creative Commons Attribution 2.0 Generic license: any reader is free to share – to copy, distribute and transmit the work, or to remix – to adapt the work, under the following conditions: you must attribute the work in the manner specified by the author or licensor, but not in any way that suggests that they endorse you or your use of the work); from William Morris Davis, *Elementary Physical Geography* (Boston, MA, 1902): p. 95 (photo Australian National University Library); from Euclid (ed. David Gregory), Ευκλειδου τα σωζομενα. *Euclidis quæ supersunt omnia* . . . (Oxford, 1703), photo courtesy St Mary's and Newman Colleges, University of Melbourne: p. 15; photo Famartin: p. 121 (this file is licensed under the Creative Commons Attribution-Share Alike 4.0 International license: any

INDEX